BLACK VOTE
in Four American Cities

Edited by Rod Bush
Foreword by Manning Marable

CHICAGO: **Abdul Alkalimat and Doug Gills**
DETROIT: **Ken Cockrel**
BOSTON: **James Jennings**
OAKLAND: **Rod Bush**
Interview with Congressman Ronald V. Dellums

D0067941

Synthesis Publications • San Francisco

ACKNOWLEDGMENTS

I wish to thank the Institute for the Study of Labor and Economic Crisis, and its Research Director, Marlene Dixon, for their contribution to this book, both in its conception and its theoretical direction. I would also like to thank Barbara Bishop for her editorial assistance and my other colleagues at ISLEC for their help in the preparation of this book.

R.B.

Cover design: Elizabeth Sutherland Martínez

Library of Congress Cataloging in Publication Data
The New Black Vote.
  Includes bibliographies and index.
  1. Afro-Americans—Politics and government.
2. Afro-Americans—Suffrage. I. Bush, Rod.
E185.615.N383 1984   324'.08996073   84-8850
ISBN 0-89935-038-0 (pbk.)

Published by Synthesis Publications
          2703 Folsom Street
          San Francisco, California 94110
Printed in the United States of America
10 9 8 7 6 5 4 3 2

CONTENTS

OAKLAND Grassroots Organizing Against Reagan   315

Rod Bush

LIST OF TABLES

BOSTON   Blacks and Progressive Politics

OAKLAND   Grassroots Organizing Against Reagan

Foreword

by Manning Marable

The *New Black Vote* represents a major departure from the traditional social science research on black political movements, because the authors recognize that politics implies something more than electoral phenomena. For the Afro-American national minority group, politics has always represented the utilization of resources and the mobilization of social forces in the collective effort to realize constructive change. The real targets of black political activity, explicitly or implicitly, have been systemic racism and the political economy of capitalism. To be sure, the tactics and strategies advanced by black political leaders have shifted radically over the last century, with the maturation and decline of monopoly capital and the concurrent demographic shifts of the black population in the United States. During Black Reconstruction in the 1860s and early 1870s, black politicians focused their energies on securing the right to vote for black males, and subsequently obtained major institutional reforms in public education and legal rights that benefited the poor of both races. Aligning themselves with Northern capital and the Republican Party, they sought to redefine the nature of American democracy to include blacks, women, and other exploited sectors of society. Following the Depression of 1873 and the Compromise of 1877, black politicians were sacrificed by their white capitalist partners in order to restructure the political economy of the South along capitalist modes of development. Soon after came segregation, the proliferation of lynching, and the loss of black voting rights for over a half century. Nevertheless, between 1869 and 1901, 816 black men were elected to Congress and state legislatures from the South. South Carolina, second only to Mississippi as the crucible of Southern racism, elected 218 blacks during this period.

The second basic black electoral strategy in the battle against racism and economic underdevelopment can be termed "clientage politics." Beginning in the late 1880s, Cincinnati blacks who were nominal Republicans in national elections began to support the Democratic machine of Boss Cox in local elections, in exchange for petty patronage and increases in public service. For the next 50 years, similar quid pro quo relationships between conservative political and corporate forces and the black electorate developed across the country, particularly in the small but growing Northern and Midwestern ghettos. In Kansas City, Missouri, the Democratic machine of Jim Pendergast manipulated black votes for decades. In Chicago, Republican boss "Big Bill" Thompson was elected mayor three times, largely by the black vote in the city's South Side. The Virginia segregationist machine of Harry F. Byrd tapped support from Richmond's black electorate from the 1920s through the end of World War II. Viewed historically, the clientage system was part of an overall strategy of political accommodation to Jim Crow segregation, prominently advanced by black educator Booker T. Washington. In economics, the counterpart to clientage was represented by Washington's National Negro Business League, and by independent efforts by small entrepreneurs to carve out markets within the segregated subeconomy of the ghetto. The inadequacy of the accommodationist approach to black political development was first clearly countered by W.E.B. Du Bois, co-founder of the National Association for the Advancement of Colored People (NAACP) in the early 20th century. But accommodationist-style black politicians continued to be the rule rather than the exception. The long career of Chicago black Congressman William L. Dawson, who played absolutely no role in desegregationist or reform struggles, stands as a prime example.

The terrain of black politics was changed primarily by two interrelated events: the rise of black workers' political organizations and trade-union activism, and the flowering of the modern civil rights movement. As late as 1940, 77% of all Afro-Americans still lived in the South: two out of five blacks were farmers, sharecroppers, or farm laborers. But in the 1940s, 1.6 million blacks left the South, to be followed by yet another 1.5 million in the 1950s. The size of the black industrial working class soared. Black labor leaders such as A. Philip Randolph emerged to develop new protest vehicles—the National Negro Congress in the mid-1930s and the Negro March on Washington Movement in 1941. The NAACP increased its membership from 50,600 in 1940 to almost 450,000 in 1946. New and more activist-oriented civil rights organizations emerged, including the Congress of Racial Equality in 1942, led by social democrats Bayard Rustin and James Farmer, and the Southern Christian Leadership Conference in 1957, initiated by Dr. Martin Luther King, Jr. The social upheaval of the desegregation movement of the 1960s eradicated Jim Crow, and created the legal reforms essential in the construction of a truly biracial democracy in the South. Yet by 1964, only 103 blacks were elected officials across the entire nation, and only 16 were in the South.

In the last two decades, the historic pattern of racial exclusion within the American electoral apparatus has been steadily reversed. Ten years after the passage of the Voting Rights Act by Congress, there were 3,503 black elected officials. Of these, there were 18 in Congress, 281 state legislators, and 135 mayors. For the first time in U.S. history, black women began to assume a visible leadership in the political process. In 1975, 12.5% of all blacks elected to state legislatures and 15.1% of all Afro-American elected officials were women. In national politics, blacks were the principal electoral bloc responsible for the election of Jimmy Carter to the presidency in 1976. In 13 states—including Ohio, Mississippi, New York, Pennsylvania, Texas, and Alabama—the black vote provided Carter's margin of victory over the incumbent President, Gerald Ford. In municipal elections, black mayoral victories began with Carl Stokes's triumph

in Cleveland in 1967. With the critical assistance of black nationalists, Kenneth Gibson was elected mayor of Newark, New Jersey;
attorney Maynard Jackson defeated a white corporate "liberal"
to become Atlanta's first black mayor in 1973; Coleman Young,
a political figure with deep roots in both leftist and black working-
class politics during the Cold War, became Detroit's mayor in
1973. Even Birmingham, the "citadel" of racial segregation in
the Deep South, elected Richard Arrington mayor in 1979.

The central dilemma confronting this first generation of black
mayors in the post-civil rights period was created by the crisis
of late capitalism. Most of the cities they managed—Newark,
Hartford, Chicago, Detroit, Cleveland—suffered from an exodus
of industry and a declining tax base. Essential city services
gradually deteriorated in the 1960s, as public capital was not
reinvested into the basic economic infrastructure. The white
upper-middle class fled to the suburbs by the millions, as the
urban cores rapidly began to reflect the images of Dresden—
bombed-out buildings, crumbling city streets, faulty sewage
systems, disintegrating public transportation systems. Federal
reductions in urban aid and social services to the poor made
the situation worse. Leaders of the corporate sector demanded
that black urban officials implement austerity policies towards
public employees and advocated sizable tax incentives to promote private investment within the central cities. Many black
officials capitulated to their demands—notably Maynard Jackson,
who in 1977 ruthlessly crushed a strike of black sanitation workers
who earned an average annual income of $7,400. Others, most
prominently Los Angeles Mayor Thomas Bradley, a former police
official, had always been enthusiastic proponents of corporate
interests. Increasingly, black mayors were placed in a quasi-
neocolonial posture: they depended upon black votes to
guarantee their success at the polls, but once elected, they
often implemented public policies that contradicted their constituency's material interests. They had assumed "electoral responsibility," yet they had no power to resolve the crisis created
by capital.

By 1983, there were more than 5,500 black elected officials.

Yet their rapid increase in numbers did not correspond to any
meaningful improvement in the socioeconomic plight of the
black working class. Despite the marginal growth of a small
black middle class, the living standards of the majority of low
to moderate income earners within the black community declined
in the 1970s and the early 1980s. As late as 1975, one million
black families lived in housing units that had no toilets or incomplete plumbing facilities. Mortality rates for black women during
childbirth are still over three times higher than those for white
women. Black youth unemployment exceeds 50% nationally,
and in some impoverished urban areas, joblessness reached
80% for youth in 1984. Black adult unemployment averages
have doubled in the past decade. More than half of all black
children under the age of 18 now live in single-parent households.
Black elected officials, particularly in urban areas, have little
choice except to respond to the urban crisis by pressing for
socioeconomic reforms that would be viewed as on the liberal
or left spectrum of American politics. A socioeconomic profile of the 435 congressional districts shows that black and
Hispanic congressmen represent 6 of the 10 districts that the
Census Bureau has placed in its lowest per capita income
category, and 8 of the 10 districts with the most families living
below the poverty line.

The recent instances of harassment of black elected officials
must be comprehended against this steadily deteriorating
socioeconomic profile of the national black community. For
example: the imprisonment of former Tchula, Mississippi Mayor
Eddie Carthan, and New York City Councilman Samuel D.
Wright; the murder of Pertis Williams, former city alderman
in Brookhaven, Mississippi, on August 22, 1983; the indictment of Theodore McFarlin, South Carolina's first black sheriff
since Reconstruction, in October 1982; and the indictment of
Kenneth A. Gibson, Mayor of Newark, New Jersey. While these
cases may not constitute a specific "conspiracy" or coordinated
campaign to undermine or circumscribe black elected leaders
in narrowly legal terms, the majority of recent instances of
harassment, indictment, and even executions of black elected

officials indicate a clear pattern. First, the majority of these
cases since 1975 have occurred in congressional districts or political
units with a high density of blacks or national minorities. As
a rule, these districts have abnormally high unemployment
rates and deteriorating housing, and suffer from a lack of adequate social services.

Tchula, Mississippi and Newark, New Jersey, for example,
do not appear to have much in common at first glance. Tchula
has a population of 3,000 and is located in the rural Mississippi
delta; Newark is the largest urban center of a highly commer-
cialized state. Yet Tchula's population is 85% black, over twice
the black percentage for the state; 30% of the town's adults
are unemployed; over 80% of the housing units are classified
as "deteriorating"; and 66% of the population is eligible for
public assistance. Holmes County, Mississippi is the 10th-poorest
county in the United States. The black sections of Newark that
make up the electoral base of Mayor Gibson are almost identical in terms of socioeconomic condition. Only 18.2% of the
Newark metropolitan area's 2,928 black-owned firms have a
single paid employee. Newark's major black-owned firms, which
fall into the category of selected services, have average annual
gross receipts of only $17,778. Youth unemployment is higher
than the national average, and many major employers have
left the downtown area, intensifying the problem of jobs. Both
Carthan and Gibson were political "mavericks"—that is, both
developed a political base outside of the traditional Democratic
Party organizations in their respective counties. Both were identified with social reform programs that attempted to address
the socioeconomic problems of their black and low-income constituents. And both were the first black mayors to be elected
in their respective towns. Other parallels in dozens of cases
can be cited: the harassment of black elected officials is part
of an unambiguous process of intimidating the black vote and
negating the institutional gains achieved by the civil rights movement two decades ago.

In the 1980s, a new current of black politics began to assert
itself, largely outside the institutional framework of bourgeois

democracy. It was evident in the streets of Liberty City, the black ghetto of Miami, when thousands of outraged youths, poor people, and even members of the black petty bourgeoisie took to the streets in rebellion in May 1980. It was expressed in the development of a politically advanced program calling for "Jobs, Peace, and Freedom" at the March on Washington, D.C., on August 27, 1983. A clearly anti-corporate, anti-racist politics began to crystallize across the nation, expressing itself not only in direct opposition to the ruthless policies of the Reagan administration, but also in a level of direct political participation heretofore unknown in recent American history. Millions of black people of different classes—but led chiefly by the urban working class—had begun explicitly to reject the institutional barriers that perpetuated high black unemployment, police brutality, poor health care and educational systems, and the near-total lack of justice within the courts. A new black social movement, far more class-conscious than ever before, was struggling to be born.

The authors in this volume address the dynamics of the new black social protest movement in the context of electoral politics. However, capital is quite unambiguously aware of the radical portents inherent in this latest wave of black activism. For example, in the 1983 Chicago mayoral election, corporations invested over $10 million in incumbent Jane Byrne's campaign against black Congressman Harold Washington. Their gift was no expression of civic charity. Byrne had already given $205 million to subsidize the city's real estate developers; hundreds of millions of dollars were therefore cut from essential services to black and white workers and the unemployed. Corporate executives recognized that the Washington campaign was in essence an anti-corporate movement, a proletarian-driven protest that created the possibility of unprecedented links across the color line in that racially divided city. Similarly, the Mel King campaign in Boston revealed the profound institutional racism within the city's political economy. King's campaign as a publicly identifiable socialist was one of the first instances in recent years in which a left mayoral candidate was able to obtain sizable shares of both national minority and liberal-left white votes.

The 1984 presidential campaign of Jesse Jackson was the logical and inevitable by-product of the Washington and King campaigns the year before. Viewed historically, the campaign represented one of the most remarkable events in modern American political culture. Without much money, virtually no television or newspaper advertisements, and against the nearly united opposition of the black political establishment, Jackson swept the national black electorate and a surprisingly high percentage of Hispanic and white voters. The essential factor in Jackson's success was the fact that the campaign became a broadly democratic social protest movement, initiated and led by black people, which *assumed an electoral form*. The most dramatic evidence of this can be found in black voter participation rates. In the Southern primaries, 45% of all black voters went to the polls, while barely 30% of all whites voted. In Illinois, black voters compose only 13% of the total electorate—but 28% of the Illinois vote in the March primary was black. Atlanta's Voter Registration Project estimated that Jackson's campaign was responsible for registering approximately 150,000 voters in Alabama, Louisiana, Georgia, North Carolina, and South Carolina. Nationally, roughly one fifth of Jackson voters had *never* gone to the polls before.

The initial caucus voting in Virginia on March 25 illustrated that Jackson's campaign, unlike that of Mondale and Hart, was a grassroots protest movement. In Norfolk, a city that is 35% black, a huge black turnout gave Jackson all 163 delegates from the city. In Virginia Beach, a town with only 10% black voters, black participation gave Jackson a plurality victory of 62 delegates, versus Mondale's 50 delegates and Hart's 30 delegates. One *New York Times* reporter noted, "At some sites party leaders ran out of registration forms. At others, participants had to stand in line for a couple of hours before they could get in. Throughout the Tidewater area, Jackson supporters filled the streets, using bull horns to exhort people to vote and distributing fliers and maps." Statewide, Jackson won 31% of Virginia's vote in the early delegate selection process.

The Jackson campaign began to successfully bridge the color line, and despite gross misinterpretations from the media, it never was solely a black campaign. In Montana, for instance, with a population less than one half of 1% black, Jackson won 5% of that state's votes in Democratic caucuses. Despite the predictions of polls in Connecticut that Jackson would receive less than 5% of the vote, he won 12%, or 26,388 votes. Significantly, only 6% of Connecticut's population is black. In Vermont and Rhode Island, Jackson won third place with 8%. And in California, only half of the 8,000 participants in Jackson's Democratic caucuses were black: 28% were white, 14% Hispanic, 7% Asian, and 1% American Indian. The numbers of white liberal-leftists, peace activists, environmentalists, and feminists who actively supported Jackson were surprisingly large, given the profoundly racist character of American political culture. Jackson attributed the problem of winning white support to "whites' lack of regard for the intelligence and hard work of black people. It remains a moral challenge, however, to white leadership to make judgments based on character and not based on race."

Jackson's race clearly illustrated the *lack of democracy* within the Democratic Party and within the American political system. In Mississippi, Jackson trounced Democratic candidates Walter Mondale and Gary Hart, winning almost half of the votes in the March 17 caucuses, but because of the state's regressive caucus rules, Jackson and Mondale received roughly the same number of delegates. In Illinois, Jackson won a fifth of the statewide vote, but obtained no delegates. In Arkansas, Mondale narrowly defeated Jackson in statewide caucuses, 6,411 votes to 6,011, while Hart ran a poor third—but Mondale was given 20 delegates, Hart received 9, and Jackson only 6. In South Carolina, white Democrats blocked efforts to endorse Jackson as their "favorite-son" presidential candidate. One frustrated Jackson supporter, Clarendon County party chairman Billy Fleming, told the press, "If Jesse Jackson were a white man this would not be happening." Even the House Democratic Study Group, meeting after the New Hampshire primary, drafted a joint fund-raising letter to aid House candidates with Mondale's and Hart's signatures. After mailing 60,000 letters, someone finally noticed that Jackson was *still* in the race, and hadn't been invited to sign!

Between caucus gerrymandering and repeated snubs from national Democratic officials, the Jackson campaign represented a genuine challenge to democratize the Democratic Party. The Jackson race also demonstrated the failure of leadership within the national black community, and the ineptitude of the majority of its elected officials to express the interests of blacks. In Alabama, Birmingham Mayor Richard Arrington and Joe Reed, chairman of the all-black Alabama Democratic Conference, urged blacks to "be realistic" and not to "throw their votes away." A majority of Alabama blacks still voted for Jackson. In Georgia, Atlanta Mayor Andrew Young and Coretta Scott King championed Mondale's credentials—but over two thirds of the black electorate went with Jackson. In Illinois, 79% of Afro-American voters supported Jackson. The "lesser-of-two-evils" line offered by black Mondale proponents was effectively defeated.

Finally, something must be noted about the internal contradictions within the campaign that modified, if not entirely negated, its full progressive potential. Most of the principal advisers in the campaign—including Mayor Richard Hatcher of Gary, Indiana, national campaign director Arnold Pinckney, Congressman Walter Fauntroy, New York businessman Eugene Jackson, and former Manhattan Borough President Percy Sutton—were moderates within the black political spectrum. Other than New York State Assemblyman Al Vann of Brooklyn and California Assemblywoman Maxine Waters, most of Jackson's key aides tried to keep the mobilization within the safe boundaries of status quo politics. Most had no desire to "burn their bridges" with the Mondale forces, since their conceptualization of Jackson's campaign was clouded by their own parochial ambitions. Thus, when Jackson was debating whether to accept an invitation to travel to Nicaragua in February 1984, his advisers overwhelmingly urged him not to go. Pinckney finally had to fly to New Hampshire to insist that Jackson stay home. Despite these moderating factors, the Jackson campaign became something larger than the candidate himself. It represented a new stage of political history that transcends the limitations of the civil rights and desegregation era. No longer will any white liberal Democratic presidential candidate take the black electorate for granted. No genuine coalitions across racial barriers can occur unless they are forged on the basis of equality—and the Jackson campaign created the terms for such coalitions.

No one can predetermine the patterns of black urban politics in the near future. It seems certain, however, that black socialists like Detroit's Ken Cockrel and Boston's Mel King represent the next generation of class-conscious, activist-oriented leaders who, in increasing numbers, are emerging from black workers' struggles. The recent Jackson presidential campaign has served not only to register several million black and poor people, but has served as a necessary training ground for thousands of politically committed young black activists. The road to black political power, as these essays suggest, lies in the fundamental restructuring of the capitalist political economy, and in the empowerment of historically oppressed classes, national minorities, and women. The recent struggles in Boston, Chicago, Detroit, Oakland, and hundreds of other cities across this country are simply the first chapter in that fundamental process to create effective grassroots democracy in America.

Introduction

Black Enfranchisement, Jesse Jackson, and Beyond

Rod Bush

Black Enfranchisement, Jesse Jackson, and Beyond

No matter what your political persuasion, it hardly seems debatable that the rise of the black electorate as a force in local and national politics is one of the most important phenomena of the 1980s. It is not that black people are becoming a political force for the first time, but the dramatic impact of black electoral strength now being revealed has extremely important implications for the future of American politics. The purpose of this study is to analyze the significance of this "new black vote," beyond the personalities that it has thrust into national and international prominence. Any such study must begin with an analysis of the significance of the Jesse Jackson candidacy for President of the United States.

From the time that Jackson announced his intention of running for the presidency of the United States in 1983, there was heated debate among progressive political activists about the merits of a Jesse Jackson candidacy. Some argued from a pragmatic point of view that it did not make sense to support Jackson, that black people must maximize their political investment, which meant supporting Walter Mondale, whether we liked it or not. Others argued, especially in the initial stages, that Jesse Jackson could not be trusted, that he was a political chameleon who moved with the opportunity of the moment, and that more than likely he sought personal gain rather than the enhancement of the political strength of the black community or the movement of national politics in a progressive direction. A third position, probably the dominant one among black progressives and on the left, was that it was important to support the Jackson campaign because of its potential progressive impact on the political process, the Democratic Party, the involvement of progressive political activists in a national movement, and the building of an independent political movement at the national level.

I would like to come down on the side of a variant of the third position. It seems useless to me to get involved in a guessing game about what Jesse Jackson would do as an individual. Everyone has a political history, and I would presume that many of us have changed our political definition of ourselves over time, including our attitude toward pragmatic politics. What seems to me to be most important about the phenomenon of "Run, Jesse, Run" is the response of the black electorate, and what that tells us about where black people are at politically. Why did 89% of the black vote in New York go to Jesse Jackson? Why did 74% of the black vote in Pennsylvania go to Jesse Jackson? Why did 74% of the black vote in Illinois go to Jesse Jackson?[1] How indeed did Jackson win in Louisiana (which does not have a black majority)? All of this in opposition to the black political establishment! And why, in opposition to the endorsement of the AFL-CIO and contrary to the vote of white trade-union members, did 77-82% of the black trade unionists in Illinois, New York, Pennsylvania, and Ohio vote for Jesse Jackson?[2]

It seems to me that something is going on here that we ought to understand, and it is a separate point from the "bowing to spontaneity" of the left. Perhaps the left was so intoxicated by being presented with the opening to be involved in a "relevant" national movement that it did not do an independent analysis. I agree with the sentiments of friends who say that this must be done if we are to build a movement with broader aspirations than the Jackson campaign.

Nonetheless, I do not think that we can dismiss the response of the black community to the Jackson campaign by calling it a "spontaneous moment" in history. We need to understand why black people turned out in such numbers for Jackson, just as we need to know why they did so for Harold Washington in Chicago, for Mel King in Boston, for Ken Cockrel in Detroit, and for a number of progressive black politicians in Oakland, California.

It may in fact be true, as some argue, that the reasons are different, that local campaigns like the Harold Washington campaign build from the ground up, that they represent the construction of a political movement from concrete instances of organized protest, and thus represent a real groundswell from the grassroots. But if Jackson is not perceived as having a "real groundswell from the grassroots," it does not follow that the only way to view his campaign is within the context of Jackson's motives, which are presumed to be the classic case of a rising petty bourgeoisie seeking its place in the existing social order of the United States.

It seems to me that there are a number of reasons why black people gave such overwhelming support to Jesse Jackson in the Democratic Party primary. First of all, he is a credible candidate. He is poised, reasonable, and witty. He is charismatic and carries a certain moral authority. He can play to the media even better than Ronald Reagan, which we all knew. He is politically smart, and can seize the time, as he did with the Syria intervention. If Jackson were not black, there would be no contest from the standpoint of popular commercial politics as they traditionally have operated in the United States. Even many whites have expressed admiration and respect for Jackson, although few are voting for him. Many middle-class and older black people support him because they see him as a positive role model for black children, as an alternative to Michael Jackson and Mr. T. Even if Jackson says that he is trying to restore hope among black people in the democratic system, that is beside the point. Jackson himself speaks to the purpose of his campaign. He has remarked that voting for Mondale or Hart in the primary means "getting off a Republican elephant and onto a Democratic donkey going in the same direction, just a little slower. We need a new direction. It is better to

lose an election going in the right direction than to win going
in the wrong direction."[3]

My point here is that we must appreciate and learn from
the "spontaneous" motion of the majority of black people and
use it to inform our analysis. I believe that the level of discussion must be raised beyond whether or not we are being "Jackson
symps," for black people have learned a great deal from our
collective struggle for freedom, justice, and equality in America,
and are not about to be dupes for Jesse Jackson or anyone
else. Even the black middle-class readership of *Black Enterprise* magazine, in a 1980 poll of 5,000 respondents, failed to
express confidence in the established black leadership.[4] The
poll showed that 73.3% of the respondents did not think that
there is effective black leadership. If this is true of those segments
of the black population who are "making it" and who believe
in the system, it takes no special genius to deduce what must
be the attitude of the majority of the black population, who
are not "making it." Case in point: When Jesse Jackson, Ben
Hooks, Andrew Young, and Joseph Lowery rushed to Miami
in an attempt to calm the angry black community from avenging
the brutal murder of black insurance executive Arthur McDuffie,
they were told to go home. From their own experience with
politicians and political activists, black people have become
very careful scrutinizers.

I don't think that there has ever been a question in the
minds of most people in the black community that the Jackson
campaign is somehow "the" answer, or that black people are
pinning all of their hopes for attaining justice and equality
in America on the outcome of this campaign. It seems to me
that black people see the opportunity to advance our collective situation in the United States through support for this
candidacy, and are acting in accordance with that understanding. It is not "revolutionary"—but then neither was the civil
rights movement, which was extremely significant for American
politics in the postwar period, especially in the sense that it
broke through the silence imposed by McCarthyism and provided the space and inspiration for the revival of progressive

politics in the United States. The essence of my argument is that the black community's support for the Jackson candidacy is a continuation of the black struggle for justice and equality in America and beyond.

Throughout history, black people have rebelled against their domination—from insurrection on the slave ships and plantations, to sabotage by slaves, to sit-ins in the 1960s, to rebellions in the inner cities. The list could go on. Black people have also petitioned the government to act in a responsible way toward us, to grant us our due democratic rights, to end our status as second-class citizens, to fulfill its duties toward promoting the general welfare. Many analysts have noted that there is a duality among black people, that there have been two separate thrusts in response to the racist and inequitable social order confronting us. One thrust has been toward greater integration into American society (the NAACP, Urban League, the Niagara Movement, the civil rights movement, Martin Luther King, etc.). The other thrust has been toward separation from American society: black nationalism (Garvey's United Negro Improvement Association, the Nation of Islam, Malcolm X, etc.).

Many observers are disturbed about what seems to be the inability to reconcile the chasm between the nationalist tradition and the integrationist-assimilationist tradition. I would argue that these two traditions simply reflect the duality of black reality in the United States. It is crucial for us to get beyond the debates about whether black people are part of the American nation or whether we are a separate people. It seems to me that we are both a part of the American nation and a people apart. We are different from the Irish, Italians, Germans, Poles, and others because we did not come to America voluntarily; we were enslaved. And we were not merely subjected to ethnic discrimination, but to a systematic and institutionalized racism, and further were deemed to be subhuman. Black nationalism is not *simply* a political strategy chosen by some actors because they feel that it is the best way to advance their interests (although this is certainly true of some black nationalists). It arises from the community of interests developed by black people in resisting the degradation of a racist society, and from a particular culture that enabled black people to exist with dignity and to survive under very difficult conditions. At the same time, the black working class is part of the great multinational working class, and its aspirations represent the most advanced form of the historic thrust of the entire U.S. working class for equality and social justice.

If we can agree that the duality expressed in the black struggle reflects a real duality, it is also important to understand the significance of the existence of black people as a people apart. The fact that we are a people apart in U.S. society makes it easier for us to avoid the white male American nationalism that infects large sections of the organized, skilled working class in the United States, as well as large parts of the American people, black and white, as a whole.

The point here is that as part of the legacy of being a people apart, especially as a people who did not fully share in the "unlimited prosperity" of the "American Century," as second-class citizens, black people identify much less than most with the interests of the American state as the policeman of the world. Moreover, as a dispersed people, as members of a black diaspora, it is easier for us (like immigrant workers) to comprehend that what we confront is not just the American state and national economy, but a world social order.

I cannot go into detail here, but would like to point out that the importance of nationalism within the U.S. working class is in its attachment to what has been a hegemonic power in the world-system, one that plays the role of keeping the world safe for imperialism. This is not at all to imply that nationalism within the U.S. working class is an exception. The fact that workers' movements act within a national context is the material basis for this nationalism. One of the most clever deceptions of the system is to maintain the focus of its working classes—especially the working classes in the advanced capitalist countries—on the nation-state, and to insist that this is the proper unit of analysis. In reality, the world is a social whole; it is a capitalist world-economy; and states, peoples, and classes are all institutions of the world-economy. Viewing the nation-state as the unit of analysis has been one of the most important sources of the promotion of status quo politics by the organized working class of the advanced capitalist countries and of reformism within the workers' movements of these core capitalist countries. In the United States, the socialist movement tried to build militant organization within the trade and skilled sections of the working class, whereas superexploitation of workers in the Third World and of sectors of the U.S. working class made possible the most state-regulated and class-collaborationist unions, resulting in workers who were both pro-capitalist and pro-imperialist.

In the postwar social order of the United States, it has been precisely the combination of Cold War liberalism and a class-collaborationist and pro-imperialist labor movement that is the basis for the weakness of the progressive political movement. At this historical conjuncture, black people represent a threat to status quo politics because they were excluded from the benefits of the "American Century" of unlimited prosperity, although not totally. Furthermore, the period of unprecedented economic expansion that made possible many of the concessions made during the 1960s has come to an end, and it is unlikely that any future recovery will restore the relatively high wages associated with that era—not for the traditional blue-collar working class, and certainly not for the black working class.

Jesse Jackson's concept of a Rainbow Coalition is a recognition of the deep alterations in the U.S. political economy that will be necessary if black people are to achieve justice and equality in the United States. Furthermore, it is a recognition of the potential for the black movement to inspire class unity among the lower and deeper working class, even if Jackson does not use this kind of language. What else could be the unity of blacks, Latinos, Asians, women, and immigrant labor, if it is not their status as superexploited members of the work force?

But again we should not lose sight of the fact that the world is a social whole. That is why we should not look at such a movement as the movement of a minority and thus limited in what it can achieve. For not only should we see the potential for class unity within the United States, but also the potential for making alliances with political forces beyond the U.S. border, as some of Jackson's foreign policy positions suggest.

I would like to look at a segment of black history from an aerial view to suggest the possibilities in viewing both black history and the future evolution of black politics within the context of a world-systems perspective. As we all know, in the War Between the States, black people sided with the Union, and contributed in no small measure to the ensuing victory of the Union forces. In the immediate postwar period, the alliance between black people and the Union was consolidated by the radical policies of the Reconstruction period. As a matter of fact, the Reconstruction period was one of the first indications of the profoundly democratic impact of black people on the United States.

Indeed, W.E.B. Du Bois describes Reconstruction as the "most magnificent drama in the last thousand years of human history...the transportation of ten million human beings out of the dark beauty of their mother continent into the new-found Eldorado of the West. They descended into Hell; and in the Third Century they arose from the dead, in the finest effort to achieve democracy for the working millions that the world has ever seen. It was a tragedy that beggared the Greek; it was an upheaval of humanity like the Reformation and the French Revolution....Yet...we discern in it no part in our labor movement."[5]

Furthermore, the reforms attendant to Reconstruction threatened to jeopardize the supply of cheap labor that was the foundation of the South's economy (based on King Cotton). And the disruption of the cotton economy threatened to stop the smooth flow of cheap cotton on which the textile mills of the Northeast and the American export economy had come to depend. So, increasingly, theories of racial equality were summarily unconvincing to Northeastern industrialists in the face of rising prices of raw cotton.

This contradiction provided the context for the Compromise of 1877 and the subsequent dismissal of the sociopolitical status of black people from the national agenda. Along with the relaxation of the radical Reconstruction policies came the gradual establishment of Jim Crow, which essentially was a system to reconstitute and maintain a pool of cheap black labor.

The harmony of interests between the Southern agricultural capitalists and the Northern industrial capitalists was not permanent. When World War I interrupted the flow of European immigrants into Northern industries, just as war production was pushing the demand for labor to record levels, black workers were among those sought to fulfill that demand. At the same time, the movement of the United States from semi-peripheral to core status in the world-economy, and consequently from debtor to creditor nation, undermined the importance of King Cotton and the need for black labor in the South.

This set of circumstances set in motion the most massive migration of people in the country's history. During the period from 1910 to 1960, nearly 5 million black people left the South. It is significant, moreover, that this out-migration was drawn disproportionately from the states with the lowest black registration percentages, and that black people settled mostly in seven key Northern states: New York, New Jersey, Pennsylvania, Ohio, California, Illinois, and Michigan. According to Brink and Harris, "No candidate for president in modern times has won without a significant share of the vote from the big seven."[6]

The increasing sophistication of the black electorate, its key location in the heart of industrial America, and its potential for establishing a political agenda beyond that of the old liberal coalition is the drama that is being played out before our eyes. Furthermore, within the context of our understanding that we confront a world-capitalist social order, we should not simply view the struggles of black people as a minority. This does not mean, however, that we do not see the development of a massive movement in the United States against the oligarchic power of our ruling elite. This brings us back to Jesse Jackson's point about going in the right direction.

The truth of the matter is that the American people as a whole play a very minor role, in proportion to our numerical strength, in the social direction and commitments of the nation. The rules of the game of political life are heavily biased in favor of those who own or control the resources to fashion or use them. The requisite resources are money, property, and control of information and communication. Nonetheless, one of the sources of stability of the great nation-states of North America and Western Europe is the belief held by the majority of the people that they can make democratic decisions about the course of the nation. Marlene Dixon's essay on electoral politics in a pre-revolutionary period points out: "The Constitution and the pretense of popular sovereignty and democracy are the vulnerable underbelly of an oligarchic rule otherwise awesome in the breadth and depth of its control over society. To enable the rulers to rule in such a context, every effort has been made to assure the exclusion from the process of the most exploited lower and deeper working-class populations."[7] If Jesse Jackson's campaign contributes to the mobilization of this sector of the electorate, then why not support it?

The point of my argument is that the participation of the black community in the Jesse Jackson campaign represents a continuation of the black struggle for peace, justice, and equality. I believe that the studies in this book on the Harold Washington campaign in Chicago, the Mel King campaign in Boston, the experience of Ken Cockrel in Detroit, and the Black Panther Party and the Peace and Justice Organization in Oakland demonstrate this same truth. Now I will briefly review the studies of black and progressive electoral activism in these four cities.

THE HAROLD WASHINGTON CAMPAIGN IN CHICAGO

Alkalimat and Gills's study of the Harold Washington campaign dramatically illustrates the way in which the "new black vote" has become a dynamic force in American politics. The electoral defeat of the infamous Democratic Party machine in Chicago is surely one of the most significant political events of the decade. For that reason, the political lessons drawn by Alkalimat and Gills from their participation in and analysis of the Washington campaign are invaluable. Their starting point is that independent black politics emerged in the wake of and interrelated with the massive civil rights movement of the 1960s.

Their study begins with the long period of machine domination of Chicago politics during which there was no attempt to mobilize the black community in any serious way because machine politics did not work when there was a large voter turnout. The operation of the Democratic Party machine in a city with multiple ethnic groups like Chicago was very simple: each interest group was co-opted and held together by exchanging material rewards for delivery of votes, based on precinct organizing within the wards. Jobs and other economic benefits were provided partially in proportion to voting strength and partially in proportion to the status of the ethnic group.

The purpose of the Alkalimat and Gills study is to describe the groundswell of opposition to machine-backed and elite policies that formed the basis of the victorious Washington coalition. The black community and their rejection of what Alkalimat and Gills characterize as "plantation politics" formed the center of the coalition, but the involvement of the most active sectors of the grassroots white and Latino communities was critical to putting Harold Washington into office.

According to Alkalimat and Gills, one of the key organizations in the development of the Washington coalition was a group called POWER (People Organized for Welfare and Economic Reform). This group was formed in response to the Reagan austerity program, to an equally rapacious attack on the living standards of the working class by Illinois Governor James Thompson, and to Mayor Jane Byrne, who was a silent accomplice. The social base of POWER was among the growing number of skilled and unskilled workers being added to the ranks of the poor white, black, and Latino unemployed, and the expanding number of welfare-dependent family heads in the Chicago area.

POWER was instrumental in the development of the political base that fueled the spontaneous upsurge of protest and electoral participation in the summer and fall of 1982, and in the winter of 1983, the period directly preceding the Harold Washington campaign. In the various reform movements that arose to deal with specific conditions, POWER's leadership played an important role in politicizing them to focus on increased electoral participation. POWER also spearheaded the voter registration drives that eventually resulted in 180,000 new voters being placed on the rolls.

The key to the forging of the victorious Washington coalition was the creation of linkages of organizations and community activists involved in struggles around basically "economic issues," building citywide networks. When these networks targeted City Hall, it signaled the beginning of the demise of the Democratic Party machine from its position of unchallenged dominance in the Chicago political arena.

A careful study of Chicago's demographics by the Chicago Urban League alerted Chicago political activists, if they did not already know, that since black people were approaching a numerical plurality in the city, the 1983 mayoral race could give black people the opportunity to determine who controls resource allocation through city administrative departments, boards, and commissions. The Urban League study also noted that shortly afterwards, control of the City Council would be at stake. The Urban League, however, was pessimistic about black people taking advantage of their numerical strength by participating in the election in sufficient numbers. It held the position that lack of electoral participation in the black community was a long-term, deeply rooted structural problem.

As we all know, this did not turn out to be the case. However, I think that it is important to point out that the Urban League's analysis could be interpreted to mean that a long process of political education would be needed before blacks would be willing to participate in electoral activity in sufficient numbers to take advantage of their numerical strength. I disagree with the implication that the reason for lack of electoral participation in the black community is that black people do not know how to move in their own interests, which seems to be the implicit assumption of most liberal analysts. It stems more from a sober and prudent assessment of the real possibilities. Of course, getting the word out is important, but I would argue that what we are designating as the "new black vote" is proof that the black electorate are considerably more sophisticated than most political analysts (and many black and white politicians) think they are.

The implicit assumption of the groups who organized the massive voter registration campaign that added 180,000 new voters to the rolls seems to have been that the black community would take advantage of an opportunity to increase their political strength. Newer groups like Chicago Black United Communities (CBUC), Citizens for Self-Determination, POWER, People's Movement for Voter Registration, and Vote Community joined with old-line groups like PUSH in this massive voter registration drive, nearly doubling Harold Washington's condition that 100,000 new voters be added to the rolls before he would run.

The next question for any practical politician was: would they turn out to vote, given that only 27.5% turned out in the black community in Harold Washington's 1977 run against Bilandic and Pucinski, and only 34% had turned out in the 1979 race between Byrne and Bilandic. In November 1982, Chicago political activists received their answer when the black community turned out overwhelmingly against Illinois Governor Thompson and provided the margin of victory for a non-machine candidate for the Cook County Board of Supervisors.

Alkalimat and Gills characterize Harold Washington as a political standard-bearer of the black community, with whom community leaders from all sectors of black Chicago had to keep in step, or be cast aside. First as an Illinois state assemblyman, then as a state senator, and finally as a U.S. congressman from Illinois, Washington consistently compiled an outstanding record. Although he was a member of Congress for less than two terms, he led the successful fight for the extension of the Voting Rights Act and the fight against

Reagan's proposed MX Missile program. He also introduced legislation for an emergency jobs program in the winter of 1982 and worked with the Congressional Black Caucus to propose budgetary alternatives to Reagan's fiscal plans, among other things.

And the proof that the black community would move in their own interest when the opportunity was ripe is that black voter turnout increased from 52.2% in 1979 to 73.7% in the 1983 primary election. Washington won 77.7% of the vote in the wards that were more than 90% black, but only 1% of the vote in the wards that were more than 90% white.

After the primary, the white backlash started with a vengeance. Byrne attempted to mount a write-in candidacy that eventually had to be torpedoed by the national Democratic Party, which feared that the defection of the local Democratic Party from the Washington campaign would be disastrous for the party in the 1984 presidential race. But although the local party organization endorsed Washington, they did little to support his candidacy and several of them supported Bernard Epton, the Republican candidate for mayor. As far as Epton himself was concerned, he had a solid reputation as a liberal Republican, but was overcome by his ambition to win and capitulated to the temptation to take advantage of the white backlash. Thus the theme of his campaign was a thinly disguised racist appeal: "Vote for Bernard Epton before it is too late." In the course of the campaign Epton stopped dealing with any substantive issues and focused solely on attacking Washington.

In the general election campaign, Washington focused on jobs and economic development, opposition to the machine and patronage politics, and opening up the process of government decision-making to neighborhood activists. Washington declared that the refutation of Epton was a step toward the defeat of Reagan in 1984. Yet Alkalimat and Gills caution that, despite Washington's militant attacks on patronage and his avowal of open government, his fiscal policies are conservative (i.e., rigid fiscal controls, balanced budget, attention to bond ratings, positive relations with lending institutions, etc.). They believe that Washington's program contains some elements of an austerity program that blacks would not find acceptable under a white mayor.

Washington won the general election by less than 50,000 votes in one of the closest mayoral races since the advent of machine politics in Chicago. Washington received 98% of the votes in the black wards, 74% of the votes in the Latino wards, and 12% of the votes in the white wards. Alkalimat and Gills point out that the key here is the dramatic increase in support for Washington among the Latino electorate. Most revealing, on the other hand, was the low level of support for Washington in the nominally liberal and progressive Lake Front wards, where Washington only received 24% of the vote.

What then do we make of the Washington victory? Alkalimat and Gills describe five factors that have been adduced to explain the electoral success of black mayors: 1) mobilization of the black community, 2) building broad support, 3) campaign organization, 4) candidate viability, and 5) the city's need for crisis management. The Washington campaign represented a repudiation of business and politics as usual by the black community. In the midst of fiscal crisis, reduction in federal assistance, a decline in the industrial tax base, a decline in public services, and increased attacks on the basic standard of living— at such critical junctures in local politics, a Harold Washington is drafted, not in the corporate headquarters of LaSalle Street, and not in the smoke-filled rooms of the Democratic Party machine, but by the black community itself.

A brief note about the campaign structure should give the reader a sense of the social base of the campaign. The formal campaign structure was initially controlled by black nationalists and community activists. Renault Robinson of the Afro-American Patrolmen's League was the first campaign manager. He was replaced by Al Raby, a civil rights activist who had broad ties with black institutional leaders and the white liberal community. Outside of the formal campaign structure was a group called the Task Force for Black Political Empowerment, composed of the leaders of some 50 community organizations, ministers, politicians, and professionals. Organizations included PUSH, CBUC, the Black United Front of Chicago, the Chicago chapter of the National Black Independent Political Party, Vote Community, People's Movement for Voter Registration, Peoples College, and others. Individuals from organizations as diverse as the CPUSA and the Black Methodist Ministers Alliance were involved. Alkalimat and Gills clearly had hoped that such a body could have advanced the movement as a whole beyond the limitations of the Washington campaign, but do not believe that it accomplished that goal. The Task Force did play a major role in mobilizing the black community in the primary, a process that played an important role in reinvigorating organizations like PUSH and CBUC.

In conclusion, Alkalimat and Gills characterize what happened in Chicago as a black power vote against a white power structure, but not as a fundamental challenge to the social system that government administers. Nevertheless, the white backlash results from the contradictions of pursuing equality of opportunity in a period of economic decline. This is unlike the 1960s, when reforms that opened the society up for blacks were possible because of an expanding economy.

What Alkalimat and Gills see as the significance of the Washington campaign is precisely the way in which it represents a groundswell from the grassroots. They note that,

> The pre-campaign period was marked by an increase of community-based protests around several concrete issues (private housing, jobs, health, education) and status-representational issues (appointments of officials to the School Board, Chicago Housing Authority Board, and other boards and City Council selection). Under the Byrne administration, welfare and status goals were pursued by various segments of the Black community, joined by popular elements among Latinos and whites. These neighborhood forces targeted Jane Byrne as the symbol of both the machine and the conservative alignment of social and political forces (Reaganomics and Thompson welfare cuts) at the federal, state, and local levels. Policies had become increasingly racist in character. Thus, in order for there to be any new redistribution of resources for Blacks, the machine had to be dismantled. "Black Power," Black electoral empower-

ment, became a tactic for reform, dictating the transformation of the economic goals of struggle among the masses into a political struggle for a Black mayor, a symbol of Black power in City Hall.

This study of the Harold Washington campaign by Alkalimat and Gills is extremely important because it moves beyond cheering about the success of the Washington campaign to explaining how it happened and asking what political lessons we must draw from this campaign to inform our future efforts.

KEN COCKREL IN DETROIT

The experience of Ken Cockrel in running for and winning a seat on the Detroit City Council, and in his subsequent battles with liberal black Mayor Coleman Young, helps us in historically situating the "new black vote." The "new black vote" is in fact a historical continuation of the black struggle and is not entirely new with the Harold Washington campaign, when it most attracted public attention. Cockrel, an avowed Marxist who had been publicly associated with the Dodge Revolutionary Union Movement (DRUM), the League of Revolutionary Black Workers (the League), and the Black Workers Congress (BWC), among others, was elected to the Detroit City Council, according to his own analysis, because he had been associated with struggles around issues of material interest to the community, especially the black community. He says that he was elected in spite of being a Marxist, but at the same time pointed out that because of the history of working-class organizing in Detroit, the notion of black people flirting "with those perverse European communist ideas isn't that offensive." Cockrel points out that there has been a tradition of political struggle in Detroit by black people associated with leftist ideas. Even Mayor Coleman Young has socialist roots, given his involvement in the National Negro Labor Congress (NNLC), and issued a scathing denunciation of the House Un-American Activities Committee when it came to Detroit to investigate the NNLC's communist ties. George Crockett, who was a judge and is now a congressman, was involved in the Smith Act trials, and so forth.

The Cockrel campaign and the organization that was founded in its wake (the Detroit Alliance for a Rational Economy—DARE) were in many ways the crowning achievement of a group of political activists who had been involved in a considerable amount of political activity in Detroit in the 1960s and early 1970s in organizations such as DRUM, the League, and the Motor City Labor League, the film *Finally Got the News*, and the election of Marxist Judge Justin Ravitz to the Detroit Recorder's Court. With a campaign organization that included more than 1,000 volunteers, according to Cockrel, they ran seventh (out of nine elected seats), although Cockrel's candidacy was not endorsed by the key decision-making institutions of the black community—in particular, not by the United Auto Workers (UAW), Rev. Albert Cleage's Black Slate, the Democratic Party, or Mayor Coleman Young. Yet despite his lack of support from the black political establishment in Detroit, and the presence of six other blacks in the race, 85% of the people in the black community voted for Cockrel.

That the black community of Detroit voted so overwhelmingly for Cockrel, despite the opposition of the popular black mayor, the Democratic Party, and the UAW, illustrates the political sophistication of the "new black vote." This is why we must pay attention to the overwhelming support for the Jackson campaign from the black community. To be sure, it is always a matter of judgment when to stand on principle and when to make practical compromises (*realpolitik*), but those who always stand on political principle, regardless of the rapports-de-force, stand a fairly good chance of opting for irrelevancy rather than being a serious political force.

Cockrel's analysis of his experience clearly indicates a grasp of this; he also seems to understand that such judgments are not always so easily made. He points out that people at the local level thought that he was a "pain in the ass" because he was always raising the issue of tax abatements. Yet he "would go to congressional hearings and hear international UAW representatives talking about how cannibalistic it was for jurisdictions to be raiding each other, and so forth; how the worker loses in the regional competition. But in Detroit...these same officials were not on your side." The problem Cockrel points to is that when it gets specific, it is not a matter of speech. When the representative of the multinational corporation says " 'Do this or we will move to Oklahoma,' it breaks down a lot of rhetorical cant. . . ." Despite his acute awareness of the political realities of day-to-day politics, Cockrel is critical of some white progressives and leftists who take a "sympish" attitude toward Mayor Coleman Young, simply because he is black.

Nevertheless, it was the press's playing up of Cockrel as a "challenge to Mayor Coleman Young" that undermined DARE as a powerful organization in the black community. This occurred despite the fact that Cockrel and the DARE leadership took great care not to directly challenge the mayor. Coleman Young, however, interpreting Cockrel and DARE as a threat to his base, let it be known that support for DARE would be seen as hostility to him, thus undermining DARE's support among the black institutional leaders and eventually undermining its grassroots support. Cockrel notes very sardonically: "There's a lot of grease there when you have a one-and-a-half-billion-dollar budget...Nobody ever said we were wrong or that we sold out...They all said, 'It ain't time.' You're in trouble when you're messing with the black mayor."

It comes down to limited options, Cockrel observes. This is clear to him from listening to the speeches of the national black leadership; but he also notes that there is an impulse, expressed in "Run, Jesse, Run." Then we have Coleman Young, saying "It doesn't make any sense, Mondale's our guy." "Is he stifling the aspirations of black people or is he trying to maximize the return on the black political investment?" Cockrel does not think that this is a simple answer, but offers that while what Jackson is saying is more appealing, Coleman Young might be right (note that this interview was in August 1983), which, he adds, "is a sad comment on our options today."

Indeed, the experience of Ken Cockrel seems to be a classic

illustration of the limits of the old liberal coalition (of liberals, organized labor, and minority groups). At least a part of Cockrel's problem and that of the forces that made up DARE is that the established workers' movement in the United States, both social democratic and Marxist, has become fairly entrenched within varous sectors of the old liberal coalition, and thus represents powerful vested interests who can be expected to defend their "turf" against upstart groups such as DARE and individuals such as Cockrel. In addition to the "turf" issue there is probably some genuine concern about defending a popular and "left-leaning" liberal like Coleman Young, whom they perceive to be a "natural" leader of the community.

It is important for us to understand that we are no longer in the 1930s and that the class forces within the United States are no longer the same. As the proletarianization of the U.S. working class has proceeded, there has emerged an increasing polarization between the higher-status ethnic groups (increasingly consolidated as a white male working class after 1945) and lower-status ethnic groups (largely nonwhite and increasingly female—what Jesse Jackson refers to as the Rainbow Coalition). The "class consciousness" of the higher-status ethnic groups tends to be largely defensive, seeking to preserve their status vis-a-vis the lower working class. These strata tend to meet with elements of the professional and managerial strata of the middle class in center-left organizations, such as trade unions and liberal or socialist parties. This then forms the basis of the "nationalist" rejection of these center-left institutions among the black and brown working class, and the formation of organizations like DRUM and the League of Revolutionary Black Workers.

I do not think, and neither did Cockrel and the DARE leadership, that there are easy answers to the contradictions that we face in developing a progressive political movement, which at the same time can achieve practical benefits for those who reside at the bottom of the socioeconomic ladder in the United States. Yet we must not confuse the interests of the working-class majority of the black community with the interests of the middle-class leadership, no matter how "natural" they may appear to be.

THE MEL KING CAMPAIGN IN BOSTON

James Jennings's study of the Mel King for Mayor campaign in Boston, like the Alkalimat and Gills study, is more than a study of a political campaign in one city. Jennings's thesis is that the political thrust of black people over the next period of time will pose a serious, if not fatal, challenge to the assumptions of pluralist politics. The reason for this is that black people are at the center of the basic conflicts in most Northern cities, and their interests have been most antagonistic to established institutions.

He argues that the traditional approach to black politics is based on seeing black people as just one more ethnic group that should have the opportunity to rely on group resources to climb the socioeconomic ladder. What this conception comes down to, according to Jennings, is replacing white politicians with black politicians. He believes that the ferment of the 1960s has given rise to a new conception of black political power in which black political activism is a tool for mobilizing not only black people, but other poor and working-class people in American cities as well.

Traditional black politicians, Jennings argues, are grounded in the pluralistic assumptions of American politics and thus are content with seeking "influence" rather than "power." They accept the present system of distribution of wealth, and they only seek to be in positions to influence the powerful in one direction or the other regarding the flow of wealth and resources. Jennings calls for a new agenda wherein progressive black politicians would not seek the traditional patronage, but would confront a system of wealth distribution that is partially built on high unemployment within the black community.

Particular scorn is reserved by Jennings for the paternalistic and objectively racist role of Kevin White as Boston's mayor during his 16 years in office. Jennings asserts that under White's leadership, City Hall represented a political front for powerful and wealthy interests, and as such continually discouraged the development of progressive politics, not only in the black community, but anywhere in Boston. Kevin White, like most mayors in the post-World War II United States, served to provide a stable environment for banking, real estate, academic, commercial, and media conglomerates to actualize their political and economic goals.

Jennings provides a very compelling picture of the "metropolitan establishment" as a network of power centers, including government officials, corporate managers, law firms, accounting firms, wealthy individuals, professional associations, chambers of commerce, union leaders, dependable academics, think tanks, media executives, and, last and sometimes least, the leaders of some of the political machines in a given area. This "metropolitan establishment" is invisible and unelected, and exercises power through its control of institutions, money, property, and the lawmaking process.

So why be involved in electoral politics at all? Jennings argues that the structural position of the mayor's office would allow a progressive elected official an opportunity to initiate decisions that favor the less powerful majority in the nation's cities. In order for this to take place, however, members of the black community, who occupy strategic positions because of their socioeconomic circumstances, must be organized around a progressive agenda.

But there are a number of pitfalls for the unwary. Jennings catalogues a number of practices used by former Mayor White to thwart the development of a progressive agenda among Boston's black political activists: 1) selective use of City Hall patronage and public dollars for purposes of rewarding those who went along with his policies and punishing those who differed with him; 2) manipulation of public relations techniques to preserve his image as a liberal mayor; 3) manipulation of various electoral processes, such as voter registration, and city elections; and 4) the nurturing of "cooperative" black political leadership.

In addition to these stock techniques, Mayor White was a master of defining situations in ways that discouraged public discussion of issues that might threaten the structures and processes supporting his base of power. The overall outcome was that prior to the Mel King campaigns of 1979 and 1983, the predominant pattern of interaction between City Hall and the black community was that between the mayor and his hand-picked leaders, who played an essentially gate-keeper or buffer role on behalf of the white power structure.

This study also shows how the anti-poverty program in Boston has served to distract activists in that city from the local electoral arena. Although the Boston anti-poverty agency has had a stormy relation with City Hall, it has also meant that the focus of people's energy has been getting funding for programs, instead of acquiring positions of governmental power. In this way the institutionalization of black political power has been undercut by people's energy being devoted to managing the human services programs of the anti-poverty agency.

It was against this long legacy of political disenfranchisement that the Mel King campaign was directed in 1979. It is important to note, however, that Mel King ran on a progressive political agenda, not just as a black candidate. The significance of this fact is that King had to do more than meet the standard prerequisites for successful electoral activism. In addition to having numbers of supporters augmented by group cohesion, leadership, political consciousness, and organization, he had to develop a strategy for challenging the entrenched power of the "metropolitan establishment." What this translated into was that Mel King had to develop ways to bring black, Latino, and white people together, and that he had to sacrifice certain principles of "good organization" in order to allow a democratically based campaign to flower. These additional requirements are the key to the development of a progressive campaign, but they make it more difficult to win.

The Mel King for Mayor campaign was based on five basic principles: "1) the 'empowerment' of black and Latino people;

2) racial and ethnic cooperation on common socioeconomic problems; 3) conservation and improvement of neighborhoods, and community-based institutions; 4) economic development that balances the interests of poor and working-class people with those of middle-class citizenry; and 5) redefinition of the values citizens act upon in the electoral arena." The campaign sought also to affect the Boston political arena beyond the particular election, and did so in numerous ways, which included spawning citywide organizations such as the Boston People's Organization and the Committee for District Representation.

One of Mel King's primary obstacles in the 1979 race was that substantial sections of the electorate, including the black electorate, did not view him as a serious candidate. Reasons for this were varied, but the most important ones were the fact that King did not act like a politician; the acceptance by many in the black community of the notion—pushed by the media and the political establishment—that Boston's black community was too small for a black person to be elected mayor; and the lack of support for his campaign among black professionals. When black students and a few black civic leaders and ministers publicized their support for Mel King, the 1979 campaign received its greatest momentum.

But in 1983 things were different. The candidate and his campaign organization had learned valuable experiences in the 1979 campaign, including the need for long-range planning in mobilizing at the grassroots level in the black community, and the importance of voter registration in producing sympathetic new voters as well as in educating the electorate about the issues. Mel King got 47,800 votes in the preliminary election to come in second place, some 400 votes behind Ray Flynn, a white populist candidate. David Finnegan, long recognized as the leading contender for the office, spent $600,000 in the campaign only to go down to defeat. The turnout for the election was an enormous 63%, nearly unparalleled for a preliminary election. And in the predominantly black wards like 9, 12, and 14, voter turnout was a whopping 79.1%. In these wards Mel King received 95% of the vote. Over all, King received 13.4% of the white vote.

In the general election, however, Mel King was decisively defeated by the white populist Ray Flynn. Jennings bitterly observes that Flynn received substantial support from progressive whites who argued that he could achieve more than King because white people would be less likely to oppose his policies. Jennings sardonically agrees with this observation, because Flynn would not challenge their racism, given his past positions on the racist practices of some of Boston's white working-class communities.

Where do we go from here? Jennings's conclusion is clear and unequivocal, although he seems to have more faith in the ability of electoral means under existing conditions in Boston than the circumstances seem to bear out. He points out that the black community stands at the center of the basic conflicts of our modern society, and have little to gain from the crumbs that are offered via the traditional black political gate-keepers for the urban executive coalition. The only choice for black people as a whole is to opt for a progressive agenda. The questions that are asked by traditional politicians are well known and repetitive: "How can we attract big business for 'downtown' economic development? How can we build more office spaces and highrise luxury hotels?. . .Which human and social services can be reduced in order to relieve. . .fiscal pressures? How can the public schools be more responsive to the needs of the business community?" We've heard all of this before, ad nauseam.

Jennings concludes with an admonition that issues for a progressive agenda must not be approached exclusively within a managerial or technocratic framework, or one that takes for granted the existing system of distribution of wealth. In his opinion:

> America has reached a critical stage in the struggle against racism and class exploitation. This study suggests that the electoral arena—especially at the local level—will be ever more crucial in challenging the holders and managers of wealth in this country. Black-led progressive campaigns are introducing a new force upon American politics. This black electoral activism will have significant impact on such developments as the nature of the political coalitions at the local level, and on the question of black-Latino political relationships. It will also encourage public debates and discussions of issues usually not raised in local electoral campaigns.

Jennings's point, of course, is well taken. Nonetheless, we must pay attention, especially at the local level, to the concrete mechanisms that will go into the construction of such a coalition. The case in point being: how do we build such a progressive agenda against populist candidates like Ray Flynn, who will accommodate the defensive use of racism by some of the white working-class communities in Boston? It seems that this process of coalition-building must be done via the route taken in Chicago, where the black community led a number of protests around concrete conditions, which the leadership of a progressive coalition then pulled together into a political movement.

GRASSROOTS ORGANIZING AGAINST REAGAN IN OAKLAND

It should not have been a surprise to anyone that Jesse Jackson won all eight delegates in the Eighth Congressional District in California, which is represented by Congressman Ron Dellums, and includes most of Berkeley and much of the black working-class community in Oakland. This congressional district includes both the historical legacies of the anti-war movement of the Vietnam era and the militant black working-class movement represented by the Black Panther Party. The study included here focuses on the decades of progressive electoral activism in the black community of Oakland, especially recent electoral organizing by a multinational working-class organization that followed in the tradition of the Black Panther Party.

Oakland is a city with a rich history of progressive and organized working-class resistance to the domination of our cities by conservative and corporate-dominated political groups. In 1911 the Socialist Party came within 2,000 votes of gaining control of Oakland's city government, gaining 45% of the vote. In 1946 the city of Oakland was paralyzed by a two-day general strike involving 100,000 union members. In some ways this study of progressive politics in Oakland is clearer in its lessons, because it is much less a story of prominent individuals (the prominence of Dellums notwithstanding), and much more the story of a militant working class with strong grassroots leadership. Although Detroit is probably the only American city with a cadre of progressive elected officials comparable to Oakland (Congressman Ron Dellums, Alameda County Supervisor John George, and City Councilman Wilson Riles, Jr.), Oakland is particularly interesting because of the role of strong grassroots organizations, in this case the Black Panther Party and the Peace and Justice Organization, in mobilizing black voters in their own interests.

The story of progressive politics in the post-1965 period in Oakland is inextricably linked to the story of the Black Panther Party. Needless to say, the story of the Black Panther Party cannot be told here, but we should pause to refresh our historical memory. In many ways, the Black Panther Party represents the crowning achievement of an era when a proud and militant black movement marched to center stage in American life. This movement was an inspiration for other excluded and repressed groups in American society and for groups in other parts of the world who fought for justice and equality. Unlike some (many?) organizational forms that developed within this period, the Black Panther Party both saw the bigger picture of a world of institutionalized inequality and injustice, and acted on what it felt should be the role of the black working class and its organizations in galvanizing and uniting the disparate social groups who had interests in abolishing this system. Because of their understanding of the longer view and their courageous stance against the brutality to which the black community was subjected, the Black Panthers electrified the nation and struck fear in the hearts of those whose duty it was to maintain control within the oppressive network of social relations. What was particularly important is that they came into existence at a time when massive opposition was developing to the domestic and foreign policies of the government, as at no time since the 1930s. Unlike the militant advocates of Black Power who followed the separatist politics of leaders like Stokely Carmichael, Imamu Amiri Baraka, and Ron Karenga, the Panthers were enthusiastic advocates of the need for class-wide unity and were a strong unifying force for progressives during the late 1960s and early 1970s.

The Black Panthers also built a strong base within the black community in Oakland, initially among working-class black youth, through their strong stand against police brutality and their bravery in standing up in a dignified way to the brutality and racism of the Oakland Police Department. They extended their base among the black working class in Oakland through development of survival programs, which provided some of the basic necessities to sectors of the unemployed and underemployed black working class in Oakland.

Huey Newton's 1972 declaration that the Panthers were embarking on a drive to register voters opened a new era in Oakland politics. Although one might think that Elaine Brown's explanation of their electoral involvement as part of a campaign to start taking power in Oakland, New York, and Texas was somewhat overly optimistic, the involvement of the Black Panther Party in the Oakland electoral arena did significantly transform Oakland politics, and was an indicator of the significance of the participation of black working-class communities (and other lower working-class communities) in electoral politics. Heretofore Oakland had been dominated by a conservative white political machine headed by the Knowlands of the *Oakland Tribune*.

During the campaign in which Bobby Seale ran for mayor and Elaine Brown ran for the City Council, the Panthers registered 30,000 new voters for the Democratic Party. They stressed the need to open the government up for public scrutiny, community control of the police, creation of jobs that served Oakland residents, and other programs from the Panther platform, such as rent control and adequate public services.

The election results stunned the political estalishment. Bobby Seale finished second in the primary in a field of five "serious" candidates. What was astounding about this is that through their get-out-the-vote effort the Panthers had pulled out 63% of the vote in the black community—in the primary! In the general election, Seale added more than 20,000 voters to his primary vote, but by now the well-to-do upper-middle-class and middle-class voters in the Hill area of Oakland were terrified about the prospects of the people at the very bottom of the socioeconomic ladder gaining such influence in the city government that they turned out in unprecedented numbers, 10 to 1 against Seale.

Nevertheless, the performance of the Panthers was decisive in breaking the dominance of the conservative white machine over Oakland politics. The following term, liberal black Judge Lionel Wilson, with the help of the Black Panther Party and a progressive coalition, swept to victory in the mayoral race. Despite the assistance that was given to Wilson by the progressive coalition, people in the black community certainly knew that Lionel Wilson was no Bobby Seale. Consequently Wilson's winning total in 1977 was less than Seale's losing total in 1974. And in 1981, after one term in office, Wilson's winning total was even less. But Wilson was much more in the liberal tradition than in the progressive tradition of such elected officials as Ron Dellums and John George. In the end, Wilson turned out to be acceptable to the downtown corporate interests, and indeed came to identify himself as the political representative of all the people, a centrist who could talk to the corporate leadership, the black middle class, and the unemployed and underemployed black working class. Nonetheless, progressive political forces in Oakland feel that they were mistaken in believing that Wilson could be held accountable to the working-class and progressive coalition that put him into office, and view him as essentially representing the interests of the corporate establishment and the black middle class.

It is within this context, shortly after the election of Ronald Reagan, that the Peace and Justice Organization (PJO) began working in Oakland to organize people in opposition to Reaganism. PJO was an outgrowth of the Peace and Justice Coalition, a broad-based coalition composed of churches (largely from the black community), democratic clubs, elected officials, community organizations, labor unions, women's and civil rights groups, anti-war and anti-nuclear groups, socialists, and students. The coalition was initiated by people who had organized the Grass Roots Alliance and the Tax the Corporations initiatives in San Francisco. The reason for the shift in strategy was that the coming to power of the Reagan administration represented a shift in the fundamental antagonism that progressive and working-class political forces had to confront. The politics of austerity capitalism that had become increasingly prevalent within the political establishment of the 1970s was augmented by the attempt of the ruling elites in the U.S. to overcome the Vietnam syndrome and reassert the role of the U.S. as the policeman of the world. With the decline of detente, this move greatly increased the danger of nuclear war. In recognition of this, the essentially anti-austerity strategy that had been pursued by the Grass Roots Alliance (GRA) was altered to emphasize the need to fight both austerity and militarism, and to show how they were intertwined in the policies of the Reagan administration.

This analysis struck a familiar chord in Oakland's black community. The rally organized by the Peace and Justice Coalition against the Reagan war machine brought out a surprisingly large crowd, which was at least 50% black. The slogan for the demonstration was based on the sentiment that PJO organizers encountered on the streets of Oakland: "money for jobs, not for war." According to veteran Oakland politicos, there had not been a turnout for an anti-militarism demonstration like this from the black community since the days of the old Black Panther Party.

Throughout the period in which PJO did political work in Oakland, it cooperated very closely with the office of Congressman Ron Dellums, whose cadre of committed staff thought that it was very important to keep in touch with and be accountable to their constituency. PJO was very appreciative of Dellums's role in national and local politics and had in fact approached him before beginning to organize in Oakland, to discuss the necessity of alerting members of the black community to the dangers of militarism and of activating them in the anti-war movement of the 1980s and beyond. He very much agreed with this contention, and stated in no uncertain terms that he appreciated the efforts of groups doing the kind of mobilizing activity that PJO was undertaking, that this was the only way to stop the militarism of the Reagan administration, and that black and Third World people had to learn that the bomb was an equal opportunity destroyer.

Subsequently, the Peace and Justice Organization, which had learned a great deal about electoral organizing and the importance of mobilizing the working-class vote in the Tax the Corporations campaigns across the bay in San Francisco, was invited to organize a number of political campaigns in Oakland. These included the campaign of Dellums's aide Sandré Swanson for the Alameda County Board of Supervisors, the re-election of Wilson Riles, Jr., to the Oakland City Council, and the election of Darlene Lawson as the first black woman on the Oakland School Board. PJO's approach was to stress the need for the electorate to vote their class interests against all those who would collude with the Reagan program. Although PJO encountered a great deal of cynicism (wisdom) about the efficacy of participation in electoral politics among the black working class in Oakland, it was able to establish a direct line of communication between these progressive politicians and the working-class electorate. PJO was also able to establish an attitude within the areas where it worked that working-class voters had to look at the issues and not just personalities. In this way it was able to overcome some of the racial antagonisms that the established political forces attempted to use to defeat progressive politicians.

PJO also worked very closely with John George, chairman of the Alameda County Board of Supervisors, whose political outlook was very similar to that of Dellums. John George, like Dellums, was an uncompromising champion of the politics of peace, equality, and social justice. He was also in a league apart from his fellow supervisors on political issues. That is why PJO committed such substantial resources to the attempt to elect Sandré Swanson to a seat on the five-member Board of Supervisors. Although this attempt to place a powerful George/Swanson bloc on the board was not successful (Swanson was barely defeated by the 12-year incumbent), John George continues to play an extremely important educative role on the board. He labors tirelessly to inform the people of Alameda County, especially the working-class people of Oakland, Berkeley, and other parts of the county, about how county resources are decimated by military spending, thus placing local politics within its proper national and international perspective.

The effectiveness of the Peace and Justice Organization was based on its understanding of the political-economic conjuncture that established the framework for political organizing at that time, and on the creative methods of working-class electoral and non-electoral organizing developed by the Grass Roots Alliance in San Francisco. PJO built a strong political movement consisting mainly of grassroots people from the Oakland black community who saw the need for strong organization and for classwide unity in the fight against the domestic austerity program, the militarist program of the Reagan administration, and those who went along with those policies. Furthermore, PJO was not just an electoral organization but had also developed a Full Employment Program that mobilized hundreds of people from the East Oakland black community to fight for jobs. In doing this, PJO activists had to utilize many creative techniques that enabled them to establish a real presence in the black community as tough, sensible, and innovative organizers, who also had the sophistication to develop programs and talk directly to the downtown establishment.

In the course of its various activities in the East Oakland black and Latino communities, PJO was able to build a strong and politically conscious movement, which could then be mobilized in various degrees to support candidates who truly articulated their interests, in opposition to the voting patterns that traditionally have been foisted upon them by the political establishment. It was not so much that PJO was the great savior, but that it established communication with the working-class electorate in a way that had not happened since the days of the old Black Panther Party.

Unlike the Black Panther Party, however, PJO was a multinational organization. There were both long-run and short-run advantages to this mode of organization, and there was one particularly difficult short-run disadvantage, born of the historical practice of certain parts of the old liberal coalition in the United States. First, in the short run, a multinational organization is more effective in reaching out to all sectors of the working class and to the liberal/progressive community. Second, in both the present and in the longer term, the black working class is highly conscious of the need for multinational unity, much more so than some other strata of the population, including the black middle class. This is true in spite of the failure of other sectors of the working class to fully champion its cause and the betrayals of the liberal white middle class when its interests are perceived to be threatened.

But despite the willingness of some people in black working-class communities to involve themselves in multinational organizations and not dwell on past injustices, the historical legacy of involvement with elements of the old liberal coalition must be a source of mistrust and bitterness for some (many). First, there is the shameful history of organized labor, which has consistently stood for the interests of a minority of skilled white men in opposition to the interests of the majority of the labor force. Second, the black electorate has been one of the most steady supporters of the Democratic Party, yet it has repeatedly been taken for granted because turning to the Republican Party has not been an option since the 1930s.

Beyond the legacy of some elements of the old liberal coalition, the demise of the Black Panther Party itself must be deeply ingrained in the minds of black working-class people in Oakland and around the country. I fully agree with Marlene Dixon's observation that "the political consciousness of black people outside of the South has been permanently marred by the state set-up, penetration, and subsequent slaughter of the Panthers."[8] That this could take place in full public view, without massive indignation, led Dixon to conclude that only one lesson could be drawn by the black political movement from the fact that the state was able so easily to decimate the Panthers: "...the fight for civil rights was far from over. America was *not* a democracy for black people." But then it is also obvious to most, although not all, members of that movement that armed insurgency by groups in the black community in a "massively racist society" is also not a viable strategy.[9]

So, although multinational organization is the most effective form of opposition to the political and economic elites who dominate our society, in the short run it is extremely tenuous. It seems that multinational organizing has to be augmented by inter-organizational forms of cooperation as a means for overcoming this legacy. Nonetheless, anti-white nationalism is much less significant among members of the black working class than it is among their middle-class political leaders (even those with militant postures and/or radical ideologies).

Utilizing the concept of "vote working class," PJO was able to offset the attempt of the political establishment to use racial antagonisms to divide the electorate, and focused people's attention on the issues. In the campaign of Dellums's aide Sandré Swanson, this approach was used to familiarize people with Swanson as a person with progressive stands on the issues and to educate people about the role of the Alameda County Board of Supervisors (with which most people were not familiar). Of special importance in the Swanson campaign were the issue of black enfranchisement and the way in which the white incumbent, through his manipulation of a few favors for a handful of people in the black community, was able to maintain his position as political representative of the community, while he spent most of his time wheeling and dealing for wealthy interests outside of his district. Against the opposition of much of the black liberal political establishment (such as City Councilman Carter Gilmore), as well as a solid white middle-class and upper-working-class vote in the city of Alameda portion of the district, Swanson won 47.5% of the vote, coming within less than 3% of winning the election.

Similarly, it was by focusing on the issues and not personalities that PJO was able to offset the strategy of the business community and conservative political interests of unseating City Councilman Wilson Riles, Jr. They had targeted Riles as a pest on the City Council, and feared that he would one day pose a more serious challenge to their interests as a mayoral candidate. Their strategy was to run a large number of candidates, representing the various ethnic and interest groups in this very heterogeneous district, against Riles in the primary. This, they hoped, would prevent Riles from winning the primary; they could then throw all of their resources behind the challenger and wage a highly commercial and slanderous campaign that could not be responded to in the short period of time between the primary and the general election. However, PJO ran a highly effective grassroots primary campaign, which resulted in a landslide vote of 66% for Riles in a field of seven candidates.

The election of Darlene Lawson as the first black woman on the Oakland School Board utilized the same approach. Lawson, a working-class woman, was running against a middle-class Latino, considered by some to be anti-union. The district included a large Latino population, which the Latino candidate claimed to represent. PJO, however, urged people to vote their class interests and not on the basis of race. The consequence was that Lawson won a very close race, in which she was not considered to have a ghost of a chance before PJO entered the campaign. What is remarkable about this campaign is that PJO was asked to work on it by progressive Supervisor John George, and within only four days had changed the situation around. Since PJO was well known in the area, it could mobilize people to whom PJO organizers had already talked about the by-now familiar theme of "voting working class."

Despite the successful efforts of the Black Panther Party and the Peace and Justice Organization to mobilize the black and working-class vote, Oakland politics is still dominated by the corporate establishment, with the black middle class making a big push for its share of the pie. Even with progressives like John George and Ron Dellums in powerful positions, the limits of electoral activism cannot be ignored. After all, the Black Panther Party was not wrong in its perceptions about the source of power, although I would add that force is augmented by great ideological legitimacy in the eyes of large sections of the population.

My point here is not that it is time to pick up the gun, but that serious opposition to the political and economic power that dominates our cities requires a long-range, sophisticated, and multifaceted strategy. Since we are dealing with a world-system (as Dellums constantly reminds us), our strategy therefore must be both national and international in scope. This is a strategy that must be developed—it does not exist in some blueprint ready for us to discover. Meanwhile, we should strive to learn from all of our efforts, for all that we do is a vast educational workshop and we should be ever mindful of the lessons contained in victory, and in partial defeats.

While the "new black vote" does not represent the final victory of the forces of progress over the political and economic forces that dominate our lives, clearly we can see in the experience of the Jackson, Washington, and Mel King campaigns, Cockrel's experience, and the experiences of the Black Panther Party and the Peace and Justice Organization in Oakland, that this political force foreshadows the tremendous potential provided by classwide unity in changing the political complexion of this country and changing the role of this country in the world. Clearly Jesse Jackson's foreign policy stands owe much to Dellums and the political movement that spawned him. Likewise the Rainbow Coalition, spearheaded by the "new black vote," most certainly represents the wave of the future, and is a harbinger that foretells the failure of the old liberal coalition to stand up to the strength of the conservative thrust of Ronald Reagan and those who support him. More clearly now than ever, as Jesse Jackson says, "We need a new direction."

NOTES

1. *Time* (May 5, 1984), p. 32.
2. *New York Times* (May 13, 1984).
3. *Time* (May 7, 1984), p. 33.
4. Francis Ward, "The Black Leadership Elite," *First World* 9, 4 (1980), p. 4.
5. W.E.B. Du Bois, *Black Reconstruction in America* (New York: Atheneon Press, 1962), p. 727.
6. As cited in Arnold Anderson-Sherman and Doug McAdam, "American Black Insurgency and the World Economy: A Political Process Model," in Edward Friedman (ed.), Ascent and Decline in the World System (Beverly Hills, Calif., Sage, 1982).
7. Marlene Dixon, "Strategies of Electoral Politics in Prerevolutionary Times," *Our Socialism* (March 1983), p. 53.
8. Marlene Dixon, "Thoughts on Multinational Organizing" (unpublished manuscript, 1984).
9. Ibid.

CHICAGO

Black Power vs. Racism:

Harold Washington Becomes Mayor

Abdul Alkalimat and Doug Gills

1.
Chicago History
and Mayoral Politics

Although mayoral elections are held every four years in most cities, some of these elections are more important than others, or at least a lot of people think so. In 1983, when Harold Washington was elected the first Black mayor in the history of Chicago, people were following this political process all over the world.[1] Chicago is a city accustomed to having its political life discussed throughout the nation and the world. Of course, it has been more generally used as an example of graft, corruption, gangsterism, and political/police violence. However, this time around, the focus of attention was on a positive movement, a movement based on the stated goal of changing the Chicago political scene. It was the movement of a previously powerless or oppressed group—the Black community. The drama of this Chicago story, as a microcosm of the entire U.S., is the historical dynamic of demographic and socioeconomic change, the changing reality of race, nationality, and class. Further, the political struggles waged in Chicago might well be understood as a preliminary stage of bigger developments now unfolding on the national scene.

Thus, it is necessary to have a clear analysis of events in Chicago, and toward that end at least 10 major book-length studies were in preparation within the first few months after the election. In the following pages, we will address four key questions:

1. What historical developments in Chicago led to 1983?

2. How and why did Harold Washington get elected?

3. What difference will it make in Chicago, or to electoral politics generally?

4. What are the lessons of this experience for progressive movements working for basic change?

OVERVIEW OF CHICAGO HISTORY

In its own specific way, Chicago's history follows the general dynamic patterns of capitalism and urban development.[2] We can distinguish four stages of development in the history of Chicago and identify the relatively characteristic dates for each:[3] Indian territory (1770), commercial town (1850), industrial city (1920), and monopoly metropolis (1970).

The terrain around the southwestern shore of Lake Michigan was largely inhabited by Indians of the Potawatomi, Ottawa, and Chipewyan tribes. They were at an early horticultural stage of development, relying on a great deal of hunting and gathering. Thus, a small population required the support of a relatively large area. Although European explorers passed through in the 17th and 18th centuries (e.g., Pere Marquette and Louis Joliet in 1673), the first permanent settlement was established in the 1770s by Jean Baptiste Pointe DuSable, a Black man.[4] Fort Dearborn was built as an early military outpost for the old Northwest Territory in 1803, burned down by the Indians, and built up again. By 1833, the city was incorporated. As a result of a forced treaty with Indians in 1835, full control of the area was attained by 1837 with a grant of a city charter from the state legislature. During this period, the central dynamic was the imposition of military force, led by the trappers and traders, who subordinated the local indigenous economic activity to the consumer tastes of European and American women back East for furs.

Chicago emerged as a commercial town because of its key location as a regional marketplace, serving the frontier settlers with goods to support their farms in exchange for farm products. The city grew in population from 4,470 in 1840 to 29,963 in 1850; and from 112,176 in 1860 to 298,977 in 1870. Over 50% of its population in 1860 was foreign-born. This was the period of significant canal building and railroad construction (e.g., the Illinois-Michigan Canal, 1848; Illinois Central Railroad, 1851; and the Rock Island Line in 1854) that opened up Chicago to increased East-West and Mississippi River trade. By 1854, Chicago was the center of the largest corn and wheat market in the United States. Chicago's famous commercial district developed in 1867, when Potter Palmer bought three quarters of a mile of State Street, widened it, built his still-famous hotel, and recruited other businesses to the enterprise that turned State Street into "that great street."

While the early industrial development of Chicago was mainly for local consumption, the Civil War produced conditions for the distribution of Chicago's products throughout the country. Further, the famous Chicago Fire in 1871 was an impetus to economic development. It cleared out over 1,700 wooden buildings of pre-industrial origins. Chicago's rebound from "the fire" was climaxed by its hosting of the World Columbian Exposition only 20 years later in 1893. Great industrial giants began to develop: McCormick built a large farm machinery factory; Armour, Swift, Wilson, and others used the Union Stockyards (1865) to build Chicago into the world's largest center of meat-packing; and Pullman built an industrial community (1884) to produce railroad cars for the nation. Chicago also began to emerge as a great steel-producing center, rising from a zero rank in 1860 to fourth among U.S. cities in steel production by 1880.

The high point of Chicago's industrial development was reached during the World War I years. In 1906 Gary developed as an industrial suburb in which the giants of steel (U.S. Steel, Inland, etc.) flexed their muscles for the world.[5] By 1914, Chicago ranked second only to New York in manufacturing, especially in men's clothing, meat-packing, and furniture, and in baking, printing, and publishing.

Perhaps more indicative of how this industrial development

changed life in Chicago is to be found in the development of working-class struggle. There was a brutal recognition by the owners of capital of the need to control labor. In 1886, the fight for an eight-hour work day led to the Haymarket Massacre and established May 1 as a *world* working-class holiday. The flip side of the 1893 World Columbian Exposition was the violent repression of Pullman Company strikers by federal troops supplied by President Cleveland. In May of 1937, police and company goons of Republic Steel massacred workers while they marched for the right to organize a union and demonstrated at their South Chicago plant. The working class paid in blood for Chicago's pre-eminence as an industrial center.

Black people have been part of Chicago history since the 18th century, but a Black community only took shape during the period of industrial advancement.[6] During the 1840s, Chicago was a major "depot" of the Underground Railroad, and soon Black people founded such basic institutions as Quinn Chapel AME Church in 1847 and Olivet Baptist Church in 1850. By 1920, Chicago's Black community had become a Black city itself: it had a hospital (Provident Hospital, 1901); a newspaper (*Defender*, 1905); a bank (Jesse Binga's State Bank, 1908); a thriving business community, and an expanding population (1885: 323; 1870: 3,686; 1890: 14,271; and 1920: 109,458).

The convergence of two processes—the decline of labor-intensive land tenancy in the South, and the peaking of U.S. industrial expansion during the World War I period—produced a "push-pull" dynamic that generated the dramatic immigration of Blacks into Northern industrial cities and their absorption into the industrial work force. It is significant that the proletarianization of Black workers came on the "downside" of the peak of Chicago's industrial development.

The stages of Chicago's history represent cumulative developments that interpenetrate and, together, constitute the structural fabric of city life. Chicago remains a commercial center, but the character of its sales has changed with overall changes in the city. With new transportation and communication developments, it became a mail-order center (e.g., Montgomery

Ward began in 1872). With the automobile and roads, its commercial activity was decentralized from a central business district to a network of suburban shopping centers. (In 1969, 11 suburban shopping centers had sales of $775 million, while Chicago's downtown had $906 million.) Further, 20th-century changes in Chicago's industrial development reflected both its growing dominance and its eventual decline. The main aspect of its decline is the loss of jobs at the rate of 20,000 a year since World War II. Factories first relocated from the central city to the suburbs, and then left the region altogether. Symbolic of this loss of jobs was the closing of the Union Stockyards in 1971 and the original McCormick Works of International Harvester in 1961.

Our understanding of Chicago's transformation up to and after World War II is informed by a 1950 study by the Chicago Workers School, *Who Owns Chicago? A Study of the Chicago Groups and the Economy.*[7] This study focused on the relative standing of Chicago capital after World War II, based on an assumption that this war might have propelled Chicago onto the world scene. They found the following: 1) An intimate connection remains between Chicago capital and Midwest agriculture; 2) Chicago capital does not control basic industry (e.g., steel, oil, auto, heavy machinery; 3) Chicago capital plays a negligible role in the export of capital, particularly to Europe (New York banks handled 93% of the business of the Marshall Plan); and 4) the great Chicago banks have developed a certain degree of independence from the dominant American banking trusts (Morgan and Rockefeller).

By the 1950s, Chicago was undergoing manifest changes.[8] In 1950, 78% of all employment was in the city, and there were only 56 miles of expressways. By 1972, there were 506 miles of expressways, and by 1980, a majority of jobs were in the suburbs. It is still a center of industry (one third of the GNP of the U.S. is produced within 300 miles of Chicago), but its character has changed to that of a giant metropolis dominated by finance capital.[9] The five financial exchanges in Chicago now comprise 80% of the world's commodity futures trading.

There are 240 banks and savings and loans institutions in downtown Chicago, and those banks generate more business loans than the banks in any other city. By 1980, Chicago had been pulled firmly into the integrated core of U.S. monopoly capitalism with its imperialist character.[10]

This general historical sketch of Chicago is reflected in its population profile (see Table 1). Until 1950, European ethnics dominated the city with the increase of manufacturing. However, the data for 1970 and 1980 reflect the relative dominance of Blacks, a decline in the number of production workers, and a rise in professional workers. This suggests that Chicago was increasing its role as a center of finance capital, including administrative headquarters, higher education, and research and development. Further, these dynamics provide the structural basis for understanding the turbulence of Chicago politics in the 1960s.

Table 1 HISTORICAL TRANSFORMATION OF THE CHICAGO POPULATION: NATIONALITY, RACE AND CLASS, 1890-1980

Date	Nationality		Race	Class	
	% Foreign Born	% Foreign Stock[1]	% Black	No. Workers in Manufacturing (in thousands)	% Professional
1890	41.0	77.8	1.3	191	2.4
1910	35.9	77.5	2.0	298	5.7
1930	25.4	64.4	6.9	391	6.8
1950	14.5	45.0	14.0	645	8.8
1970	11.1	29.8	34.4	477	12.6
1980	14.5[2]	[3]	39.8	241	11.4

1. Foreign stock includes people foreign-born and children of foreign-born, so in 1890 41.0% were born outside of the U.S. and 36.8% were their children.
2. This increase in percent of foreign born reflects the new immigrants from imperialist contradictions in Central America, the West Indies, Southeast Asia, and the Middle East.
3. Data not available.

The entire history of Chicago politics reflects to some extent the changes just discussed in its economic development. There have been three broad groupings of mayors (for this purpose we are not examining some of the historical transitions and exceptions to this model).[11] (See Table 2.) City Hall seems to have become increasingly stable, dominated by the Democratic Party, and led by native-born politicians. While mayoral leadership was once mainly recruited from business, over time this source of recruitment has increasingly been shared with professionally trained lawyers. Three examples of Chicago mayoral types will make the historical transition clear: 1) William Ogden (1837) was an enterprising land speculator and railroad magnate from New York who established a business and political career. 2) William "Big Bill" Thompson (1915, 1919, 1927), a colorful, corrupt mayor during the high tide of gangster activity in Chicago, illegally became a millionaire. He built a large Black following on his way to becoming the last of the big-time Republican mayors. 3) Richard J. Daley (1955, 1959, 1963, 1967, 1971, 1975), trained as a lawyer, dominated the city as chair of the party and mayor for over 20 years.

Table 2 HISTORICAL STAGES OF CHICAGO MAYORAL LEADERSHIP

Types of Chicago Mayors	Avg. No. Years in Office	No. of Mayors	% Mayors Democrats	% Mayors Chicago-Born	Type of Mayor % Years in Office, by Occupation:	
					Business	Lawyer (N = years)
Commercial Elite (1837-1875)	1.7	23	48	0	86.8	13.2 (N = 38)
Factional Fighters (1876-1930)	4.7	12	50	25	57.1	42.9 (N = 56)
Machine Administrators (1931-1983)	8.7	6	100	67	51.9	48.1 (N = 52)

This development of Chicago mayoral administrations has been summed up by Donald Bradley:

> The type of men recruited for the mayoralty changed over the 125 years of Chicago's history. The office was initially (1837-1869) the prerogative of the early promoters and original business elite of the community. Alteration in the economic structure

of the city, the proliferation of public services and official responsibilities, the qualitative and quantitative changes in the population, however, all created a new trend in political recruitment.
The rapid change experienced by the city in all of its aspects
produced an atmosphere conducive to the cult of the personality
that obtained between 1880 and 1930. The 1930s saw the stabilization of the community and the ascendency of a dominant party
machine. Thus, between 1931 and the present, the chief elected
office in the city has been held by a group of political
entrepreneurs who came up through the ranks of the party
organization.

When viewed in the broad perspectives of the changes that
have taken place in Chicago, two factors stand out as responsible for the observed trend in political leadership: the desirability
of political office for those differentially situated in the community fabric, and the type and distribution of political resources
within the community. Related to, but analytically distinct from,
the ambition to hold political office is the ability to muster
the necessary support.[12]

Black politics fits this model to some extent.[13] Early Black
politicians were strong individualists who built political careers
during the first stage and within the second mayoral stage
in Chicago. These included the following: John Jones (first Black
official elected as county commissioner, 1871-1875); Oscar de
Priest (first Black on the City Council, 1916, and the first Black
in the U.S. Congress after Reconstruction, 1928-1934); and Ed
Wright (first Black ward committeeman, 1920). These political
leaders attached themselves to a political faction when it served
their ends, and frequently changed sides as political expediency
dictated. They were "race men" in that their overriding concern, as individuals, was to work for the good of Black people,
or the community.

A second stage in Black politics emerged with the building
of the Black submachine. James Q. Wilson identifies its origins:

> The Negro machine owes its existence in part to the existence
> of a city-wide Democratic machine; it is, to use a clumsy phrase,
> a "submachine" within the larger city machine. Although Negroes
> have held important political office in Chicago since 1915 (when
> Oscar de Priest was elected alderman), in Cook County since
> 1871 (although continuously only since 1938), and in the Illinois

State Legislature since 1876, the rise of the present Negro machine did not begin until 1939. In that year, Dawson, an independent Republican who had served in the City Council, switched parties and, with the active support of Mayor Edward Kelly, entered the Democratic Party as committeeman of the second ward. Real political power in Chicago is vested in the ward committeemen. Although nominally they are elected by the voters of each ward, in fact they are selected by the party leadership. All political matters, including the control of patronage, are decided by the ward committeemen, either individually on matters within each ward, or collectively on matters concerning the party as a whole. Negro political strength is coterminous with the number of Negro ward committeemen, and the existence of a single Negro machine is dependent on the extent to which these Negro ward committeemen can be led as a group by one of their number.[14]

Beginning in the 1960s with massive civil rights demonstrations, a third stage of Black politics in Chicago began to emerge—independent politics. Rooted in radical movements, and including activists who would later rise to prominence (e.g., Harold Washington, Gus Savage, Bennett Johnson), this phenomenon began as a movement often discussed as "Protest at the Polls," which became the first organized thrust for Black political power. At times this motion supported regular Democrats, but by the time of the militant anti-Daley demonstrations in the 1960s, a stream of independents began banging on the door of City Hall.[15] Despite these actions, little substantial benefit accrued to the masses through local changes.

The 1960s were characterized by sustained mass protest and struggle, but without a great degree of lasting change in the lives of the majority of Blacks. Middle-class Blacks did win some benefits. Since mass demonstrations rather than voting had won these gains, the middle class lost interest in voting.[16] (This was the opposite of the pattern in the South, since middle-class Blacks did have hopes of material gain from voting.) Further, the machine did not work for a large voter turnout, so the majority of Blacks were not encouraged to vote en masse. An independent politics had been developing since the 1960s, but it had yet to become organized sufficiently to mobilize and consolidate the mass vote beyond the boundaries of given wards. The mid-1960s in Chicago witnessed an explosion of mass political participation and various forms of social action. Malcolm X had said that change would come from the "Ballot or the Bullet."[17] During Black riots of the 1960s, Daley gave orders to shoot to kill, while he planned for the Democratic machine to maintain order and political control. Although it seems important to keep the Malcolm-Daley positions clear, the following study is on one additional case of using the ballot.

DALEY AND THE MACHINE

From 1955 until 1976, Chicago was run by Richard J. Daley, the undisputed dominant figure in City Hall and in the Democratic Party.[18] The pattern of Democratic rule in Chicago can be clearly seen in the history of the Democratic mayoral primary since Daley's election in 1955. Daley's political dominance is best indicated by his being unopposed for four of his six elections. He was a formidable opponent who could scream four-letter words on national television, order police to shoot to kill looters during riots, and force prominent civil rights leaders to give him the Black-Power handshake. In fact when he did these things, working-class ethnics loved him even more. As point man for the Irish, Daley administered their disproportionate control of power and jobs despite their declining numbers and percentage of the population. When Daley was first elected, the Irish were 10% of the population, but held one third of the City Council positions. Irish mayors have been in office from 1933 to 1983, except for 1976-1979 (when Daley's floor manager in the City Council, a Croatian, was installed after Daley's sudden death). This domination of City Hall by the Irish has been a source of gripes from the Polish community (although they are the largest white ethnic group in Chicago, they have never had a mayor).

Mike Royko, a well-known Chicago journalist, quotes former State's Attorney Ben Adamowski about Daley's early career while they were young state legislators in Springfield, Illinois:

I remember those walks. Abe Marovitz was always saying, "Some day the three of us will run Chicago, a Pole, an Irishman, and a Jew." Abe was always saying that. But Daley never said anything. I never once heard him say a word about where he wanted to go. Actually, he didn't say much of anything. He rarely said anything on the Senate floor. He was very quiet, humble, and respectful of everyone, and he developed a reputation for being good on revenue matters, but that was about all.

Most of the time he kept to himself, stayed in his hotel room, and worked hard. In Springfield, you could tell real fast which men were there for girls, games, and graft. He wasn't. I'll tell you how he made it. He made it through sheer luck and by attaching himself to one guy after another and then stepping over them. His ward committeeman in those days was Babe Connelly. Babe was always pushing Daley out front. He sent him to Springfield, pushed him for the better jobs. Then, when Daley got a chance, he squeezed Connelly out.[19]

Daley was great if he could use you—his concept of friendship— and was a ruthless enemy to his opponents. For years, his power was damn-near absolute.

Table 3 CHICAGO DEMOCRATIC MAYORAL PRIMARIES, 1955-1979*

Year	% Voter Turnout	Candidates	Votes Totals	% of Total
1955	52.7	Richard Daley	369,562	49.0
		Martin Kennelly	266,946	35.4
		Benjamin Adamowski	113,173	14.0
1959	44.1	Richard Daley	471,674	Unopposed
1963	47.3	Richard Daley	396,473	Unopposed
1967	46.5	Richard Daley	420,200	Unopposed
1971	45.7	Richard Daley	375,291	Unopposed
1975	57.6	Richard Daley	463,623	57.8
		William Singer	234,629	29.3
		Richard Newhouse	63,489	7.9
		Edward Hanrahan	39,701	5.0
1977	47.1	Michael Bilandic	368,409	51.1
		Roman Pucinski	235,790	32.7
		Harold Washington	77,345	10.8
		Edward Hanrahan	23,643	4.0
1979	60.5	Jane Byrne	412,909	51.0
		Michael Bilandic	396,134	49.0

*Chicago Board of Election Commissioners, "Mayoral Election Returns, 1955-1979."

Things began to change in 1975 when Daley was challenged in the primary by an independent (William Singer), a reform-oriented Black (Richard Newhouse), and an out-of-favor machine hack (Edward Hanrahan, the infamous butcher who ordered the murder of Fred Hampton of the Black Panther Party for Self-Defense in 1969). However, an even more important change occurred with Daley's death on December 20, 1976. As in all political regimes run by a strong leader, the question of succession was a central issue, and here the seemingly invincible machine revealed its factions, internal tensions, and fundamental weaknesses.

A critical issue in understanding Chicago politics is the way interest groups were co-opted and held together by the machine.[20] This was achieved through an exchange of material rewards for delivering the vote based on precinct organizations within the wards. Jobs and economic favors were differentially and disproportionately allocated, based upon voting strength, which in turn was based on which ethnic groups were represented. Irish votes counted more than those of Blacks, and Blacks were given jobs on the lower levels, in the less well-paying agencies. The Black middle class was given honorific positions with status but little control of jobs, because they could not be trusted to hire "right"—meaning, hire mainly loyal Democrats and Blacks who would work for the organization.

The position of president pro tem of the Chicago City Council had been held by three Blacks (Ralph Metcalfe, Claude Holman, and Wilson Frost) up to Daley's death. When Daley died, Frost had the mistaken notion that conventional constitutional precedent would elevate him to the position of acting mayor. Armed Chicago police met him at the mayor's office and rudely turned him away. Power was seized by using the armed force of the state, and Blacks on the City Council were forced to swallow pride of self and community in exchange for a powerful but considerably less meaningful trade-off. Frost became chair of the Council's Finance Committee, while Michael Bilandic, a Croatian who was Daley's Council leader, was made the fourth consecutive mayor from the predominantly Irish 11th ward.

The special election in 1977 attracted some challengers.[21] Bilandic, a Croatian, beat Roman Pucinski (running for the Polish), Harold Washington (replacing Newhouse as the Black reform candidate), and Edward Hanrahan (the machine renegade). This was the last race to be controlled by the old machine regulars. Blacks were now less reliable, and no charismatic white candidate who could rally the old coalition was in sight.

Bilandic was not an exciting mayor. He presided over factional fights and simply tried to hold things together. Powerful forces were given key posts: Edward Vrdolyak was made president pro tem; Edward Burke became chair of Police, Fire, and Education Committees in City Council; and Ed Kelly maintained Parks with its large patronage "army."

Academic insider Milton Rakove, in his book *Don't Make No Waves, Don't Back No Losers*, sums up the end of the Bilandic administration:

> In the winter of 1978, one year into Bilandic's mayoralty, there was, however, a minor upheaval of some consequence. Jane Byrne, who was Commissioner of Consumer Sales, Weights and Measures, a small city department, accused Bilandic in the media of "greasing" the city's taxicab companies with regard to a projected fare increase. After a short brouhaha in the press between Byrne and Bilandic, the mayor fired the Commissioner.
>
> Byrne, aggrieved by her sudden dismissal, convinced that the new regime headed by Bilandic constituted "an evil cabal" that had corrupted the political organization and city government built by her mentor, Richard J. Daley, and bent on revenge for the wrongs done to her and Daley, announced that she would run for mayor against Bilandic in the February 1979 primary.
>
> Byrne had some assets as a candidate. She had a sharp intellect, good "gut" political instincts, a long-time familiarity with the political workings of city hall and the ward organization, an ability to communicate effectively at street level with the voters, and a demonstrated knowledge of how to use the media effectively, a talent she had acquired as Commissioner of Consumer Sales. But neither Bilandic nor the machine took her candidacy seriously.
>
> Under normal circumstances Bilandic and the machine would

not have suffered from their political mistake. But the winter of 1978-79 was not normal. The worst snowstorm in the city's history paralyzed the city and aroused the citizenry. The city government's inability to clear the snow away, the breakdown of public transportation and garbage collection, the anti-city hall posture of some key media figures, and Bilandic's handling of the public all combined to encourage a massive anti-machine turnout on primary day. Byrne received all of the normal anti-machine vote in the city plus an outpouring of normally lethargic non-voters who trooped to the polls to register their anger and vent their frustration on the machine's candidate, Mayor Bilandic. Byrne won the primary by 15,000 votes. Six weeks later, with the assistance of the machine she had defeated in the primary, she also won the mayoralty with 82 percent of the vote, a higher percentage than even Daley had received in any of his six mayoral victories.[22]

Rakove, as an academic apologist for the machine, paints Byrne as a powerful figure. Byrne ran against the machine and won—then the machine took power after the election. The "evil cabal" became her closest advisers, and the people she feared most were those who had elected her. Further, her protest vote had also elected new young Black Democrats to the City Council—Danny Davis, Niles Sherman, Timothy Evans, and Marian Humes—all with independent postures. She had to deliver, or be challenged as she had done to Bilandic. Byrne blew it. She gave virtually every aspect of the movement fuel for building a protest against the machine. More decisively, she did this when Black and progressive forces were conscious that they had created her with votes and could eliminate her the same way.

ISSUES OF STRUGGLE

First, it is necessary to describe the concrete struggles in the city's poor, Black, and Hispanic communities that built this movement. Then, we will examine how these "economic" struggles were transformed into a "political" movement. Seven issues characterized the anti-Byrne momentum leading up to the mayoral race: health, education, public housing, political representation, business and job opportunity, unemployment and welfare, and private housing development.

Cook County Hospital Struggle

The cost of private health care has tripled in Cook County over the past five years. It is estimated that 600,000 people within the Chicago area cannot afford adequate medical treatment. The infant mortality rate in Chicago (17.9 per 1,000) is one of the highest in the U.S. The infant mortality rate for Blacks is 23.7 per 1,000, one and one-half times the white infant mortality rate.[23] Clearly this factor is associated with the fact that two thirds of all heads of households below the poverty line are Black, and over 80% of these households are headed by women.

The relationship between class and health care is highly correlated. In Chicago, Cook County Hospital is by far the most widely used hospital for Blacks, especially for poor Blacks. Its facilities are outdated and at the time of this struggle the county preferred to close the hospital rather than renovate and upgrade its services. Blacks would then be forced to seek more expensive treatment within the private research hospital facilities in the city or get no treatment at all because of restrictive admissions practices of the private hospitals. Such a move would have resulted in a health catastrophe for Blacks in Chicago.

The struggle to save Cook County Hospital was a result of the fiscal crisis affecting the county. The white middle class and political elites wanted to close Cook County Hospital rather than respond to Black community pressures to expand and upgrade its facilities. The struggle sharpened in the spring and summer of 1981 following the federal and state budget cuts that drastically reduced the quality of life among Chicago's urban poor. Dr. James Haughton, chief administrator of the hospital, became identified as a symbol of Black neglect and the subordination of the Black poor and working class with regard to health care. His dismissal as chief administrator was demanded; part of the controversy stemmed from the fact that the leading opposition to this Black professional came from white progressives.

In response to the crisis, health professionals such as Dr. Quentin Young and Lea Rogers, a longtime health and community activist, provided the leadership of the Coalition to

Table 4 RESURGENCE OF MASS PROTEST DURING MAYORAL ADMINISTRATION OF JANE BYRNE, 1979-1983

Issue	Problem	Affected Population	Protest Leadership	Protest Action (Dates of Greatest Intensity)	Outcome of Protest
Health	Deteriorating health services and facilities. Problem becomes more critical as cuts in health services increase.	Most working-class Blacks, and large segments of general assistance recipients. Over 250,000 inpatients are treated at Cook County Hospital annually.	Coalition to Save Cook County Hospital. Black community leaders and health professionals and health activists.	Spring 1980, mass demonstrations are held. State officials are brought in to hear local community testimony in 1979, 1980.	Hospital is saved temporarily; fight becomes part of the increasing anti-Reagan, anti-Thompson fiscal policy resistance. Young plays major role in Washington's health program.
Education	Black representation on Board of Education. Struggle for democratic control over education.	Over 500,000 students are in public school system, of which 61% are Black, 20% Latino. Chicago district has largest enrollment in country.	Parent Equalizers and CBUC lead mass struggles. SUBS coalition provides popular exposure through newspaper.	1979-1980, mass protests, petition drives are launched. During 1982, CBUC leads opposition to Byrne's appointment of two whites to Board replacing Blacks.	Successful in opposing selection of Ayers as Board President. Palmer becomes a leading advocate and adviser in Washington's campaign. Tillman runs for alderman, placing second in 3rd ward. Palmer runs unsuccessfully for Congress in First District.
Public Housing	Black representation diluted by Byrne on CHA Board. Conditions in public housing worsening.	144,000 people reside in CHA housing developments. Over 90% are Black, 68% of families are headed by women, two thirds are on public assistance.	Chicago Housing Tenants Organization and other tenant/community activists.	Spring-summer 1982, stormy series of protest actions escalate, leading to arrest of many activists.	Swibel is forced to resign as chair. Replaced by Mooney, a Swibel/Byrne protege. Community leaders call for boycott of Chicago Fest. Stamps runs for alderman in 43rd ward. Robinson becomes campaign manager for Washington, is appointed CHA chair after election.

Streeter Campaign: 17th Ward Politics	Byrne attempts to unseat Streeter for opposing her appointment of Janus-Bonow to School Board.	The 17th ward is 97% Black, voting against machine positions and opposed to "Plantation Politics."	CBUC joins forces with other West Side community groups to oppose Byrne, along with other white reformers and liberals.	May-July 1982, with the support of a Black-led citywide coalition, Streeter defeats Byrne's candidate in the primary and runoff.
Black Businesses and Jobs	Underpinning the status issue of Black representation are issues of inequality of job and contract opportunities for Blacks.	Blacks are 40% of population, yet have only 27% of the policy positions and 27% of total jobs. Blacks get less than 20% of city contracts.	A broad coalition both within the Black community and citywide supports the Chicago Fest protest. Key organizations are PUSH, CBUC.	August 1982, a 14-day boycott of Chicago Fest led by Coalition to Stop Chicago Fest and supported by a white-Latino "Committee of 500."
Unemployment, Welfare	The economic crisis and the Reagan-Thompson budget cuts represent a direct attack on the standard of living.	Over 600,000 people in poverty; 200,000 GA recipients. Unemployment is over 12.4%. The overwhelming majority are Blacks.	POWER, spearheaded by community activists across the city. An all-Chicago Summer Congress is held in August 1982.	August-September 1982, exposures of Reagan-Thompson-Byrne links to domestic cuts and diversion of public resources into politicians' coffers
Private Housing Reform	A large percentage of federal Community Development funds are retained to support machine politicians and patronage, as well as investments in central business district.	City receives over $110 million in Block Grant funds to support housing rehabilitation, neighborhood development, and revitalization.	Chicago Rehab Network, a coalition of housing development organizations, is joined by other community-based organizations.	August-September 1982, administrative complaints made; protest at Mayor Byrne's office and media campaign launched against repeated "reprogramming" of CD funds to meet other political objectives of Byrne's administration.

The Streeter victory is termed a "people's victory" and a defeat for Byrne and the regular party. Serves to further weaken the machine in the Black community.	
Leads directly into mass voter registration push. The leadership become key supporters of Washington's mayoral bid.	
Leads to mass voter registration drive based upon mobilizing the disenfranchised among Blacks, Latinos, and poor whites.	
Leads to a general and widespread anti-Byrne motion being developed in the neighborhoods. Undermines Byrne's base of support. HUD rules funds must be restored.	

Save Cook County Hospital. This coalition led the fight for Cook County Hospital amid disclosures of administrative mismanagement, overbillings of patients and the state, and of health suppliers such as American Hospital Supply Corporation overstocking and overcharging the hospital for its basic inventory. The Cook County struggle was integrated, in part, into the broader struggle developing in opposition to Reaganomics and state budget cuts by Governor James Thompson. This broader motion had a citywide scope, taken up by organizations such as the Illinois Coalition Against Reagan Economics (I-CARE) (dominated by white liberals, social workers, and municipal employees), and the more grassroots POWER (People Organized for Welfare and Economic Reform) headed by Slim Coleman, Nancy Jefferson, Clarence Probst, and Bob Lucas, all community activists.

While Cook County Hospital was not closed, its director James Haughton—the highest paid public official in the U.S.—was dismissed and the hospital turned over to a hospital conglomerate controlled by the wealthy Pritzker family of the Lugent chain.

Public Schools

In Chicago over 500,000 children are enrolled in the public schools, making Chicago the second-largest school district in the United States. Chicago's school system, like those of most large Northern cities, is shackled with a persistent fiscal crisis. Struggles over sources of revenues, pay increases for teachers, quality of education, and control over allocation decisions are related to the budgetary crisis, and the fact that 61% of the students are Black and 82% are Black and Latino.[24]

Within the context of the fiscal crisis two issues are predominant: representation and the deteriorating quality of education children receive in the public schools. On the latter point, 1982 data indicated that Chicago students' average reading scores were at the 43rd percentile nationally, and those of Black students were at the 19th percentile. The deterioration of educational standards, coupled with keener competition in the job market, has sparked widespread concern in recent years. One of the

most prominent actions had been led by a coalition of parents
and community activists called Parent Equalizers, headed by
Dorothy Tillman, a longtime South Side activist.

But the most dramatic issue growing out of the conditions
of the Chicago schools has been policymaking representation.
Blacks, while only a plurality of the city's population (39.8%),
are an overwhelming majority of the public schools' enroll-
ment (60% Black students). Blacks have been underrepresented
on the School Board: only 27% (3) of the 11 School Board positions were held by Blacks at the time of the 1983 primary. The
Byrne administration became the focus of sharp representational struggles. The first of these struggles was over her attempt
to appoint, as president of the School Board, Thomas Ayers,
one of Chicago's ruling elite, who serves on the boards of Sears,
Zenith, First National Bank, Commonwealth Edison, and Chicago
United (a group of leading businessmen). A broad unity coalition
headed by Lu Palmer of the Chicago Black United Communities
(CBUC) opposed Ayers's appointment and blocked it with a
massive petition drive, demonstrations, and a court challenge.
But the issue of representation obscures the broader issue of
who runs the schools. Following the school crisis of 1981-1982,
the control over the public school system budget was taken
out of the hands of the School Board and placed in a "receiver-
ship" of bankers called the Public School Finance Authority,
patterned after "Big Mac" in New York.

The second of these struggles was over the selection of a
Black Superintendent to replace Joseph Hannon and his temporary replacement Angeline Caruso. Most of the Black leadership supported Manfred Byrd, Deputy Superintendent, for
the post. When Ruth Love, a Black woman, was appointed
in Byrd's stead, the movement was temporarily dissipated.
However, a new upsurge resumed in the spring of 1981 when
Byrne replaced two Blacks on the School Board with Rosemary
Janus and Betty Bonow—both white—who were leading
neighborhood activists opposed to further school desegregation. Again, the CBUC led a citywide, multinational coalition,
with significant support among white and Latino community

leaders; this coalition included Tillman, Marian Stamps, Operation PUSH (People United to Save Humanity), and Slim Coleman on the North Side and Arturo Vazquez in the near West
Side Pilsen community. This coalition-building process, featuring
broad Black community unity, supported by white and Latino
progressives and neighborhood activists, typified the 1983 mayoral
campaign and the substantive and representational issues underpinning the mayor's race.

Public Housing

In Chicago, 90% of the 144,000 residents in the Chicago
Housing Authority (CHA) units are Black; 85% of all CHA
households are Black; and 68% of all CHA families are headed
by women. Throughout the United States, government efforts
to provide decent, affordable housing and to subsidize the
occupancy of housing have been under increasing attack since
the mid-1970s. Historically, public housing has always been
an arena of sharply contested struggles: first to get into it (1940s
and 1950s), and then to maintain and transform it (1970s and
1980s). Throughout both periods, tenant-residents have had
to do battle with public housing policymakers and administrators
over the right to participate in decision-making. As the social
character of CHA residents shifted to become mainly those
on public subsidy, the fight for tenant management on all levels
of CHA activity increasingly took on the character of a fight
for Black power.[25]

Public consciousness around CHA was broadened considerably during the spring of 1981, when Jane Byrne gained
national attention by moving into Cabrini-Green, a near North
Side housing development. Byrne's move into Cabrini brought
with it intensified police/political violence, wholesale evictions,
and generalized deterioration of maintenance in other CHA
developments to compensate for the short-term improvements
that were made in Cabrini-Green. These all occurred at a time
of growing conservative sentiment that public support for housing
should be curtailed. Public opinion was sharply divided along
class lines, overlaid by racial polarity.

During the Byrne administration, the fight to maintain Black representation within CHA policymaking circles intensified amid disclosures that CHA properties would be converted into private housing (condos and middle-class apartments) by real estate investors like Charles Swibel. Swibel has figured prominently in all disclosures about city housing/business deals. A leading member of the machine's "evil cabal," he chaired the CHA Board until the summer of 1982, when he was forced to resign under massive protest, led by a coalition pulled together by Marian Stamps and the Chicago Housing Tenants Organization. Moreover, Renault Robinson, the most vocal Black on the CHA Board (and later to be named CHA chair under Harold Washington), called for a federal (HUD) investigation of CHA administrative practices. HUD recommended that Swibel resign his position as chair in order for CHA to continue to get its funding. In order to "save face" for the corrupt but influential Swibel, Byrne led a fight in the state Legislature for the CHA chairmanship to become a paid position so that Swibel could refuse the position as a "conflict of interest."

Byrne also played a direct role in an upsurge of CHA tenant protest when she replaced three Blacks on the CHA Board with three whites during the spring of 1982. She enraged the Black community further in the summer of 1982 by replacing Swibel as CHA chair with another white, Andrew Mooney, a protege of Swibel and a product of the ward bosses, who had only been appointed to the CHA the previous spring. The citywide protest targeted Jane Byrne at City Hall and at her 42nd ward home, linking her to both the political cabal and the large corporations. (One of her appointees was a junior executive with Prudential, and the wife of a judge with strong machine ties.) The CHA protest action during the summer escalated with attempts to take over CHA Board meetings and a series of acts of civil disobedience that resulted in the jailing of several protesters, including Lu Palmer.

Ward Politics

The 17th ward, located on the far South Side, has a population which is 97% Black. Its social class composition is 76% blue-collar, with a relatively large concentration of single-family homeowners.

They have voted independent of machine-slated candidates and opposed machine-backed positions in the City Council they believed to run counter to the interests of the Black community.

In April 1982, in a special ward election, Jane Byrne attempted to unseat 17th ward alderman Allan Streeter, whom Byrne had appointed to fill the ward vacancy the year before.[26] In City Council, Streeter had become a popular hero by opposing Byrne on four major issues: the seating of Thomas Ayers as School Board president; the appointments to the School Board of two white segregationists with Northwest and Southwest Side constituencies; the appointment of three whites to the CHA Board and Andrew Mooney's selection as CHA chair; and Byrne's plan for remapping the city ward boundaries. All of these issues represented systematic attempts on the part of the regular Democratic Party leadership to dilute Black political representation and/or voting strength within local government.

The issue that most provoked Byrne's wrath was Streeter's public criticism of her for replacing Leon Davis and Michael Scott—both Daley supporters—on the School Board. Until then, Streeter was little known outside his ward and within the Democratic Party leadership. Supported by a broad coalition of Blacks, white independents, and community activists (CBUC, PUSH, the newly formed POWER, and white progressives like Jody Kreistman and Hal Baron at Associated Colleges of the Midwest), Streeter bested 13 other candidates in the April primary and then won a special runoff election, to retain his City Council seat.

The Streeter election was significant in several respects. First, it laid to rest the notion of machine invincibility *at the level of ward elections*, just as Byrne had demonstrated that City Hall could be wrested away from the ward committee slaters. Second, Streeter's victory represented a major political defeat for Jane Byrne. By supporting Streeter, Black community leadership had retaliated against Byrne's political insults of replacing Black leadership. Finally, it was a significant mass victory for the 17th ward electorate, who registered a major blow against "plantation politics" by repudiating the Byrne-endorsed candidate and the machine selection process.

This election showed that unity among the Black community leadership was a prerequisite for citywide coalition-building. Streeter, like so many other politicians, grasped the motion of his electorate toward increasing independence from the white/ethnic-dominated leadership of the regular Democratic Party, its paternalist attitude, and outright racist practices.

Black Businesses and Jobs

The Chicago Fest boycott of 1982 was an immediate aftermath of the CHA struggle.[27] However, the actual material basis for the boycott was certain economic realities of the Chicago scene. In Chicago, the city budget approximates $2 billion ($1.96 billion overall budget for fiscal year 1983). The city has nearly 44,000 employees, only 26.9% of whom are Black. The average employee earns $24,000, and Blacks earn some $3,500 less, according to a recent study.[28] In addition, the city purchases $500 million in goods and services with less than 15% contracted with Black firms and individuals. Moreover, the city has nearly $2 billion in time deposits, with over 80% of these deposits held by the five largest banks, including Continental Bank, First National Bank, etc.; only 7% of these deposits are held in all Black banks combined.

It has been conservatively estimated that 25% of the city employees are patronage workers (and 20% of these are from four wards: 11, 18, 19, and 23) on the near West and Southwest Sides of the city. A recent *Chicago Reporter* study of the contracts negotiated by all Chicago area public construction agencies in 1982 reported that of the $121 million in construction contracts issued by these agencies, less than 15% were let to Black contractors and subcontractors. Moreover, Black and Latino workers have long claimed discriminatory hiring practices by the city and broken promises by city officials. During the summer of 1982 Black workers and community activists led by Nancy Jefferson, a Black West Side activist, protested discrimination in the construction of Presidential Towers, a near-Loop luxury highrise, in which Charles Swibel and the Democratic Party chair of Cook County, Ed Vrdolyak, have considerable interests. Finally, Black vendors claimed that the city systematically excluded them from equitable participation in the sponsorship and opportunities generated by the city-sponsored mass festivals and cultural activities. Chicago Fest is the most popular of a series of festivals promoted by the Byrne administration and Festivals, Inc. (The private promoter of these festivals had arranged for lucrative contributions to the campaign funds of leading party officials—Byrne, Vrdolyak, and Ed Kelly, the Park District Superintendent, among them.)

Thus, when Jesse Jackson of PUSH called for a boycott of Chicago Fest, it had a social basis of support not immediately grasped by many of the leading forces in the CHA struggle, who saw it as a media-oriented diversion from the main issues raised by that struggle. However, when community activists like Tim Black, Ish Flory, and Bob Lucas joined the boycott, many of the CHA protesters saw in this motion a further attempt to target Byrne and end City Hall policies that allowed party elites and loyalists to rob the public blind.

The Chicago Fest boycott started as a Black protest headquartered around PUSH and later CBUC, then expanded more broadly to include a coalition of community-based groups and activists among Blacks. The boycott quickly gained support from many segments outside the Black community, including a "Committee of 500" headed by Slim Coleman and Arturo Vazquez. The "Committee of 500" included white and Latino community and labor leaders, as well as liberals and activists involved in various reform struggles. The main point of unity was the need to expose the fact that the "evil cabal" in City Hall had linked the system of patronage to the major firms with which the city did business. Indeed, the City Hall cabal was identical in many cases with these same firms.

Out of the Fest boycott was generated the momentum leading to the mass voter registration drives in September and early October 1982, preceding the statewide November elections and the primary campaign. Politically, the Fest boycott expressed the basic coalition-building process that underpinned Washington's election victory: the Black community as the main force, with critical support from the most active sectors of the white and Latino grassroots communities.

Unemployment/Welfare

In December 1982 the unemployment rate in Chicago was 13.7%. For Blacks as a whole it was 20.4%, and for Black youth (ages 16-24) the unemployment rate was a staggering 40.1%. In addition, it was estimated that some 900,000 persons in 240,000 households were eligible for food stamps in the Chicago area in June 1981—30% of those persons and 40% of the families were Black. Moreover, the number of people below the poverty level in Chicago has been variously estimated at between 600,000 and 800,000.[29]

As a result of the Reagan budget cuts in the past two fiscal years, more than 15,000 CETA jobs had been eliminated and cutbacks to public assistance had affected over 800,000 persons and 240,000 households in the Chicago area. A sizable number of jobs lost were held by social welfare employees, who formed the base for the Illinois Coalition Against Reagan Economics (I-CARE). This group was most representative of the leadership of the anti-Reagan coalition in Chicago. In Illinois, Governor Thompson's fiscal austerity program has, as part of its significant social impacts, meant marked reductions in both the eligibility and in the level of assistance for health care, daycare services, education, and public aid. In the Chicago area the people hit hardest have been a large number of general assistance recipients, who now find it more difficult to survive; the prospects for finding self-supporting jobs have become increasingly unrealizable (especially given the transformation of the economy and the fiscal policies of the Reagan and Thompson administrations).

In contrast with I-CARE, the social base of POWER (People Organized for Welfare Economic Reform) was the growing number of skilled and semi-skilled workers swelling the ranks of the poor white, Black, and Latino unemployed, and the expanding number of welfare-dependent family heads in the Chicago area. POWER was organized in immediate opposition to Governor Thompson's austerity program of the winter and spring of 1982. It was also a grassroots response to the failure of I-CARE to develop a program and build a coalition that reflected the needs and aspirations of the grassroots poor. Moreover, many of the founders of POWER were acutely aware that Jane Byrne was the only large-city mayor who had not publicly criticized Reagan's general domestic policies and their specific urban impacts upon the poor and politically disadvantaged. POWER organizers were persistent in their efforts to link Reagan, Thompson, and Byrne as an unholy alliance, who victimized the poor and unemployed—both the more visible Blacks and Latinos and the less visible poor whites—and whose policies propped up the rich and the super-rich.

During the early summer, POWER made plans, including mass meetings and local ward organizing, developing the unity that fueled the spontaneous upsurge of protest and electoral participation in the summer and fall of 1982 and the winter of 1983, the period immediately preceding the 1983 mayoral campaign. First, POWER leadership built for an All-Chicago Community Congress, whose basic purpose was the development of a political platform that could be used as an organizational and educational tool in the November statewide elections (targeting Thompson), the February 1983 primary (targeting Byrne), and the 1984 presidential elections (targeting Reagan and the Republican Party). Second, POWER's leadership played active and supportive roles in the reform struggles around particular issues, politicizing them to focus on increased electoral participation. Third, POWER elements were involved in the particular tactics of the electoral process underpinning Harold Washington's campaign: monitoring election law enforcement, ward remap struggles, and litigation, along with the Political Action Committee of Illinois (PACI), headed by Sam Patch and Charles Knotts. PACI's main role was to use the courts to defend the interests of the Black community in federal, state, and local redistricting issues. Fourth, POWER spearheaded the citywide coalition build-up to push the voter registration of anti-Reagan, anti-Thompson, anti-Byrne forces to "protest at the polls" against their policies and government practices.

The role of the *All Chicago City News* (*ACCN*) must be mentioned. Initiated in the spring of 1981, *ACCN* became the citywide newspaper of the independent opposition and pro-reform forces. On a biweekly basis, *ACCN* provided timely political exposure, agitational and mass propaganda, linking particular issues of struggle with the need for local and national political reform and making a populist critique of the capitalist system as a whole. Wherever there was an issue, *ACCN* reporters were there. *ACCN* is an excellent source of background material and documentation of the pre-campaign build-up to the Chicago mayoral elections.

Private Housing Reform

In Chicago there are approximately 1,200,000 units of total housing stock. Some 240,000 of these units, mainly multifamily rental property, are in need of moderate to substantial rehabilitation. Each year the city has received over $120 million in federal funds for urban and community development (CD). In 1982-1983, the city received about $110 million in CD funds. Only a small fraction of those funds were actually expended for community and housing development in the neighborhoods. In fact, during the four years of the Byrne administration over $500 million in federal funds were received, and less than 25% of the monies reached the neighborhoods. When administrative costs were included, nearly 80% of these funds were spent to support the development of the city's central business district (the "Loop") and agencies based inside it.[30]

During the last two years of the Byrne administration, Byrne "reprogrammed" (i.e., diverted for unplanned purposes) over $36.8 million in funds previously allocated through the CD process for housing and neighborhood redevelopment. These reprogrammed allocations were made to meet other fiscal needs ($16.8 million to the Board of Education's teacher pension fund, which was indirectly political, and $10 million into a temporary youth jobs program during the midst of the primary campaign). During the previous year, she had diverted $8.8 million in housing program funds for a "clean and green" cleanup campaign and for purchase of expensive snow-removal equipment for the Department of Streets and Sanitation, although that department is supported by the regular city budget.

The opposition to Byrne's reprogramming efforts was spearheaded by the Chicago Rehab Network, a coalition of many of the most politically active of the housing community development organizations throughout Chicago's neighborhoods. The Network provides a forum for the public critique of city housing policy, and has been a leading force for the actual rehabilitation of over 2,600 units of housing in the most economically depressed community areas of the city.

The peak of the reprogramming struggle came during the pre-primary period from August 15 through October 1982. The widespread public exposure around the diversion of CD funds led many opinion-makers to note that Byrne had lost the neighborhood electoral base that had made it possible for her to defeat Bilandic in 1979. Moreover, it would not be difficult to argue that the groups targeted for CD fund cuts by Byrne were active Washington supporters.

In sum, local activists, involved in a series of welfare and substantive issues, targeted City Hall and the mayor's office— particularly Jane Byrne's administration—as the focal point of attack to address the deteriorating conditions faced by Blacks, Latinos, and poor whites in Chicago. Struggles took place within the areas of neighborhood services, housing, health care, employment, welfare distribution, educational opportunity, political representation, and enforcement of affirmative action standards for Blacks, Latinos, and women. These struggles around seemingly isolated and discrete issues were transformed into citywide policy issues as networks were forged, bringing activists together. A developing consensus emerged around: 1) issues (reform programs); 2) the problem (Jane Byrne and the machine); and 3) the solution (a reform candidate). Thus, an important dimension of the pre-campaign build-up to the massive voter registration drive of fall 1982 was the linkage of organizations and community activists involved in struggles around basically "economic" issues into citywide networks, with their protest demands aimed at City Hall. The voter registration drive was the first phase of the political expression of this united citywide movement—based among Blacks and led by Blacks.

2.
The Primary:
The People Choose
A Candidate

The economic struggle waged in the 1982 mass protests had a direct relationship to the control of City Hall. Mayor Byrne and young Richard Daley, son of the late mayor, had their followings and were expected to declare as candidates for mayor in 1983. The people had no champion to challenge the Democratic Party regulars; however, a movement to find a Black mayor began again (prior efforts were the "Committee for a Black Mayor" formed in 1974 by Harold Washington, Charles Hayes, Larry Bullock, and Lemuel Bentley, and also Washington's bid in the 1977 primary).

Table 5 shows three of the efforts to identify a Black candidate by community draft or by poll of community leaders. It was obvious that only with a high level of Black unity behind a viable candidate would there be a chance of winning. By the summer of 1981 the one person who had the credentials and the developing consensus was Harold Washington. A serious movement to "draft" Washington to run for mayor was the expression of this consensus.

Harold Washington had been a Democratic Party regular, the son of a precinct captain whose position he assumed, but in 1975 he bolted the party machine and evolved as a consolidated independent. He achieved national visibility as the popularly elected replacement for Ralph Metcalfe (after the machine appointee, Bennett Stewart, served out a term), and he was elected national vice president of the liberal Americans

**Table 5 SELECTION OF A BLACK MAYORAL CANDIDATE:
THREE CITYWIDE SURVEYS, 1980-1983**

Survey by the Chicago Reporter Newsletter (August 1980)	Survey by AIM Magazine (Summer 1981)	Community Vote Organized by CBUC (May 1982)
1. Harold Washington	1. Cecil Partee	1. Harold Washington
2. Roland Burris	2. Harold Washington	2. Lu Palmer
3. Richard Newhouse	3. Roland Burris	3. Danny Davis
4. Wilson Frost	4. Jesse Jackson	4. Roland Burris
5. Cecil Partee	5. Richard Newhouse	5. Jesse Jackson
6. Warren Bacon	6. Wilson Frost	6. Lenora Cartwright
7. Clifford Kelley	7. Tom Todd	7. Renault Robinson
8. Earl Neal	8. Clifford Kelley	8. Anna Langford
9. Kenneth Smith	9. Manfred Byrd	9. Manfred Byrd
10. Jesse Jackson/ Clark Burrus	10. Danny Davis	10. Margaret Burroughs

for Democratic Action. Other candidates to run for mayor were less appealing because they: 1) were still party regulars, 2) were not known well enough throughout the city, or 3) had never held public office. Washington was the best-qualified candidate.

Washington had demonstrated his viability as a candidate by winning every election in which he ran except his 1977 bid for mayor, and even then he did better than all previous Black mayoral candidates in Chicago. As a successful Chicago politician, he called for the real lifeline of any serious citywide race— Black voter registration. He announced that the main condition for his running for mayor was that the "draft" movement become a voter registration movement, and that 50,000 voters be added to the rolls.

VOTER REGISTRATION

The Chicago Urban League had issued a report on Washington's problem in September 1981: "Why Chicago Blacks Do Not Register and Vote." It began with a focus on the 1983 mayoral election:

The Black population is steadily approaching a numerical plurality in the city. In 1983, the mayoralty—and with it control
of resource allocation through city administrative departments,
boards and commissions—might well hang in the balance. If
Black political participation could be increased 5 percent to
10 percent, Blacks might effectively determine the outcome
of this crucial election. Within a year after that, control of the
City Council and most services of city government also may
well be at stake.[31]

Of course, the Chicago Urban League was trying to find out
if the 5 to 10% increase was possible. They presented eight
reasons why Blacks do not register and vote. Heading the list
of reasons were "not interested in any of the candidates" (49.4%)
and "fed up with the whole political system" (32.2%). They
combined a controversial point of summation with a call for
a serious review of political strategy:

Lack of electoral participation appears to be a long-term, deeply-
rooted "structural" problem—one for which electoral reform
and other superficial stopgap measures can only have very
limited and temporary success....Sizeable, sustainable increases
in Black registration and voting are unlikely without a rather
fundamental effort to make politics and public affairs a much
larger part of Black family and community life.[32]

An extensive citywide voter registration drive peaked between
August and October 5, 1982, setting the stage for the Democratic
mayoral primary. While many of the traditional institutionalized
organizations (i.e., the National Association for the Advancement of Colored People, Chicago Urban League, PUSH) had
attempted to build a mass Black community registration as
far back as 1981, the most significant aspect of the pre-primary
voter registration drive was the entrance of new entities into
voter registration. For the most part, these new entities
represented grassroots community efforts both within and outside
of the Black community. First, there was Chicago Black United
Communities (CBUC) headed by Lu Palmer, a leading community activist and a Black professional journalist opposed
to Jane Byrne and the machine. Second, there was Citizens
for Self-Determination, a far South Side organization, headed

by Mercedes Maulette, a noted organizer in electoral politics, and sponsored by Al Sampson, who emerged early as a significant figure in the mobilization of the Black church and the organization of ministers to support Washington's candidacy. A South Side youth social service group, Concerned Young Adults, promoted nonpartisan registrations. Moreover, the Independent Grassroots Youth Organization, dominated by a local street gang, claimed to have registered 5,000 youth. Then there were two campaign-specific coalitions that emerged in anticipation of the Black community fielding a candidate for the 1983 mayoralty. They were Vote Community, founded by Ed Gardner and Tim Black and promoted by Robert Starks and influenced by his associates in the coalition known as the "African Community of Chicago," and the People's Movement for Voter Registration and Education (People's Movement) under the leadership of longtime independents such as Lu Palmer and Tim Black, a former labor organizer; Nate Clay, a Black journalist; and Sam Patch, prominent in PACI. The leadership of all of these groups became the principal actors in forming the Task Force for Black Political Empowerment as the informal arm of Harold Washington's campaign organization. Added to these groups was the significant infusion of money from Black businessmen. Most notable was a cosmetic industry millionaire, Ed Gardner (Soft Sheen), who was the principal financier of the "Come Alive, October 5" media blitz leading into the final voter registration weekend before the November election as well as the encore rendition, "Come Alive, January 25," which closed out the pre-primary election registration.

While these united community efforts represented one of the indispensable preconditions for mobilizing the Black community for a Black mayoral success, what was unique about this voter registration movement was its citywide character. POWER provided the framework for formal and informal coalition-building across lines of race and national origin. POWER also provided the organizational context for community activists and political reformers to coordinate citywide, and to plan organizational tactics (for voter mobilization and education).

By September 1982, the goal of 50,000 new registered voters had been reached, through POWER's use of the tactic of mobile registrations, i.e., taking registration stations to welfare and unemployment offices within the city's South, West, and North Sides. Washington's response was to increase the call to register 100,000 new voters! The leadership of this movement answered him. Under the combined efforts of POWER, PUSH, Vote Community, People's Movement, CBUC, and Citizens for Self-Determination, an all-out campaign was launched to meet this challenge. Churches were targeted, library centers were established, and an extensive absentee ballot thrust was coordinated by PUSH and CBUC. Gardner announced that he would put up $50,000 to sponsor a media blitz targeting the Black community for the weekend of October 5. Through *ACCN*, POWER announced that 180,000 registrations needed to be on the books by the final weekend. Over that weekend some 60,000 registrations were made, principally in the Black community and mainly independent of the regular party apparatus.

The increase in Black voter registration placed the total Black registration at 565,000. An additional 76,000 registrations were added between December 1982 and January 25, 1983; 36,000 were Black registrants. This brought the combined total of Black registration to 600,000 out of an estimated 665,000 eligible Black voters. The total primary registration was 1,582,000. These potential voters had to be protected from challenges by the machine-controlled Board of Elections Commissioners. This was done successfully, mainly through strong community monitoring and vigilance.[33]

When community representatives approached Washington with 180,000 registrants, his response was, "Yes, they are registered but (1) will they turn out, and (2) will they support the independent candidates in the November 2 state election?" These were no trivial questions, given that in the 1977 primary only 27.5% of all eligible Blacks voted when Washington ran against Bilandic and Pucinski. In 1979 (Bilandic vs. Byrne) only 34% of all registered Blacks cast ballots out of 490,000 Black registered voters.

In Chicago, the November 1982 election was characterized by an anti-Republican vote. While the Black community leadership was lukewarm about the Adlai Stevenson III candidacy for governor,[34] the Black turnout against Thompson was overwhelming. This overshadowed the fact that the three independents targeted for support for state Assembly seats (Monica Faith Stewart, Art Turner, and Juan Soliz) lost because of the machine's "Punch 10" campaign for a straight Democratic-ticket vote, which cut into the votes of these independents. The opposition to Thompson demonstrated to the Black leadership, and to Washington supporters in particular, that the Black community would unite to support a viable Black candidate for mayor. Second, George Dunne's victory in the Cook County Board president's race against Bernard Carey was attributed to the Black independent orientation, since Byrne publicly opposed Dunne, a longtime supporter of Mayor Daley.[35]

On the strength of these developments, the sentiment for a Washington candidacy grew to a fever pitch. Following the successful registration drive and the outcome of the November 2 elections, CBUC and a delegation of Black community leaders presented Washington with his "draft." Washington had only one course of action: to postpone his official announcement to the week following the announcement by Richard M. Daley, son of the late mayor. Daley announced his candidacy on November 4, ensuring that there would be two strong white candidates and a viable Black candidate in the battle to head the municipal government.

The Washington strategy had been predicated on at least two strong white Democratic Party candidates vying for the primary nomination. With Daley safely announcing, Byrne's forces would turn their attention to her formidable rival from the Bridgeport neighborhood, home of the Daley machine. The theory was that Byrne and Daley would split the white vote and neither could afford to attack Washington for fear of alienating the Black vote.

On November 3, columnist Mike Royko noted in the *Sun Times* that the real race was now beginning. He was correct.

Streeter's aldermanic victory, the boycott of Chicago Fest, the strong anti-Byrne sentiment in the neighborhoods, and issues of redistribution policy for sharing wealth and power (housing, jobs, education, CD funding, and the closing of the Jackson Park "El") all indicated that the 1983 Democratic primary would be unique, having major implications for the alignment of mainstream political forces in Chicago.

The three prime candidates who entered the field were going to war for the mayoral seat. Before the 170-day campaign was over, dated from Daley's announcement on November 4 through April 12 (Washington announced on November 10), it would be the most expensive ($18 million spent), the most corrupt (Byrne's blatant payoffs to street gangs), the most polarized among race/nationality lines (Byrne and Epton share the laurels),

Table 6 CANDIDATES FOR DEMOCRATIC MAYORAL PRIMARY: FEBRUARY 1983

Candidate	Harold Washington	Jane Byrne	Richard Daley
Birthplace	Chicago	Chicago	Chicago
Date of Birth	1922	1935	1942
Race	Black	white	white
Nationality	Afro-American	Irish-American	Irish-American
Gender	male	female	male
Father's Occupation	minister/lawyer	corporate executive	lawyer
Education	Roosevelt University, Northwestern University	Barat College, University of Illinois	Providence College (R.I.), DePaul University
Occupation	lawyer	housewife, civil affairs	lawyer Son of Mayor Daley
Political Experience	Father was a precinct captain. Served as apprentice to the Dawson organization, held elected office for 18 years in state Legislature and U.S. Congress	Campaign volunteer, close associate of Mayor Daley, appointed to positions in party and city government, only elected office as mayor of Chicago (1979-1983)	(terms 1955-1976), committeeman of 11th ward, held elected office for 10 years as state senator and State's Attorney of Cook County

and the most publicized (internationally, nationally, and locally) mayoral race in Chicago's political history.

More people participated in the primary and general election than in any other election in Chicago history, and more white people voted on the losing side than in any two successive elections in the city's history. In the 1983 Democratic primary, the Chicago electorate had three choices: Byrne represented the present, Daley the past, and Washington was identified with their aspirations for the future.

THE INCUMBENT

Byrne's campaign strength was among middle-class and working women, the neighborhoods, and seniors.[36] She had not been able to hold her electoral coalition together for very long after her election for several reasons. First, she was saddled by a deepening fiscal crisis that affected her relations with city employees (teachers, police, fire, lower-level department administrators). In order to keep spending in line to satisfy creditors and to protect her base among white homeowners, Byrne was forced to hold down salaries and block further increases in social expenditures, as well as taxes.

Second, in order to govern, she had to accommodate the machine leadership, who demanded a free hand with patronage and the opportunity to make deals that, once exposed, revealed corruption and caused a further loss of credibility, especially among the liberal opinion-makers in the media. Byrne apparently was willing to accept this accommodation so long as she was able to swell her "war chest." She raised some $10 million for political campaigning by the primary opening. A large proportion of this money came from city workers (a source of resentment to those out of power) and from agents with city contracts.

Third, she reorganized the Office of Neighborhoods to be a legitimating device to promote her image and secure her re-election instead of a vehicle for mass input into changes in community development policy. Moreover, she alienated community leaders by reducing and then rerouting the flow of money into development programs at the neighborhood level.

Fourth, while leaving her doors open to real estate developers and business contractors, Byrne lost credibility with many of the corporate elite, who viewed her as politically unstable and prone to quick changes of both policy and personnel. Thus, she contributed to an unfavorable business situation by failing to provide a climate for continuity of program, personnel, and policymaking in government leadership.

Fifth, while Byrne consolidated her alliances with the most reactionary and irresponsible wing of the Democratic Party, she alienated herself from the mainstream of the party. On one hand, not having strong connections with the corporate and declining industrial elite, she was forced to build up her coffers by repeatedly "tapping" city patronage workers, in addition to contractors doing business with the city. On the other hand, Byrne encouraged further fragmentation of the Cook County Democratic Party and, instead of uniting the party, she undermined her most organized potential base of support. She did this by: 1) dropping Carter after earlier endorsing him in order to support Kennedy during the 1980 presidential campaign; 2) opposing Daley as State's Attorney in 1980; 3) closely identifying with Reagan and becoming the only mayor of a large city not to oppose his domestic and urban policies; and 4) opposing George Dunne and supporting Bernard Carey, the Republican candidate for Cook County Board president.

Finally, Byrne made a series of tactical blunders that undermined her brittle support among Blacks and Latinos.[37]

She attempted to play off Blacks against Latinos on the one hand, while exploiting the nationality differences among the various groups within the Latino population in the city, mainly through her appointive powers (i.e., replacing Kenneth Smith, a Black minister who chaired the School Board, with a Cuban, Raul Vialobos).

In a series of appointments that undermined Black and Latino representation on other boards, commissions, and within departments, Byrne replaced representatives from these blocs with whites (i.e., CHA, Board of Education, CTA, Police Department, Department of Housing).

Byrne played the role of a "sacrificing public official," appearing to learn firsthand what the people faced. Byrne is from the 42nd ward, which encompasses what Chicagoans call the Gold Coast and the slums—she is from the Gold Coast, and the Cabrini-Green housing development (known for the TV show "Good Times") is in the slum. Amid tremendous publicity, Byrne "moved in" to Cabrini. While she was there, personally protected by police in all adjacent apartments (both sides, above, and below) and by hundreds of others in the area, crime was reduced. But as she soon left, it was worse than ever—elevators would go out for weeks in 21-story buildings where senior citizens and the sick would be under a sinister form of de facto "house arrest." The gangs retaliated against families who were able to avoid the mass evictions of so-called "anti-social" elements. In the end, many of the people who initially praised Byrne for her actions in Cabrini were later neutralized by reports that services were being withdrawn from other CHA developments to support Byrne's temporary publicity stunt.

She earned the enmity of Blacks by leading the battle to dilute Black representation and voter strength on substantive issues. At the same time, she continued the tradition of hand-picking candidates for elective offices with predominantly Black constituencies. The Black community resented the appointment of Bennett Stewart for the First Congressional District seat when Metcalfe died. It was further aroused when she pitted Eugene Barnes against Washington, who two years before ran as an independent and became the first Black congressman to be elected from a central city district independent of the machine. Byrne's all-out campaign to dislodge Allan Streeter incensed the Black community. With his successful election some observers proclaimed the end of an era: "No more plantation politics" from City Hall. The "last straw" occurred in the West Side 29th ward aldermanic primary, when Byrne attempted to send Iola McGowan (a Byrne appointee who had been ruled not a resident of that ward by a district court) against

Black independent Danny Davis. The Black community viewed this challenge with a mixture of righteous indignation and sarcastic amusement at the fiasco. Despite the fact that the 29th ward boundaries had been recently redrawn to maximize the possibilities that Davis, an ardent Washington supporter, would lose, McGowan lost big—another blow against the "machine invincibility" myth.

DALEY "THE SON"

When Richard M. Daley[38] left the state Senate in 1980 to run for Cook County State's Attorney, it became clear to all that he was gearing up for a mayoral bid—perhaps as early as 1983—by testing his drawing power in a citywide election. His campaign announcement for mayor therefore came as no surprise. However, it brought panic to Byrne's camp and smiles of hope to Washington supporters. Daley had a number of credits that enhanced his viability as a candidate:

He had his father's name and his mother's blessings. "Sis" Daley is the machine matriarch who has carefully guarded the Daley legacy to be bestowed upon her sons. He also appeared to have enough support within the party to make winning against Byrne a realistic prospect. The 11th ward had control over as much as 20% of all the known patronage jobs in the city. In fact, the four contiguous Southwest Side wards (wards 11, 18, 19, and 23) control 8,000 of the patronage-held jobs in the city government. Political elites throughout the city owed their careers to Richard J. Daley, including George Dunne, John Stroger, William Lipinski, William Bowen, Thomas Hynes, Burt Naturus, Frank Stembeck, and others, as well as most veteran Black politicians in the city. Within the Black community, there was thought to be a significant political base among the old generation of business and professional people who remembered Richard J. Daley, "the Father," and saw "the Son" as one who would have influence among their constituencies. Daley was also expected to pick up substantial support among the "Lake Front liberals," city union workers, and many employees who were perceived as having nowhere to go but to support Daley, given Byrne's practices as chief administrator and as a politician.

Daley also had weaknesses, but some of these weaknesses tended not to be significant during the campaign. First, public speaking was not his main forte. Although he lacked charisma, the four-month campaign laid to rest the rumor that he couldn't talk. Second, Daley resided in Bridgeport, one of the most segregated communities in the near Southwest Side. During the summer of 1982, the Rev. Cecil Turner, a Byrne supporter, attempted to embarrass Daley by exposing him as a supporter of racism. Turner attempted to exploit a street gang attack on a Black man by holding a mass demonstration through Bridgeport to dramatize the situation and hurt Daley's mayoral chances. The event drew little support among Black leadership, who saw that Byrne would benefit and a Black mayoral success would be weakened if Daley's viability as a candidate vis-a-vis Byrne was reduced. Third, as the lines of the campaign battle unfolded, Daley was put into the position of having to compete with Jane Byrne for mainly white votes. He did not want to embarrass his liberal supporters or alienate his potential Black support by attacking Harold Washington. Thus, unable to dictate the campaign issues, Daley was forced to make a relentless attack on Byrne's mayoral record before white audiences. He had to attack her without attacking the Democratic Party. At the same time, he could not dislodge Black support from Washington, nor was he able to gain more than an even split with Byrne. Daley's campaign faltered during the final weeks leading into the election and dissipated during the period in which Washington peaked.

Pragmatically, Daley's vision of Chicago was government reform and "business as usual," but with a new twist. If on the surface most of his reform positions were shared with Washington, it is because they both are liberal Democrats. On the other hand, the line of demarcation between the two candidates was the question of patronage. Washington moved from a soft position on patronage to a hard position against it, enabling Washington to disassociate himself from Daley's platform. Daley was locked into a white ethnic base, primarily among white trade-union workers and city employees on the Southwest Side and part of the North Side of the city.[39]

Endorsed by the *Sun Times* and *Tribune* newspapers as State's Attorney for Cook County, Daley had taken strong administrative initiatives on issues relating to women, and had promoted women to positions of responsibility. This gained him endorsements of leading liberal feminists, such as Dawn Clark Netsch, a state representative to the Assembly, who became his campaign manager. However, he did not gain much support among women's organizations.

During the period they were both in the Illinois General Assembly, Daley's record tracked side by side with Washington's vote on most issues, i.e., the fight against the consumer sales tax, mental health and nursing home reforms, Equal Rights Amendment, pre-natal health care, expense of daycare centers, equal pay for equal work, medical and mental care for rape victims, and child abuse-child support legislation. His strong stand against street violence (vs. "organized" crime) had earned him the enmity of the Black and Latino street gangs, some of whom eventually became paid, active supporters of Byrne. After failing to get money from the Washington campaign, the El Rukns cut a deal with the machine leadership that netted them as much as $70,000 for "polling" assistance.[40] The outcome of the primary election indicated a rejection of both the gangs and Richard J. Daley by the Black electorate.

3.
The Harold Washington Primary Campaign

Harold Washington[41] was born into the regular Democratic Party. His father Roy was one of the first precinct captains of the old Dawson organization, having previously worked for Oscar de Priest. A Baptist minister and lawyer, his father never held public office. Washington attended public schools, graduating from DuSable High School in 1940. He spent four years at Roosevelt University and was elected president of the student body his senior year.

Among his peers at Roosevelt were: Gus Savage, later a U.S. congressman, Second District; Bennett Johnson, later a leader of "Protest at the Polls," and the late Lemuel Bentley. After earning his law degree at Northwestern University in 1952, Washington worked with the Illinois Industrial Commission (1960-64) and was Assistant State's Attorney in Chicago from 1954 to 1958. It was not until 1964 that Washington won his first elective position as a member of the Illinois General Assembly for the 26th District.

In the Assembly from 1965 to 1976 and as state senator from 1976 to 1980, Washington served on numerous committees and commissions. He drafted liberal legislation in the areas of consumer credit, witness protection, small business and minority set-asides (affirmative action programs), fair employment practices, and the Human Rights Act of 1979; he was also the prime sponsor of the Illinois Martin Luther King, Jr., Holiday Act of 1973. From 1965 to 1975 he voted generally with the Cook

County Democratic Caucus in the Assembly. After 1976, and while in the state Senate, he consistently voted his conscience and that of his constituency, which often put him into opposition to the Cook County machine.

Washington earned consistently high ratings by the liberal Independent Voters of Illinois-Independent Precinct Organization, as well as being rated one of the 10 best legislators by *Chicago Magazine*. Until his bid for the 1983 Democratic primary nomination he was repeatedly endorsed by the *Sun Times* and *Chicago Tribune* as well as the Black-owned *Chicago Defender*. During his mayoral candidacy, *Crain's Chicago Business* ran features favorable to his candidacy, although its editors did not endorse any of the three candidates during the primary.[42]

While in Congress for less than two terms, he distinguished himself as an active and generally progressive member of the Congressional Black Caucus and on the floor of the House as a sponsor or co-sponsor of progressive legislative initiatives. He led successful fights for the Voting Rights Act extension and against the Reagan-proposed MX Missile program. Moreover, he voted consistently against the Reagan budget cuts and for extension of welfare benefits. He introduced legislation in support of a nationwide emergency jobs bill during the winter of 1982. Finally, he worked with the Congressional Black Caucus to propose budgetary alternatives to Reagan's fiscal plans. On international issues, he opposed pro-South African initiatives, supported the Nuclear Freeze, opposed U.S. foreign intervention in Central America, and supported cuts in defense spending by the U.S. government.

So in Harold Washington Black people had drafted a standard-bearer with the credentials and progressive orientation to be "their" candidate for mayor. Community leaders from all sections of Black Chicago were forced to keep step with this new electoral upsurge or be cast aside.

WASHINGTON CAMPAIGN STRATEGY: AN OVERVIEW

Harold Washington emerged victorious in the Democratic primary, riding the crest of an unprecedented mobilization of the city's Black community, which includes nearly 1.2 million people, or 40% of the total Chicago population. Underpinning this campaign victory and augmenting the tremendous Black community mobilization was the significant coalition built among Latinos, white liberals from middle-class backgrounds, and poor whites from working-class origins.

In a special newspaper call for a 1983 conference on "Black People and Mayoral Politics," five key factors from research studies were cited as having the highest salience for explaining the electoral success of Black mayors. These factors are: 1) mobilization of the Black community, 2) building broad support, 3) campaign organization, 4) candidate viability, and 5) the city's need for crisis management. We can use these factors to focus on a summation of the primary campaign.[43]

Mobilization

The most important factor explaining the election of Black mayors (at the macro-level of analysis) is the percentage of Black people in the population of the political jurisdiction. The larger the proportion of the Black population, the greater the chances for election—especially since absolute population increase is typically accompanied by a greater quantity of resources (money, skills, talent pools) needed by Black candidates. This population of Blacks must be mobilized and they must cast their votes for the successful Black candidate.

In the case of Chicago, the most significant factors in Harold Washington's victory were the increases in voter registration, voter turnout, and bloc voting of the Black electorate. We examined the patterns of the electorate in the 18 most homogeneous wards in Chicago: 11 are 90% or more Black (wards 2, 3, 6, 8, 16, 17, 20, 21, 24, 28, 34) and 7 are 90% or more white (wards 13, 23, 26, 38, 41, 45, 50). In the 11 Black wards, net new voter registrations increased by 78,919 between the 1979 and 1983 mayoral primaries. By contrast, in the 7 white wards there was an average increase of only 600 net new voters. The registration drive in these 18 most homogeneous Black wards showed an average increase in registrations of over 4000 per ward! Thus the addition of 180,000 new voters to the rolls was a key tactic that led to Washington's success.[44]

In the same 11 Black wards, the average voter turnout was 73.7%, compared to 79.1% in the 7 white wards. Although the turnout rate among whites was higher, this was offset by a big increase in the number of Black voters between 1979 and 1983. The Black voter turnout in 1983 increased by 21.5 percentage points from the 1979 level of 52.2%. In the 7 white wards, the percentage increase over 1979 was only 13.9%, up from 65.2% that year. In 1983 the election was defined by the role of the new Black electorate, made up of many voters who had previously been alienated from electoral participation.

The overwhelming support Black voters gave to Washington is significant in other respects—especially given the high viability of Byrne and Daley, Washington's drawing strength was outstanding. In the 11 Black wards, Washington won 77.7% of the 276,678 Democratic votes cast. By contrast, in the 7 white wards Washington won less than 1% of the Democratic ballots cast, 2,131 of 227,327, showing the racist character of the primary election.[45] Table 7 presents a profile of the primary results highlighting the racial/national origin-characteristics of the turnout.

Table 7 RESULTS OF DEMOCRATIC MAYORAL PRIMARY, FEBRUARY 1983

	Washington	Byrne	Daley
Total Vote	36%	34%	30%
Wards Carried	40%	42%	18%
Vote from Black Wards	79%	15%	6%
Vote from Latino Wards	25%	45%	30%
Vote from Lake Front Wards (Middle-Class, White, Liberals)	8%	46%	45%
Vote from White Wards	2%	47%	51%
Estimated Total White Vote	8%	45%	44%
Estimated Total Black Vote	80%	12%	8%

Racial bloc voting was the principal characteristic of the primary returns. The white community split 88% of its vote between two white candidates, Byrne and Daley, while Washington got less than 8% of their votes. Over all in the primary election, more than 1,200,000 people turned out. Over 500,000 Blacks voted—or some 77.7% of an estimated 600,000 Black voters. It is estimated that Washington received over 80% of the Black vote; at the ward level, the higher the percentage of Black voters, the higher the percentage vote Washington received in that ward.[46] While the correlation of the percentage of Black voters with the Washington vote was significant, as many as 165,000 registered Blacks in the 18 predominantly Black wards either did not vote at all or supported a losing candidate. Consolidating these potential Washington voters would become a prime objective during the general election, since voting behavior became even more polarized around racial/ national lines than in the primary election.

Table 8 shows the relative political mobilization of racial/ nationality groups in Chicago's electorate. Significantly, the voting capacity of the Black electorate nearly doubled, from 34.5% in 1979 to 64.2% in the 1983 primary, while during that time, white voters only increased their voting capacity by 14.0% This would lead to the conclusion that the Black electorate, while numerically smaller relative to the white electorate, exercised a higher vote capacity and was more highly mobilized than the white electorate —a prime factor in accounting for the Washington primary success.

Table 8 POLITICAL MOBILIZATION OF RACIAL/NATIONALITY GROUPS: REGISTRATION AND TURNOUT AS PERCENTAGE OF VOTING AGE POPULATION, 1979-1983

Elections	% Registration			% Turnout		
	Black	*Latino*	*White*	*Black*	*Latino*	*White*
Primary 1979	69.4	31.5	77.4	34.5	18.3	50.6
General 1982	86.7	35.1	78.3	55.8	20.9	54.0
Primary 1983	87.2	36.1	82.2	64.2	23.9	64.6
General 1983	89.1	37.0	83.2	73.0	24.3	67.2

Voter turnout is a function of two other elements: material resources, such as money and facilities, and the recruitment of talent and skill. During the primary, Washington had to depend upon resources raised in the Black community. Of the $1.3 million raised during the primary, over 90% was raised in the Black community (locally and among national Black elites).[47] The Black middle class provided the main support for mobilizing skill and talent for the Washington campaign during the primary. However, his campaign also drew heavily upon the specialized skills of white professionals, especially at campaign headquarters. Moreover, the high percentage of campaign personnel from professional backgrounds in policymaking and executive positions throughout the organization is shown in Table 9.

Broad Support

As the Black Mayoral Conference newspaper stated:

> The successful Black candidates have been supported by key sectors of the White community, especially leading capitalists who contribute legitimacy, money, advice, skills, and other resources. Positive coverage of the Black candidate's campaign by major media follows if the corporate leadership give the nod. The votes of a significant number of Whites and Latinos are also critical.[48]

Washington did not receive the kind of broad support said to be necessary to win the primary. For example, both major newspapers, the *Chicago Tribune* and *Sun Times*, endorsed Daley, while the TV Channel 2 (CBS) editorial board endorsed Byrne. Washington received the endorsement of the *Chicago Defender* and many smaller weeklies. Byrne and Daley won endorsements from the leading capitalists, enabling them to amass large sums of money—over $14 million between them. Washington's support from the corporate sector was so weak that it led Edwin "Bill" Berry, a longtime civil rights leader who chaired Washington's campaign steering committee, to publicly criticize the white business elite and lament that he had worked so closely with them! The most positive corporate response was in *Crain's Chicago Business*, which suggested that Washington's strengths were being underestimated, although the paper decided not to endorse any candidate.[49] Labor in the city split three ways. Most of the leadership, especially those in the Chicago Federation of

Table 9 SOCIAL CHARACTERISTICS OF OFFICIALS IN HAROLD WASHINGTON MAYORAL CAMPAIGN ORGANIZATION: THE PRIMARY

Social Characteristics	Policymaking Bodies		Campaign Staff		
	Formal	*Informal*	*December 1, 1982*	*January 14, 1983*	
	Steering Committee (N = 42)	*Black Community Task Force (N = 38)*	*Headquarters Staff (N = 16)*	*Headquarters Staff (N = 28)*	*Field Staff (N = 20)*
Race/Nationality					
Black	71%	100%	56%	61%	45%
Latino	17%	-	6%	4%	15%
White	12%	-	38%	36%	40%
Occupations					
Professional	57%	45%	56%	69%	25%
Business	10%	-	6%	10%	-
Political	14%	18%	19%	10%	20%
Community/Labor	19%	37%	19%	10%	55%

Labor, with some controversy, supported Byrne. AFSCME (American Federation of State, County and Municipal Employees), representing the city workers, endorsed Washington, and the industrial unions' rank and file generally split between Daley and Washington. The United Food and Commercial Workers Union, headed by international vice president Charles Hayes, endorsed Washington. The most vocal women's group in Illinois, the National Organization of Women (NOW), voted to support Byrne, though not without dissension in its ranks. A strong network organized by Black women led the support for Washington in this sector. Community organizations generally supported Washington, particularly in areas of the city where their constituencies were predominantly Black or predominantly Black and Latino. A smaller percentage supported Daley and still fewer publicly endorsed Byrne.[50]

Overwhelmingly, the Black churches supported Washington, many openly and publicly. On the other hand, many churches had constituencies that supported Byrne (because of jobs) or Daley (because of past loyalties). A group of Black ministers called together to endorse Daley were not significant opinion-makers and were picketed by community activists. Byrne's efforts among the Black churches were dismal. The Catholic vote split, with a small percentage going to Washington and Daley and Byrne getting shares. The Jewish vote was split between Daley and Washington.[51]

Washington's support among whites and Latinos was critical to his plurality of 32,573 votes. Over all, Washington received about 8% of the white ballots cast, but in some wards his share was higher. In the 48th ward, with a 16% Black population, he won 21% of the vote. In three other wards Washington won 5% of the vote, although the Black population was less than 1%. Taken together, the Washington vote in these wards totaled 8,520, nearly 25% of his margin of victory. In six wards ranging from 46.3 to 75.6% Latino (and only 8% Black), Washington won 13.4% of the vote. These 12,775 votes contributed 40% of his margin of victory. Thus, while the Washington support base was not as broad as many would have hoped, it was broader than his campaign expected, and it sealed the primary victory.[52]

Organization

The general assessment of many observers is that the *movement* for Harold Washington led to his victory, and was followed by *organization*. This was perhaps to be expected, given his late decision to enter and meager financial resources. What surprised many was the failure by key black leaders and others, who for months had been discussing the viability of a Black candidate to put more of the campaign "nuts and bolts" into place. As a result, the campaign organization developed in several stages, which defined its effectiveness at critical points. We have identified four such stages:[53]

Stage 1: Campaign Build-up.

Chicago's Black community was fired up by a series of racial incidents involving Mayor Byrne. Further, many of these incidents also involved other sectors of the community, broadening the dissatisfaction. Simultaneously, this built the basis for Black unity against City Hall, and Black-white-Latino unity against City Hall. The poor led the voter registration drive (especially public housing residents and welfare recipients), and were later joined by the Black middle class. Harold Washington was drafted in the neighborhoods and the churches, and not in conference rooms in Chicago's financial district. This period ended with Daley's announcement on November 4, 1982.

Stage 2: Campaign Crisis.

After Washington reviewed the overwhelming voter registration drive and turnout in the gubernatorial race (November 2), he declared himself a candidate. However, the Washington campaign organization was slowed down by personnel, structural, and financial problems. All of this occurred while the media relegated the Washington campaign to second-level status. At this stage, which lasted through November and December, the Washington campaign remained in the neighborhoods.

Stage 3: Campaign Viability.

The main feature of the third stage was the media. The main events were the debates held in late January 1983. Byrne had millions of dollars, Daley had name recognition, and Washington had Black solidarity. But they stood with an equal chance during four public debates aired on television. Washington emerged as a strong contender after he "won" all of the debates. Further, he rebuilt his campaign leadership around "establishment," middle-class veterans (especially Bill Berry and Warren Bacon) and recruited middle-class professionals into the campaign administration. Last, Washington developed a reform program in line with the interests of the city's poor and the Black middle class, as well as some "business interests." He emerged as a candidate whom various conflicting interests "could live with." This stage began in early January and ended in early February.

Stage 4: Campaign Mobilization.

After the increased viability of Stage 3, Washington quickly got the support of national Black leadership. The best proof of this is the massive rally of 15,000 held on February 6—the largest for any candidate throughout the campaign. Further, most Black leadership in Chicago supported Washington, with machine-based Blacks splitting between Byrne and Daley. This period experienced a wave of support at the grassroots level—its symbol being the "blue button." Over one million were minted and hundreds of thousands were proudly, even defiantly, worn by his supporters. The Black masses exploded on election day, overcoming the widespread and visible disorganization of the day.

Viability

The fact that Harold Washington was eminently the most "qualified" candidate became obvious to many people: the son of a machine precinct captain and an activist in the machine since his youth, a member of the state Legislature for 16 years, and a member of the United States Congress since 1981. Clearly he was viewed as the most viable Black candidate by a broad cross section of the Black community.

In addition to these credentials, Washington had three major traits that enhanced his viability. First, he had a gift for combining polysyllabic words with a sharp wit and culturally symbolic references that appealed to the predominantly Black audiences wherever he spoke. Second, he had a tremendous oratorical presence and appearance of command of the subject that captivated white audiences as well as Blacks. Third, Washington's apparent frugality and indifference to contemporary fashion matched his ability to engage in straight, no-nonsense dialogue with the "masses" and the "elites," qualities deeply appreciated within Afro-American culture.

Leading into the four January debates, the Washington campaign appeared to be stalled. The corporate sector had taken a "hands-off" posture. The national Black elites were not excited about his chances, and the media had relegated his campaign to second-level coverage. Washington needed a breakthrough in terms of his image, and while he had addressed the major issues, he needed a way to project his message broadly. With no money for TV ads, he needed the debates as his major avenue to the white voter, as well as for free advertisement.

Washington had not been drafted by LaSalle Street (Chicago's version of New York's Wall Street), or slated by the machine as its candidate. As suggested by Table 5, he had been drafted by Black people; then his candidacy was affirmed by community activists and most political reformers across the city. In this sense, Washington had a mandate as far as the Black community was concerned. A year earlier, several polls confirmed his popularity among Blacks. CBUC conducted a two-phase poll (called a "plebiscite"). In both the mailing poll and the community straw poll, Harold Washington placed first. Yet in spite of his high accreditation within the Black electorate and among community activists, he was hardly known outside the Black community, who knew "Harold" very well. (See Table 6.)

By January 10, when Washington opened his downtown offices on Dearborn Street overlooking the Daley Plaza and City Hall, negotiations for the debates had been broken off. However, that same day, Richard Daley, who had been lukewarm toward the debates, received the results of two polls, which indicated that his leading position in the race had dissipated and that Byrne was forging ahead. Daley now saw that the debates might be just the thing to get Jane Byrne to hang herself and restore his lead in the polls. So Daley pushed for the debates, Byrne accepted, and Washington got what he wanted.

Washington benefited more than the other candidates from the debates. He received important visibility and enhanced his viability as a candidate among the local electorate outside the South Side wards and among the national political elites. He also established himself as a gladiator in command of the issues, with a credible program of reform and with a "presence" that inspired people's trust that "he would do what he said." In other words, he was convincing. Finally, Washington's debate performances pumped new life into his supporters and staff executives, pushing many of them to higher levels of effort while invoking a missionary zeal among campaign volunteers.

Need for Crisis Management

In our view, "The ruling elites no longer find it possible to continue to rule in the same way. . .and larger numbers of citizens are no longer willing to tolerate the existing patterns of politics as usual." The election of Black mayors has often signaled a critical juncture in local politics. The ruling elites become divided, the people more intolerant, and they battle in public view around substantive issues. The same developments bring both the elites and the people to the same realization: Fiscal crisis caused by the increasing loss of public resources, the reduction in federal assistance, and a decline in the industrial tax base, all result in the loss of jobs and income, greater poverty and need, decline in public services, heavier residential property taxes, increased attacks on the basic standard of living and quality of life, and increasing social unrest.

All of these elements were operative, unleashed by the social contradictions expressed in the issues underpinning the 1983 mayoral primary. For the masses, Harold Washington's candidacy became the symbolic expression of their aspirations to repudiate "business and politics as usual."[54]

POLITICAL ORGANIZATION
OF THE WASHINGTON CAMPAIGN

The Washington campaign was organized on several distinct levels and in several forms. First, there was the formal campaign organization, which was headed at various stages by three different campaign managers. The first center of the formal organization was space rented in the South Side offices of the Afro-American Patrolmen's League headed by Renault Robinson, a longtime confidant and friend of Washington with strong ties to the nationalists and South Side community activists. He had been a leading voice for public housing activists as a member of the CHA Board.[55]

On December 12, Washington replaced Robinson with Al Raby, a longtime Chicago civil rights activist who founded the Coordinating Council for Community Organizations (CCCO) as the first citywide civil rights coalition in Chicago during the 1960s.[56] Raby has since served in state government under Governor Dan Walker and as head of the Peace Corps in Ghana under President Jimmy Carter. Raby's social base was among Black institutional leadership and among liberals on the city's North and South Side Lake Fronts and in Hyde Park. Robinson's replacement by Raby reflected the politics being played out on the campaign steering committee for control over the ideology and program production of the campaign between nationalists and community activists, on the one hand, and the business/professional sector and white liberals on the other. It also reflected the real fact that a move for Black empowerment could not be won on a narrow nationalist base.

Raby's tenure was marked by a shift of campaign offices to a downtown location, close to the heart of media and other institutional supports. During January and February, the most significant developments for the Raby-led campaign staff were the planning and coordinating of a staff with expanded functions, preparation for the debates, and preparation of a field organization that would ensure a high mobilization and turnout. To do these things, Raby and his advisers moved to bring in the talent necessary to win the election.

The second level of organization was outside the formal campaign structure: the Task Force for Black Political Empowerment.[57] The Task Force had been developed the weekend prior to Washington's announcement. Its conveners were leaders from some 50 community organizations, ministers, politicians, and professionals. These included: PUSH, CBUC, the Black United Front of Chicago, the Chicago chapter of the National Black Independent Political Party (and other groups identified with the African Community of Chicago), Vote Community, People's Movement for Voter Registration, Peoples College, and several West Side and far South Side organizations. Among the individuals involved were: Robert Lucas (KOCO), Nancy Jefferson (MCC), Joe Gardner (PUSH), Nate Clay (People's Movement), Sam Patch (PACI), Ish Flory (CPUSA), Lu Palmer (CBUC), John Porter and Al Sampson (Black Methodist Ministers Alliance), Mercedes Maulette (Citizens for Self-Determination); many aldermanic hopefuls, including Danny Davis, Cliff Kelly, Dorothy Tillman, Marion Stamps, Josey Childs, Al Streeter, Anna Langford, Perry Hutchinson, and Ed Smith; professionals such as Don Linder, Conrad Worrill, Anderson Thompson, Harold Pates (members of the African Community of Chicago); and political activists Lou Jones and Elgar Jeffers. The Task Force was supported by some community-sensitive legalists, such as Yvonne King and Charles Knotts. Among the youth involved in the Task Force were Leo Webster (CBUC), Doreen Charles (PUSH), and Paul Oliver (Concerned Young Adults).

The mass base of the Task Force was relatively broad— much broader than the functional leadership, which was dominated by a group of institutional militants with limited experience in community organizing and virtually no sense of electoral politics. Their narrow perspective regarding the relationship between immediate and strategic tasks of the Washington campaign relative to the needs of the Black liberation movement and the aspirations of the popular masses set severe limitations upon the capacity of this united-front organization to advance the struggle for political reform (symbolized by

Washington's campaign) in a manner consistent with the broader goals of the movement. Realization of those goals would require a fundamental transformation of the social relations of wealth and power.

Meetings of the Task Force were most often characterized by: petty feuds among the leadership masquerading as principled opposition; the subordination of mass demands for substantive social change to matters of tactical and organizational details, instead of struggling for a program of action that would engage the community in serious political consciousness-raising and fertile debate; and the suppression of debate on central political questions concerning the relationship between the Washington campaign and electoral politics on one hand, and the struggle for Black liberation on the other hand. The issue of tactics in relationship to goals continued to surface within the Task Force but was never struggled through. Thus, the dominant practice of the Task Force for Black Empowerment was reduced to serving as an extension of the Washington campaign instead of advancing the spontaneous struggles of the masses toward political goals beyond the limitations of the Washington campaign and electoral politics.

So while the Task Force played a major role in mobilizing and politicizing the Black electorate in support of the Washington campaign, the Task Force provided little enduring leadership for the campaign. It further liquidated its capacity to provide socially responsible leadership and direction by failing to be self-critical and to sum up the political lessons that the broader community could use in subsequent struggles once the mayoral election, as an event, was over.

The Task Force was conceived and structured as a parallel organization to the formal Washington campaign. It functioned essentially as a vehicle for outreach to the Black community and as a means to articulate positions and take actions that Washington might find expedient to disassociate from his formal campaign. Of the founding 50 organizations, 25 usually had representatives at its regular meetings. Although the Task Force had been called together by a diverse cross section of community organization leaders and activists, and its meetings were usually attended by 60 to 80 people—many of them working-class and community-oriented—the functional leadership of the Task Force was dominated by professionals. Out of 38 persons identified as the core leadership of this coalition, 45% were lawyers, teachers, ministers, or institutional administrators. About 37% had community or labor backgrounds, and nearly one fifth were politicians seeking to gain elective office or to retain a seat on the City Council. While some small business people and vendors were associated with the Task Force during the primary, they were not significant in its leadership; however, they did become more prominent during the general election period and the period after Washington was elected.

The ideological and political orientation of the Task Force leadership was predominantly nationalist in perspective and reformist in character, which also accounts for its transitory impact. While the Task Force made its most significant contribution during the primary, as we shall see later, given the ideological orientation of its leadership, it could not play as significant a role during the general election—a period that required a citywide campaign and a program to attract more white, Latino, and liberal reform voters. The leadership of the Task Force had too narrow a political framework to guarantee a success of Washington's campaign, since it was not based solely on support for the demand for "Black Power."

The idea of a parallel organization that could support a citywide Black mayoral candidacy originated with the 1967 Stokes campaign in Cleveland. Such a model provided two elements essential to a Black mayoral success: 1) maximization of democratic input and grassroots participation in the campaign; and 2) a direct, immediate source of "muscle" for the campaign on the streets and a mobilization arm to provide the formal campaign with essential resources—money, talent, skilled personnel, and advanced ideas.

The Task Force provided very few funds to the campaign. In fact, it received support from the central campaign. It recruited few talented personnel who held positions of responsibility at any level within the formal campaign organization. The Task Force *was* able to provide a "strike force" and a street force to use against the opposition. For example, when the Task Force surfaced publicly in January 1983, it threatened to—and did— picket those Black churches that provided a forum to Daley and Byrne within the Black community. It also picketed a group of 75 "old guard" Black ministers who announced their intended support for Richard Daley. The media exposure accompanying the event was effective enough to cause the Black ministers to short-circuit the planned endorsement luncheon at the Hyde Park Hilton. In conjunction with a group of former civil rights activists, led by Bob Lucas, a noted community organizer, the Task Force also demonstrated against Jane Byrne's opening up a South Side campaign office on the corner of 47th and Martin Luther King Drive, the historic site where the Chicago civil rights movement was born. Finally, when the El Rukn street gang, "hired" by the regular Democratic Party to support Jane Byrne, threatened and intimidated Washington supporters in the South Side communities of Douglas (near South Side) and Woodlawn (far South Side below Hyde Park), the Task Force was mobilized under the leadership of Nate Clay to confront the El Rukns and to reassure residents that political violence by the machine would not be tolerated in the Black community.

FORMAL ORGANIZATION
OF THE WASHINGTON CAMPAIGN:
THE STEERING COMMITTEE AND CAMPAIGN STAFF

In late November 1982, Harold Washington announced an 18-member campaign steering committee to provide oversight to the campaign and make policy recommendations to Washington (as chief executive of the steering committee). The steering committee was also responsible to coordinate the efforts of various citizens' and sector committees for Washington, including the umbrella, 300-member Citizens' Committee to Elect Harold Washington for Mayor of Chicago. Of course, with a formal Citizens' Committee this large, the actual operative body was the steering committee. The Citizens' Committee was headed by Bill Berry and Warren Bacon, the ranking Black executive of Inland Steel[58]

The steering committee was chaired by Bill Berry. Berry, the former director of the Chicago Urban League, is now a leading executive with Johnson Products Company and a "principal" in Chicago United, the main coalition of elite Black/white corporate executives and corporate board officers in the city. The steering committee began with 18 members and during the latter stages of the primary was expanded to include an additional 10 people, as well as the co-chairs of the various citizens' committees. The steering committee remained predominantly Black throughout the campaign—71% of its members were Black, 17% Latino, and 12% white. The occupational background of steering committee members was predominantly professional (lawyers, ministers, and administrators constituted 57% of the committee), followed by community and labor leaders (19%), political activists and politicians (14%), and business people (10%). So the social character of the steering committee differed markedly from that of the Task Force (see Table 9). Nearly two thirds of the steering committee were professionals and business elites, while the Task Force had a smaller representation from the professionals (45%) and a significantly higher proportion of community and labor types among its leading members (37%).

During December and early January, the senior campaign staff was composed of 16 people; it was expanded to 28 after January 15, reflecting both the increased viability (qualitative) and increased resources (quantitative) of the Washington campaign. The senior staff remained predominantly Black (56 to 61%), with whites constituting a smaller proportion (36 to 38%). While Latinos constituted a much smaller proportion of the campaign headquarters staff, they were more significantly represented in the field organization (15%) as well as on the steering committee (17%).

In contrast to the other levels of campaign organization, the field staff most represented the racial/national origin and class composition of the electorate and the movement that fueled Washington's candidacy. For example, Table 9 shows that the composition of the field staff closely approximated the percentage of Blacks, whites, and Latinos in the general population, with Blacks slightly overrepresented and whites slightly under-represented. Moreover, 75% of the field executive staff positions were filled by persons whose principal occupations and orientations were toward community/labor groups and political struggles for change.

A quick overview of Washington's campaign organization confirms the pattern of open democratic involvement and influence at the bottom (reflected in the composition of the Task Force and the field staff) and the policymaking and executive positions at the top dominated by professional and business people. This pattern becomes even more apparent in the campaign organization during the general election period, when there was a significant shift in the character of the campaign.[59]

Notwithstanding this pattern, throughout all levels of the Washington campaign, Blacks not only constituted the social bases of the primary mobilization, but also were the leading force within the campaign. Nevertheless, the contributions of whites and Latinos were significant, and the roles they performed in certain skilled, technical positions perhaps may have been indispensable.

The Washington campaign organization had several "centers" of activity and locations at various stages of its development. Initially located in the far South Side headquarters of the Afro-American Patrolmen's League, the campaign headquarters moved downtown under Al Raby's leadership. The major influences in the early campaign's direction were decidedly those forces within the community and neighborhoods. During the mid-stage of the primary (the period marked by the debates and Washington's increasing viability) the influence of community activists was wrested away, as a media-oriented approach gained ascendancy. However, by February 6, the date of the big rally, the pendulum had swung back toward community forces under nationalist-conscious leadership, mainly from the Task Force for Black Political Empowerment. Thus, at each stage of the campaign, different class forces—but mainly different strata within the middle-class leadership—contested for control over the ideological orientation, strategy, and program content of the Washington candidacy.

While some degree of decision-making went on outside the formal apparatus (as indicated in campaign documents, interviews, etc.), it is difficult to demonstrate who these informal advisers were. Most inside observers agree, however, that Washington resisted attempts to be "kept" by the various factions within the diverse, multifaceted coalition that converged as his support base. It seems that he listened to many actors during the course of the campaign and allowed democratic input from many political blocs. This would account for the essentially eclectic, liberal/populist character of his campaign program, whose platform planks evolved over the course of the campaign.

Not only was there a dynamic quality to the source of influence on campaign decision-making, there was also a dynamic character to the locus of campaign activity. Besides the central headquarters, at least two other "centers" of campaign activity are important to mention. First, the PUSH headquarters, near Hyde Park on the South Side, served as a major center of campaign activity, information, and mobilization for campaign tasks (voter registration, fund raisers, and small community rallies). More often than not, the Saturday morning PUSH meetings were filled to capacity (2,000 people). Second, the Charles A. Hayes Labor and Community Education Center (also known as the "Packing House") served as the main training center for campaign workers across the city, especially for the 19 predominantly Black wards on the South and West Sides. The Hayes Center, also on the near South Side, is more central to the working class than is the PUSH location. Following the PUSH meeting, 200-300 campaign workers each week would await the "pep talk" speeches and weekly summations of Harold Washington, which pumped up workers for the next, usually monumental, task to be carried out by a field organization of people with limited experience even at voting, and virtually none at running a field operation for a citywide campaign. The Center also served as a daily distribution center for campaign literature: buttons, posters, stickers, shirts, and other paraphernalia. At the latter stages of the primary, a literal vendors' market was created, with peddlers hustling over 140 different "Harold Washington" buttons. These vendors made the Hayes Center a major stop on their rounds to other campaign sites.

Another major stop on the Harold Washington campaign trail was the Tuesday night meeting of the Task Force for Black Political Empowerment. The Task Force claimed a work force of 2,500 volunteers in the 19 wards that it was responsible to coordinate. The most sustained period of Task Force activity came during the mobilization stage of the campaign. During this period, Task Force workers provided muscle and escorts on Washington's daily transit and CHA housing stops; during two mass "literature blitz" weekends, nearly one million pieces of literature were distributed throughout the Black community. As part of the Task Force's routine, a "squad" of workers combed the community, looking for "green" (Byrne) and "red and white" (Daley) posters, which they "replaced" with Washington signs and posters, which in turn were often removed by the opposition's workers.

Finally, CBUC headquarters on 37th Street was a major source for political education on Wednesday nights, before and during the campaign. Lu Palmer and Jorga Palmer gave leadership to two auxiliary support units: the "1000 Black Men" and the CBUC "Women's Auxiliary for Harold Washington." These two units provided much of the unofficial tactical and logistical support for the formal campaign organization (postering, distribution, telephone solicitation, typing, and mass mailings). If Renault Robinson and Al Raby were *the* campaign managers, Jorga Palmer was *the* unofficial campaign monitor and publicist for the Black community. Lu Palmer had been the leading proponent of a Black mayoral bid over the past three years. He coined the expression, "We shall see in '83."

Because of the excitement and electricity generated by the

Washington campaign and the movement it represented, many organizations, including CBUC and Operation PUSH, benefited from the campaign by increased membership, revenue, and publicity. The Washington campaign reinvigorated these organizations and injected new viability into them.

Following the last debate on January 31, the attention of every camp turned to field organization. Both Byrne and Daley had citywide organizations composed of veteran field personnel. Washington had access to only a few professional or seasoned organizers, most of whom were familiar only with the terrain inside the confines of the First Congressional District, his extended home base.

An earlier attempt by Raby to test the field organization had failed miserably, because of poor planning, lack of motivation, incorrect rationalization, etc. Raby had called for a January 15 rally at the downtown Daley Plaza, stating that its purpose was to convince the national Black political leadership that Harold Washington was a serious candidate. Despite objections from community organizers, Raby had stood firm on his proposal to go ahead with the January 15 rally. He had expected 10,000 people to attend, but only 2,500 came in the cold and rain in response to a six-day notice. Now February 6 had all of the surface indications that people would not fully support the first in a series of Washington rallies at the near West Side Pavilion at the University of Illinois-Chicago Circle Campus. It was cold, and 6 to 9 inches of snow lay on the ground in some parts of the city. Yet people came out in droves from all parts of the city, in numbers officially estimated at 15,000 seated (with many others standing inside). What accounted for the turnabout?

Washington's success in the debates had raised the level of interest in his candidacy to a fever intensity. Many people were also incensed that Byrne had unleashed the gangs on the Black community, targeting Washington supporters. They supported the rally as a manifesto of their intentions to "protest at the polls." But the most important factor was that everyone in the city of Chicago knew about the rally. It was advertised on radio, discussed on talk shows, and talked about by DJ's between records. More than one million handbills were distributed in the eight days leading up to the rally, including a major distribution the day before the rally. The Women's Network, the Task Force, the campaign headquarters, and PUSH must have called everyone on their mailing list twice!

THE OUTCOME

On February 23 at 2:00 a.m., Harold Washington accepted the resounding mandate by 79% of the voting electorate in the Black community: the Democratic Party nomination for mayor. At the McCormick Inn, a throng of 30,000 to 35,000 people anxiously awaited for him to say: "It's our turn!" The Washington campaign had opened with "Harold" promising to take his campaign into every community, into every ward, and to every sector of the Black community. In response to this intensive-extensive and open campaign process, the vast majority of Black voters overlooked the mistakes, errors, blunders, and high level of disorganization of the campaign. The Black community made it a heinous crime to be unregistered, a shame not to wear a blue button—and its leadership heaped scorn on all those who sided with the opposition.

Working people held hands with the unemployed and the impoverished across racial lines. The church support was reminiscent of the energy of the 1960s, a period when the politically "dead" rose up. And there were many Lazarus-like winos and street people in the campaign who put on ties, picked up notebooks, pens, and pencils—not merely to vote, but to advocate that others do so also. Women's groups united under the Women's Network in Support of Harold Washington, where middle-class highbrows joined hands with welfare recipients. Youth joined together with senior citizens who had passed on the baton of active struggle to those younger. The elderly, many of whom had been trapped in their highrises for years in fear, walked in defiance (of the gangs) to "punch 9" and await the unfolding of their wildest dreams—a Black mayor in their lifetimes.

Finally, it was all-class unity in the Black community that made it possible to strike another blow at racism and the systematic exclusion of Blacks from power that had characterized Chicago politics for so many decades. While for many, Harold Washington's victory was the fulfillment of a dream, for others it marked only the beginning of another phase of the march in which too few knew how utterly treacherous it would be.

For the Washington victory there were three magical tactical weapons: the January debates, the blue button, and the mass rally on February 6. These innovations electrified the mass electorate and consolidated the Washington support base. They were expressions of a mass movement for political reform combining elements of political protest with cultural affinities rooted in a Black tradition conditioned by the historical oppression of Blacks. Taken together, this electrified mass movement enabled the Washington campaign to compensate for its shortcomings in formal organization.

4.
Racism vs. Democracy in the General Election

I n the aftermath of the primary, the Black community was filled with new excitement and new possibility; in general, the people's victory gave every Black person and a few whites in Chicago a positive "high." Precedents for this included Joe Louis's knock-out punches and the speeches of Martin Luther King. Spontaneously, mass celebration spilled out into the streets throughout the Black community, while thousands of people crammed into the campaign headquarters hotel. In this context, new political contradictions were emerging, relating to the three recipients of the victory: the man, the community, the party. Would the primary lead to greater unity (either the maintenance of unity in the Black community or a rapprochement to unite, on a multiracial/multinational basis, the regular Democratic organization)? Or would racism dominate the general election regardless of party or the tradition of Democratic voting?

Every Democratic politician changed posture immediately. Once again, Black people were in a position to serve the Democratic Party. White politicians particularly had been making some serious errors and were concerned that they might have alienated Black support. Blacks who supported Daley and Byrne were super-quick to get on Harold Washington's bandwagon.

A major question in the media and on the street was the role of Jesse Jackson and Operation PUSH. Two things were clear: 1) PUSH put way more than its share of effort into supporting Washington for mayor, gave exposure to virtually all

Black and progressive candidates on its radio broadcasts every
Saturday morning, and made its facility available for meetings,
workshops, and staging areas; and 2) Jesse Jackson was viewed
as opting for media "star" status as his main leadership style,
and therefore could be used by the press to dominate the campaign imagery precisely at the time when the campaign faced
the danger of racism and had to be pitched to a broad multiracial
constituency. A decision apparently was made by Washington
and Jackson. PUSH would continue to give its informal support to the campaign, and Jackson would avoid being
manipulated by the press into creating an image problem.[60]

Harold Washington's primary victory was a people's victory. It generated a community-wide "high" with effects upon
subsequent mass organization, particularly upon the Task Force.
The crescendo effect of a significant social protest is often followed
by a downturn in the level of effort and organizational discipline.
The loss of focus within the Task Force came precisely at the
point when another upsurge in activity was required, since
the general election was seven weeks away. Some people "stayed
home" or went "on vacation" for a couple of weeks. This loss
of orientation and momentum in the Task Force occurred at
the same time the campaign organization was being forced
to adjust to the new conditions of success. An expanded citywide
movement was needed, which required that political resources
be rediverted and concentrated outside the Black community,
indicated by the increased outreach efforts to Latino and white
voters. There was also a new emphasis on "top-down" coalition development that contrasted sharply with the "bottom-
up" thrust of the primary and the pre-campaign build-up: 1)
The steering committee was expanded to include more Black
elites, whites, and Latinos in formal and functional campaign
roles; and 2) a "blue ribbon" Transition Team was formed,
composed heavily of business and professional elites, the majority
of whom were white.

These readjustments in campaign orientation and activity
led to a loss of status and a role-shift for the Task Force: there
were new needs for the general election. It was no longer

necessary to use militant tactics to defend Black unity. The pervasive racism generated by Epton's campaign and the racist reaction of the machine's defeated leadership were sufficient to ensure unity in the Black community. Washington took on all the traits of a gladiator who could do no wrong in the Black community. When white Chicago Democrats decided to vote Republican, Chicago was put on war alert!

However, the Task Force leadership resisted preparing a plan to stay in front of the spontaneous mass energy unleashed by the primary victory. Hence, the Task Force's role became limited to campaign literature distribution and advance street work for Harold Washington, and it raised no new demands or program. In short, between the primary and the general election periods, the Task Force lost its capacity to innovate tactically. (Or, to quote Al Sampson, a leading member of the Task Force, "We haven't busted any new grapes since the primary.")

Thus, the primary victory and the transition in strategy by campaign leadership in the face of an expanding movement significantly altered the social character of the leading bodies of the campaign organization. The Task Force had provided a militant character to the campaign that was no longer required. The role redefinition of the Task Force was reflected in its decline and fall in status relative to other bodies and activities in the campaign organizations; included in this was the expanded use of television media and radio advertising.

CRISIS IN THE DEMOCRATIC PARTY DEEPENS

The Democratic Party was immediately confronted with a deepened organizational crisis with national ramifications for the 1984 presidential elections. It involved the ability of the party to mobilize and consolidate the growing electoral bloc of Black people as the party elites attempted to wrest control of the national government from the Reagan-led Republican and conservative Democratic alliance.

Responses of local party leaders varied a great deal from

the objective needs of the national party organization. Within the former group, the main contrast was between the behaviors of local Black leaders, who rapidly closed ranks behind Washington's mayoral bid, and white Democratic Party leaders, whose actions ranged from full endorsement and public support (e.g., Richard Daley, George Dunne) to outright repudiation of Washington's bid (e.g., Roman Pucinski, Vito Marzullo). At the national level, the call was for national party leaders and Black elites to endorse Washington immediately, while the local white Democratic Party elites hedged, being unable to reject the Democratic Party or to accept the Black Democratic nominee. But at the same time, the local elites lacked a full alternative. Given this, their only other option was to denounce the Democratic Party and to support the Republican Party candidate, Bernard Epton. It is significant that the regular Democratic Party did not endorse Washington until March 24, a full month after the February 22 primary elections. By then, every major Democratic Party presidential hopeful had endorsed him. Allan Cranston endorsed Washington during the primary; Walter Mondale and John Glenn endorsed him immediately after it. Edward Kennedy, after endorsing Washington, came to Chicago in March in order to tell Jane Byrne personally that her "write-in" candidacy would get no broad party support. The national Black political elite, who consolidated behind Washington late in the primary, now redoubled their efforts to improve the position of Blacks within the party by leveraging individual party support for Washington's campaign as a precondition for the deliverance of the national Black vote in the 1984 elections.

National Party: The Southern Strategy

The national Democratic Party, sensing an upsurge in electoral participation among Blacks and working people throughout the country, resulting from the widespread resistance to Reagan's domestic budget cuts, saw in the Washington victory the first step to Reagan's defeat in 1984—a rebuilding or reconstitution of the Democratic coalition. Therefore, recognizing the importance of Black voter strength, Democratic Party leaders, candidates, and officeholders put Chicago on their calendars and made it known that they would support Washington in "any way he desired." This comment was echoed by Cranston, Mondale, and Glenn, the early presidential front-runners. The venerable Claude Pepper (D-Florida), a leader of the senior citizens' lobby in Congress, was brought in to target the white ethnic vote among the aged. Bert Lance of the Georgia State Democratic Party endorsed Harold Washington amidst a great deal of publicity and led a delegation of Southern state party chairs to Chicago. Democratic fundraisers were held by Black and white party elites across the country, notably in New York, Washington, D.C., and Los Angeles.

The week after the primary, Washington, Byrne, and Washington's political adversary, Police Superintendent Richard Brzeczek, attempted to show party unity by leading a delegation to Washington to push the case that the 1984 Democratic convention should be held in Chicago instead of in San Francisco. While the appeal failed to land the lucrative convention, it was a significant attempt to rise above local party divisions. Everyone in Chicago would have benefited from the national attention and the money spent by Democratic convention-goers. Clearly, this event would appeal to local business owners of hotels, restaurants, taxi companies, and downtown commercial outlets.

Brzeczek, an avid Byrne supporter, had earned Washington's ire, in part, because he had mismanaged the police department, and contributed to racial polarization within the police ranks by adhering to unfair promotion policies, and by underreporting of police-crime statistics, especially crimes committed against women, Blacks, and Latinos. He further enraged Washington supporters by appearing on Byrne's TV campaign commercials, politicizing the Police Department even more. During the huge February 6 rally, Washington announced to the predominantly Black crowd that the "first thing I will do when I assume office will be to. . .fire Brzeczek!" Later Brzeczek sarcastically replied, "No he won't, I'll resign first," which he did in April following Washington's unanticipated and unwelcomed primary and general election victories.[61] Were the convention to be held in Chicago, it was obvious that such differences could explode in the party's face.

The Congressional Black Caucus represents the formalized political center of the Black elite in the U.S.[62] Since 1980, Washington had been one of its newest but most vocal and progressive members in Congress. But only during the later stages of the primary, beginning with the debates, did the Black Caucus begin to view the Washington bid for mayor as a serious one. It was at this time that Caucus members such as John Conyers, Ron Dellums, Shirley Chisholm, and Harold Ford, leaned on the national Democratic Party to support Washington, if the Democrats were to have any hope of winning in 1984. They were particularly incensed, but not surprised, by Kennedy's endorsement of Byrne in the primary. However, they reserved their sharpest criticism for presidential hopeful Walter Mondale, who endorsed Richard Daley—in a miscalculated underassessment of the level of local Black unity operative in the Washington campaign and an overassessment of Daley's support in the regular Democratic Party.

John Conyers (D-Michigan) spent nearly three weeks in Chicago and brought in his leading organizers to head up the Election Day apparatus for Washington during both the primary and the general election. Other members of the Caucus raised money for his candidacy. While over 85% of his $1.3 million in primary funds were raised locally, over 25% of the $3 million raised for Washington during the general election period came from national sources, with Black Caucus individuals serving as conduits for a large percentage of these monies. This in part substantiates the observation that the Washington campaign was "nationalized" and taken on as an agenda item of the national black political elite.[63]

The success of the Washington campaign has stimulated interest in local elections across the country. The international and national media attention generated by the Chicago mayoral election has had a major, perhaps enduring, impact upon the level of Black political participation and the nature of local electoral coalitions. This certainly was the case in Philadelphia, where Wilson Goode withstood the challenge of Frank Rizzo, the arch-villian of the Philadelphia Black movement of the late 1960s and 1970s. It has also contributed positively to local elections in Boston and Baltimore, where strong Black electoral challenges were waged. It is too early to foretell the full ramifications of the Washington campaign success for the alignment of race, nationality, and class forces. Part of this will depend on the benchmarks and limitations of Washington's reform government administration in its practice, as well as the practice of progressive and radicalized sectors of the Chicago movement. The latter have assumed the responsibility for identifying the course of march and advancing the struggle, qualitatively, past the limits of reform.

The Democratic Party leadership understood that the key to a presidential success in 1984, depended upon the mobilization of the Black vote in Northern cities and in the Southern states. While other sectors of the national electorate, such as the working class and national minorities, are critically important components of a new Democratic coalition, Blacks hold the key. Reagan's 1980 victory can be attributed to the under-mobilization of Blacks in the South and the Northeastern cities.

A Chicago election success by Washington on the basis of a multi-racial/multinational coalition could be used as a springboard and a political model for mobilization of disaffected Blacks across the United States. Hence, the significance of Jesse Jackson's presidential bid. The critical questions for Black people are these: What will be the qualitative uniqueness of a new Democratic coalition that can transform national politics and the social status and conditions of Blacks in return for their support? In other words, whose class interests will be served by Black support of the Democratic Party, and will those interests push the political process beyond the traditional limits of reform that have dominated the platform and programs of Democratic candidates and Presidents in the past?

In Chicago, a similar question could be raised. Washington had won the primary without the support of the regular

Democratic Party organization. It appeared that he would have to win the general election without broad party support. Should he lose, the Democratic Party would have blown an excellent opportunity to consolidate on a new basis. Should he win without the party support, there would be no basis for a rapprochement. From this standpoint, the national democratic leadership had everything to gain and nothing to lose by supporting Washington. In supporting him, they had an opportunity to rebuild on the basis of an upsurge in mass participation among Blacks and other disaffected segments of the electorate in an all-out effort to defeat Reagan. The Black Caucus understood this and it became easy for them to influence white Democratic leaders of the national party to put Chicago on their itinerary. So a succession of Democratic politicians and hopeful candidates were willingly paraded through Chicago to "prime the pump." They had to convince white Democrats to do what Blacks had done for 50 years: to be a decisive force of support rather than the main base of support for Democratic candidates. The main obstacle was the incipient racism that was a cornerstone of Chicago's machine politics, but that had been ignored by Democrats and historically lamented by Blacks, who foresaw no other political alternative. In the aftermath of his general election victory, Washington spent considerable time on the national Democratic circuit drumming up support for Democratic candidates.

Local Party Organization: Crisis of Leadership

At the local level, individual Black leaders who had split support between the machine candidate, Byrne, and her main political rival, Daley, now immediately came out publicly for Washington. Black Byrne supporters—Cecil Partee, City Treasurer; Iola McGowan, a party central committee member and West Side opponent of Danny Davis in the 29th Ward; state Representative Larry Bullock; and aldermanic influentials Wilson Frost, Tyrone Kenner, Bill Henry— all loyal machine politicians, immediately threw their support to Washington within one week of the primary election. It took no intricate analysis for them to see that the Black vote in their wards and districts was an anti-machine rebellion. On the other hand, party leaders representing the most politically operative white ethnic constituencies were unable to achieve unity on the issue of whom to support. As a consequence, they sent confusing signals to a cross-pressured white electorate who historically had been loyal to the Democratic Party, but loyal to the ethnic-based machine as well. Now, in the absence of a united party leadership, these white voters were momentarily immobilized. Perhaps for this reason, an expected white backlash, manifested in increased post-primary voter registration of ethnic white voters, did not occur. For example: post-primary voter registration averaged about 2,000 per Black ward, but averaged less than 500 in the ethnic white wards.[64] Had the party leadership provided an alternative prior to the closing of the post-primary registration period, there might have been an attempt at a mass mobilization of the white ethnic vote. As things stood, the Washington victory paralyzed the machine, throwing its conservative leadership into political crisis.

One major illustration of the crisis within the local Democratic Party was Jane Byrne's attempt to mount a write-in campaign outside the framework of the regular Democratic Party process. In considering this futile effort, several factors must be highlighted. First, the norm of reciprocity that normally applies in electoral politics is a hallmark of machine politics. Jane Byrne, in amassing an unprecedented $10 million war-chest, had locked herself into a number of promises in return for these contributions. Moreover, Byrne had not contemplated losing and had not calculated the ramifications that transition report disclosures might have for her long-term career ambitions.

Further, rumors had persisted since the first week in March that Byrne would try an independent bid to retain her City Hall post. Initially, it was widely held that she would negotiate with the Republicans to displace Epton as the GOP standard-bearer and "great white hope." Epton wanted no part of this deal. On March 16, Byrne announced a "write-in" candidacy bid amidst mixed reactions of shock (on the part of national

Democrats), anger (on the part of Black leadership), and alarm (on the part of the Epton camp and Republicans who could not see how Epton would benefit by her entry). Byrne calculated that Washington did not have a "green light" from the local party bosses and that, therefore, her candidacy would fill this vacuum. Byrne correctly anticipated a racist upsurge within the white ethnic wards in Chicago's Northwest and Southwest Sides and believed that she could ride the crest of a racial tidal wave to victory.

Finally, a large percentage of the white electorate had experienced a high degree of "cognitive dissonance" relative to Washington's candidacy, amidst charges of his failure to file income taxes, pay his personal bills, and meet professional obligations to his legal clients. At the same time, a large portion of the white electorate was cross-pressured between supporting the Democratic candidate or bolting the party to vote for race. Some pondered the possibility of staying home altogether.[65] In the absence of a clear signal from the party leadership to unite behind an alternative to Washington, Byrne perceived that she could be the "last hope" short of a Black Democrat or a Republican as mayor.

However, Byrne miscalculated how pragmatic considerations on the part of the ruling elite and the national Democratic Party leadership would operate to limit her base of support. The business sector did not rally to her support with money to finance a write-in attempt. Business interests undoubtedly calculated that the political costs of supporting Byrne in a racist appeal would far overshadow any benefits that might accrue as a result of a Byrne victory. *Crain's Chicago Business* weekly had already stated that in their post-primary assessment, a Washington government might not be so bad after all.[66] Most observers talked repeatedly about the tactical difficulties of launching a serious write-in candidacy, which would require a massive infusion of money for educating the electorate (how to correctly spell Byrne's name and where to write it on the ballot, etc.). The Byrne candidacy fizzled when every one of her major primary supporters deserted her. It was extinguished altogether when Ted Kennedy came to Chicago and told the family protege that she would get no national support and that any attempt to run would be politically suicidal for her. National Democrats had sent her pointed messages: "Back Washington."[67] Thus, one hour after the Kennedy visit on March 24, Byrne held a press conference to withdraw from the race. This was also the signal for the regular Democratic Party to endorse Washington publicly, although some party leaders found themselves too busy to attend the slating session. Still others released their ward organizations to "vote their consciences." Eight aldermen and committeemen eventually either came out publicly for Epton or allowed their precinct apparatus to be used by "Democrats for Epton."

Byrne reneged on her postelection promise to support Washington as the party nominee and to facilitate a full transition by opening up her government to Washington (and Epton) transition officials. However, Richard Daley, the other principal primary candidate, made his position clear that despite the disaffection of many local Democrats, "I'll stick with Washington."[68] Daley had little to gain by bolting the party, and, were he to run for other citywide office or to retain his State's Attorney's Office position, he would certainly need the support of Chicago's Black voters to win. Given the position of the national Democrats on supporting Washington, Daley would need the support of the national party should he run for a future congressional seat against a strong local rival.

With Jane Byrne running a dead-end write-in campaign, the local machine leadership divided, and the Republican Epton running a campaign with lukewarm electoral appeal and little substantive content, many observers felt that, even in this racially charged environment, Washington's chances for victory were most favorable. For one thing, Black voter interest had been sustained at a fever pitch.

When Byrne withdrew, the Epton camp was enthusiastic, since this enhanced the possibility of a serious election bid by Epton. In other words, the viability of Epton's campaign bid was established on the basis of racism becoming the dominant

aspect of his candidacy, which accounted for the subsequent
groundswell of support he received from white voters at the polls.

The local Democratic Party organization had not given Byrne's
write-in a seal of approval. The day following her withdrawal,
the Democratic central committee endorsed Washington. With
40% of its members absent, an unprecedented voice vote (instead
of a roll call) was called by chairman Ed Vrdolyak, who had
supported Byrne during the primary. While Vrdolyak had for-
mally endorsed Washington, he, like many committeemen,
did little to support his candidacy. This act drove a wedge
between the Black Democratic committee members and aldermen
and white politicians from the ethnic wards. Meanwhile, the
party became further polarized, as staunch conservatives like
Roman Pucinski and Joseph Nardulli joined with 25th ward
alderman Vito Marzullo (the first ward boss to back Epton openly)
to bolt the party position on endorsing Washington.

Following Marzullo's lead, longtime alderman Anthony
Laurino (34th ward) and Park District Superintendent Ed Kelly
(also the 47th ward committeeman) became early supporters
of Epton. Seventh ward committee member John Geocaris had
the dubious distinction of not only endorsing Epton in a racist
bid against Washington, but also letting it be known that he
supported Frank Rizzo over Wilson Goode in the Philadelphia
primary.

Some local politicians, such as 38th ward committeeman
and alderman Thomas Cullerton, remained "neutral" as did
Richard Mell in the 33rd. They took the posture that their
constituencies—and the wing of the party under their
leadership—should vote their own consciences. The most
despicable roles were played by party chairman Ed Vrdolyak
(10th ward), Ed Burke (14th), Frank Stembert (22nd), and others
who feigned public support for Washington, but in every other
way worked directly to support Epton's candidacy.

Vrdolyak must be singled out as the center of the racist
reaction to the Washington campaign.[69] On the last weekend
before the primary, he made the clearest statement of the central
campaign issue: racial power. Arguing before Northwest Side

party workers, Vrdolyak stated that the party should close ranks behind Byrne and abandon Daley, since a vote for Daley was a vote for Washington. "After all, it's a race thing," he said. Vrdolyak then bolted the post-primary unity breakfast attended by every central local party figure to show unity for Washington being the party's nominee for mayor. During the general election, Vrdolyak went to Gary, Indiana, to speak before a Democratic Party organization meeting, where he levied an implicit criticism against Washington about how racially charged the general election had become. "Fast Eddie," as Vrdolyak is called, failed to attend the major Democratic Party fundraiser for Harold Washington, a $200-a-plate affair attended by 2,500 people, sending his brother instead. Finally, Vrdolyak procrastinated in pushing for early party unity around Washington's nomination: he convened the party central committee only after national Democratic Party leadership made it clear that Byrne's write-in bid was to cease and that local party leadership should close ranks behind Harold Washington. This gesture of support came a full month into the seven-week-long general election period. It goes without saying that Vrdolyak is the leader of the current block of "29" aldermen in opposition to Washington's reform-in-government program. This group has been called part of the "Cabal-ocrats"—Republicans masquerading as "Democrats" within the party.[70]

THE EPTON CAMPAIGN

In Chicago, the electorate is not merely predominantly Democratic. Republicans are virtually non-existent. Normally, a Republican candidate for mayor must be "accosted at gun point" and forced to run.

Bernard Epton, the Republican mayoral candidate, won the Republican nomination with a little over 11,000 votes. However, as indicated in Table 10, Epton's proportion of the Washington vote was 93%, a percentage four and one-half times higher than that polled by Wallace Johnson (20% of the Democratic vote) against Jane Byrne in 1979. The fact that Washington had outpolled Epton in the primary by over 400,000 votes in an overwhelmingly Democratic city makes his campaign one of the clearest cases of racism. Vulgar, barbaric, and violent is the story of how a Jewish Republican turns into the white racist's darling candidate in opposition to a Black reform candidate with a prior history of party loyalty and service—Washington had even supported Richard J. Daley in 1975 against Richard Newhouse, the Black candidate.

Table 10 RATIO OF REPUBLICAN VOTE TO DEMOCRATIC VOTE

Daley (6 elections)	.51* (.36)
Bilandic	.28
Byrne	.20
Washington-Epton	.93

*Daley was contested in 1955 by Robert Merriam and in 1963 by Ben Adamowski (when Republicans got 80% of the Democratic vote). In his other four elections he beat the Republicans 4 to 1.

Bernard Epton had served in the state Legislature for 14 years. During his early years in the House, he had enjoyed the repeated endorsement of the liberal Independent Voters of Illinois, which had a stronghold in the Hyde Park district that he represented. Epton had teamed with Washington to sponsor a number of progressive bills. A prodigious investor, he parlayed his knowledge of insurance law to become the authority in the Legislature on insurance legislation and regulatory statutes—and was rewarded handsomely by the large monopolized insurance industry in the state. To this extent, the frugality of Washington is sharply contrasted by the style of the multimillionaire Epton.

Soon after Washington's primary victory, Epton, little known outside his liberal Hyde Park constituency before the primary election, made several statements that set much of the tone for the general election campaign to follow. First, Epton was quoted in the press as stating that Washington's Democratic primary opponents "had been too soft on Harold," a person whom he had known for two decades, mainly through their roles in the state Assembly. They had co-sponsored legislation during the late 1960s and early 1970s. This remark was a signal that Epton planned to exploit Washington's tax, professional, legal, and personal business difficulties, which his primary opponents had not raised directly.

Second, Epton called upon Washington to take a public pledge that the two would not inject racism into the election campaign. In a February 27 *New York Times* interview, Washington replied to Epton's challenge by making the following statement:

> I've known Mr. Epton for 20 years. He knows my stand on racism. I talk about it softly not abrasively. And I resent his subtle injection of racism even as he says he rejects it. He doesn't have to contact me. He should just shut up about it.[71]

Washington responded even more angrily when he heard Epton had hired the firm of Bailey, Deardourff, and that the Republicans had sent in a crack team of investigators known for "digging up dirt" on the Democratic opposition.[72] Soon afterward, racist street literature began to appear, having originated among the city's Police Department personnel. One particular leaflet featured a new Chicago police emblem labeled: "Chicongo Po-lease" and suggested that Washington would quickly hire Black comedian Richard Pryor as the Police Superintendent were he elected. In the days and weeks that followed, the racist literature became more widespread and outrageous. There were the "Honkies for Bernie" buttons, intended to counter the outstanding electrical charge generated by the blue button, worn proudly by hundreds of thousands of Chicago Blacks and Washington supporters. Finally, there was the famous "watermelon" button, which mysteriously appeared and had the effect of enraging the Black community while shaming white liberals who vacillated in giving Washington their unconditional support as the bona fide reform candidate in the race.

Finally, Epton launched his first series of TV and radio ads under the theme: "Vote Bernard Epton Before It's Too Late." Blacks were infuriated and white liberals thought the slogan too clear in its deliberate appeal to the white ethnic vote. In a statement that sent a message to Epton supporters within and outside the Democratic Party, Washington lashed out at the racists and opportunists who would exploit racial fears among the electorate and divert the substance behind his campaign and the movement that propelled it toward political reform:

> Those who would slyly, shamelessly and irresponsibly inject racism into Chicago politics and into this campaign are playing with fire. This racism business is dangerous. Racism is a dangerous thing and those who should know better should inform those who don't that they should stop it.

The central issue in the general election was racism, racism that obstructed the democratic right of a people who are the largest plurality within the city to translate their numerical dominance into electoral power by capturing City Hall. For 50 years the Irish had controlled Chicago's City Hall. By the beginning of the 1970s the Poles had thought it would be "their turn."[73] However, the marked but gradual decline in overall white ethnic voting strength relative to Blacks and Latinos, the new nationalities, forged by legacies of common struggles against oppression and political subordination, would not allow the Polish aspiration to be played out in Chicago.

On one side of the struggle was an antagonist who represented an attempt to turn back, or at least to suspend, the clock of social time, preserving the decadence of the Chicago machine. On the other side was an alignment of race, nationality, and class forces who supported the fullest aspiration of an oppressed people to have their democratic rights realized, at least symbolically, through the transfer of the political power of governance as expressed in the selection, then the formal election, of "one of their own" as mayor. This event brought to a conclusion an act denied them in 1976, when Daley died and Wilson Frost, then mayor pro tem, was locked out of the mayor's office and Blacks thereby were blocked from achieving a semblance of real political power.

Blacks were now the basis of a major convergence of racial/ national, and class forces into a movement that targeted for extinction a system of rule and dispensation of favors and rewards based upon the differential voting strength and political power of ethnic groups in Chicago. Over the years since its inception, the machine had not merely become obsolete—its problems were now making it difficult for the ruling elite to rule. The machine had more and more begun to run into contradiction with the realization of the democratic aspirations by Blacks and Latinos (who constitute a large portion of the working people, the poor, and powerless). The machine had become bankrupt as a system for selection of policymakers and for allocation of social resources. We saw this unfold most dramatically with the upsurge in protest issues under the Byrne administration. The deepening fiscal crisis of the city, intensified by federal retrenchment in urban and social expenditures, further aggravated the existing political situation. The contradictions inherent within the fiscal crisis set in motion widespread and seemingly isolated political conflicts, which collectively called into question the old system of privilege and power based upon patronage and "plantation politics." Thus, the systemic dislocations experienced in Chicago would have profound consequences on the city's politics and politicians. For in their attempts to preserve their privilege, the "old guard" had to call upon primitive, barbaric tactics of racial hate-mongering, which feeds upon ignorance and fear and arouses the most backward sentiments and passions among the white electorate.

On the one hand, Epton was an instrument whom the "old guard" would hoist to champion their cause. On the other hand, Epton's ambitions to rule made him more than willing to be their pawn. He was a conscious political actor, who had amassed the material resources and influence to come closer to realizing his "great venture" than any other Republican in more than 50 years. He tried to do this at the expense of the aspirations of Black people in Chicago and all working people, the unemployed, and dependent sectors who became the broad social base of the movement to elect Harold Washington mayor.

By mid-March, and certainly by the eve of the Washington/Epton debate (March 21) and thereafter, Epton attempted, with notable success, to make Harold Washington, the person and the candidate, the central issue of the campaign.

After it was clear that Byrne's write-in campaign had failed to capture the white voter upsurge that had been anticipated, Epton moved to fill this void. By then he had received considerable encouragement from machine politicians who had bolted the party. Epton, a politically obscure and unknown Jewish liberal, had become the "white hope."

Table 11 EPTON: THE ALTERNATIVE

	The Reform Democrat	The Maverick Republican
Candidate	Harold Washington	Bernard Epton
Birthplace	Chicago	Chicago
Year of Birth	1922	1922
Race	Black	white
Ethnicity	Afro-American	Jewish
Gender	male	male
Father's Occupation	minister/lawyer	business lawyer
Education	Roosevelt University, Northwestern University	University of Chicago
Occupation	lawyer	lawyer, investor
Profession	politician	politician
Political Experience	Father was a precinct captain. Served as apprentice under Dawson; protege of Metcalfe; held elective office for 18 years in state Legislature and in Congress; ran for mayor in 1977.	Longtime loyal liberal Republican with Hyde Park political and social connections. Served in state Legislature for 17 years; no prior city-wide campaigns.

Just as Washington had been selected as the "Black hope," the question until this time had been: who would best represent the "white hope"? Since Byrne's burn-out, many white people had become interested in the Republican candidate. Washington's past legal and personal difficulties (failure to file income taxes; spending 40 days in jail; being suspended from the Bar for three years; failure to pay gas, electric, and water bills; being "co-owner" of a slum building on the South Side), made it easy for some people to justify their support for the

Republican candidate who happened to be white—even if the negative disclosures about Epton's background were not essentially different, qualitatively.[74] As noted in Table 11, there was not very much in terms of political background that separated Epton and Washington. Most Black people were not really disheartened by the disclosures about Harold Washington. There was a generalized mass view: one cannot be within the machine for over 30 years of one's adult life and not be infected by it to some extent.

Epton tried to use his relentless attack on Washington both to consolidate whites, ethnics, and liberals around his candidacy (Table 12) and to discredit Washington in the eyes of the Black electoral base. He failed; despite the daily press coverage, he was unable to fragment the overwhelming political solidarity that emerged in the Black community. He achieved little but the creation of conditions for a deeper and broader exposure of his own social and professional background and that of his "classmates."

Programmatic Issues in the General Elections

During the primary period, racial bloc voting had been the main characteristic of the voter turnout,[75] but was not the defining characteristic of the political leadership of the contending camps. However, in the general election period of the campaign, racism became the all-pervasive characteristic and the central issue for the electorate and the political leaders alike. Racism overshadowed all other issues projected in the media, as suggested by the list of headlines presented in Table 13. Racism minimized the salience of other social issues of governance and public policy.

In contrast to Washington—who attempted to run a citywide campaign during the general election and campaigned in all 50 wards—Epton never went into the Black community and, except for a few instances, did not attempt to attract the Latino vote. In fact, the few Puerto Ricans, Mexicans, and Cubans who were initially interested in Epton became less attracted to his campaign when he admitted that he had no specific program for Hispanics.

Table 12 GENERAL CAMPAIGN CHARGES AND COUNTERCHARGES

Epton's Campaign Charges		Washington's Charges and Countercharges	
Date	**Charge**	**Date**	**Charge**
2-14	Washington didn't file income taxes for several years. Washington didn't pay local taxes.	2-26	Epton is injecting race into the campaign.
		3-1 to 3-20	Epton is a Reagan puppet.
3-11	Epton is a victim of racism: Blacks for Washington.	3-1	Epton is physically ill.
		3-1	Epton is using racism to promote his candidacy.
	Washington took money from his law clients without representing them.	3-20 to 3-30	Epton is under psychiatric treatment and is being treated during the campaign.
3-21	Washington did not file income taxes for 19 years.		
3-21	Washington lied in court that he had no lawsuits against him during his law suspension or probation.	3-15 to 3-30	Epton voted against the ERA and is generally anti-woman.
		3-15	Epton had an anti-labor record in the Assembly, voting for "right to work" laws.
3-21	Washington was "disbarred" (rather than suspended) from practicing law.	3-27	Washington erred but Blacks learned forgiveness long ago.
3-21	Washington illegally received unemployment compensation while working.	3-20	Epton was a tool of large insurance interests in the Legislature.
4-8	Washington is a slum landlord on Chicago's South Side.	4-8	Epton is spreading lies and conducting a smear campaign.
4-9	Washington was arrested on a morals charge involving a child.	4-8	Epton spent state money to travel to conferences to pursue personal business.
4-13	The Chicago media have attempted to ruin Epton and distort his campaign.	4-9	Epton is resorting to every conceivable trick to save a campaign and keep the machine in power.

Note: The major sources for all the charges, countercharges, repudiations, and concessions of prior misdoings are matters of public record (Chicago *Sun Times, Tribune, Defender* newspapers). Epton widely circulated a paper called "The Case Against Harold Washington." In addition, Epton published a 600-page compilation to document his charges. Washington supporters countered with a "record" search on Epton, which was selectively released to the press and supporters. Finally, the ads and publicly distributed campaign literature of both camps are sources of information.

Table 13 A SAMPLE OF MEDIA COVERAGE OF THE RACIST PROPAGANDA HIGHLIGHTING EPTON'S BID FOR THE MAYORALTY IN CHICAGO*

The Charges/Assertions	*The Appeal*
"Epton Sees Himself as Victim of Racism," *Chicago Tribune,* 3-11-83	"Are UNI Students Racist?" *NI Press,* 3-8-83
"Epton Fans Racism: Washington," *Sun Times,* 2-26-83	"Race Baiting Gave Byrne the Hook" *Chicago Tribune,* 3-29-83
"It's Our Turn": Jackson, Washington (2-23-83 post-primary celebration)	"Ignore the Racist Scare Tactics," *Chicago Metro Weekender,* 3-29-83
"Racial Propaganda Continues to Spread," *Chicago Tribune,* 3-7-83	"Must Racism Taint Campaign?" *Sun Times,* 3-8-83
"Epton Uses Racism, Foe Charges," *Chicago Tribune,* 3-11-83	"Cardinal Bernardin Rips Jeering Whites," *Chicago Defender,* 3-29-83
"Another Racial Schism Is Showing," *Chicago Tribune,* 3-83	"Two Bank on Racial Hot Spots," *Sun Times,* 3-15-83
"Racial Charges Fly as Epton Presses Attack," *Chicago Tribune,* 3-11-83	"Ethnic Coalition Must Avert 'Race War'," *Sun Times* editorial, 3-15-83
"Label of 'Racist' Overused, Abused," *Chicago Tribune,* 3-11-83	"Epton Hits Talk of Racial Tensions," *Chicago Tribune,* 3-17-83
"A One-Issue Mayoral Race," *Chicago Tribune* "Perspective," 3-27-83	"The Constituency of Fear," *Chicago Tribune* editorial, 3-27-83
"The Black and White Facts of Racism," *Chicago Tribune,* 3-27-83	"Chicago's 'Racial' Race," *Rockford Star,* 3-31-83
"In the End It's Quality that Counts," *Chicago Tribune,* 3-27-83	"Religious Council Plea: Epton Stop Racist Ads," *Sun Times,* 4-2-83
	"Ugly Campaign Buttons Surface," *Chicago Defender,* 4-11-83

*Authors' note: This table captures part of the character of the general election period of the 1983 mayoral campaign, both the charges and assertions, as well as the liberal appeals to avoid the racial polarization. Mass racism was fanned by reactionaries and opportunists in their search for power and privilege, and in pursuit of greed.

But the charge that Epton had no program that addressed the political and substantive issues is only partially founded. The Epton campaign generated six major policy papers and a series of press statements addressing specific areas of government affairs. What is true, however, is that he failed to make the issues addressed in his policy papers *the* major issues in the campaign. He also failed to distinguish his position clearly from his more reformist and socially conscious adversary.

Initially both candidates attempted to make matters of governance and public policy major campaign issues. Washington retained this posture throughout the campaign; Epton, however, dropped any pretense of addressing broad public issues after Byrne initiated her write-in candidacy and that became the dominant news item. The local media were now giving scant attention to Epton's campaign. By the night of his debate with Washington, and thereafter, Epton made little use of his campaign issue papers, subordinating them to his relentless attack on Washington, while his supporters encouraged the mobilization of the white ethnic vote against the Black Democratic candidate.

To Washington's credit, his campaign adhered to its promise to take the priority issues into all 50 wards (the theme, "A Mayor for All Chicago").[76] He continued to center his campaign around the issues of jobs and economic development (substantive), opposition to the machine and patronage (reform of distributive policy), and opening up the process of government decision-making to neighborhood-level (reform of allocative policy). Despite internal struggle within the campaign, Washington published 10,000 copies of a compilation entitled " The Washington Papers: A Commitment to Chicago, A Commitment to You." "The Washington Papers" addressed the concerns of constituencies in 11 substantive issue areas (see Table 14). However, as a campaign organizing tool, the content of the 52-page booklet received little exposure, overshadowed at the introductory press conference by John Glenn's endorsement of Washington's candidacy. Washington did make other attempts to consolidate his constituency around central campaign issues. In addition to a number of "street sheets" and

Table 14 ISSUES OF THE WASHINGTON CAMPAIGN

"The Washington Papers": Constituent Arenas	*Washington 12-Point Program:* Unity Themes
1. Jobs for Chicagoans	1. Open government
2. Health	2. More jobs for Chicago
3. Crime and community safety	3. Sound fiscal policy
4. Housing	4. Neighborhood involvement in revitalization
5. Neighborhoods	5. Better, more affordable housing
6. Education	6. Excellence in education
7. Women's issues	7. Secure communities
8. Seniors' issues	8. Affordable, quality health care
9. Art and culture	9. Improved race relations
10. Energy	10. Fairness and equity in governance
11. Fiscal policy	11. Strong leadership to new partnerships (between government and the people on one hand and the private sector on the other)
	12. Women's rights and opportunities in government

12 issue papers, Washington distributed some 250,000 copies of a fold-over 12-point platform entitled "A United Chicago, On the Move Again for All of Its People." These points became the over-arching themes that united the campaign speeches and issue papers and provided coherence to "The Washington Papers."

Jobs

Washington stated repeatedly that the number-one substantive issue in Chicago was: "Jobs, Jobs, Jobs." With over 12% of the city's work force unemployed and Black unemployment over 20%, Washington hammered this theme to good advantage. The issue was: how could he deliver? Washington saw in his election as mayor a signal to the Republican-corporate coalition behind Reagan that supply-side economics had failed and that people needed a government that would put them back to work. He reached out to the forces behind POWER, the coalition of unemployed workers and welfare recipients that had been so instrumental in the voter registration mobilizations. A refutation of Epton was a step toward the defeat of Reagan in 1984.

Health

The issue of quality, affordable health care was a priority in the Washington program, not only because of the high level of need among Chicago's Blacks, Latinos, and working poor, but also because of the active role of the health coalition in the campaign. Many of the health activists in Washington's campaign had also been involved with POWER, I-CARE, and the earlier Coalition to Save Cook County Hospital. The Health Coalition for Washington held a number of fundraising benefits, distributed literature, and sponsored a day-long health conference in early February 1983.

Crime and Community Safety

Washington's constituency contained many contradictory interests (Black police officers in the Afro-American Patrolmen's League, CHA protesters, seniors, small businessmen, anti-gang forces, etc.). Washington attacked the leadership of the Police Department as the main source of the problem. At the February 6 rally, mass approval for the dismissal of Superintendent Brzeczek indicated that this fragile point of unity was on target. Moreover, Black independent security firms were among those who had complained the loudest about the unfair manner in which the city contracted for special security (Chicago Fest, CHA Housing, etc).

Housing and Neighborhoods.

The housing constituents in the city are among the most organized and politically institutionalized groups in the city. While private housing (rehabilitation) interests at the neighborhood level are more organized, the public and tenant husing interests are equally vocal. Both elements were brought into the campaign in opposition to Byrne's policies and the collapse of federal housing programs. Both groups also realized that something significant had to be done about the increasing political demands for immediate relief and involvement in shaping housing policy by these actors. Washington offered CHA residents, rehabilitation housing groups, and all recipients of federal Community Development Block Grant funds the promise of a greater flow of dollars into their programs, unencumbered by the machine-patronage system and "downtown developer interests"—Swibel and Vrdolyak. It was also the neighborhood/housing constituency that had made the most sustained and comprehensive criticism of Byrne's fiscal and budgetary policies.

Education

Like the area of crime and public safety, the public education arena is very diffuse. However, the single most common denominator among the diverse education interests is their argreement that the quality of education received by children in Chicago is dismal. While Washington promised noninterventionist policy into School Board affairs, he did offer his moral leadership to advocate for the resources essential to promote excellence in education in the public schools and in the city college system. Under Jane Byrne, a School Finance Authority made up of the leading banking interests in the city was superimposed upon the School Board structure, with the authority to approve or reject the school system's budgetary plan and fiscal policy. Its members were committed to the ideology that the schools, whose students were mainly children from working-class and poor families, should be "run like a business." A reasonable translation: expenditures made to ensure educational quality and improved skills development should be subordinated to the banks' interest in having loans made by the banks to the schools repaid on time. Opposition to the banks' exercise of direct control over education policy came from three separate but interrelated sources: 1) Parent Equalizers, headed by Dorothy Tillman, a parent protest organization of grassroots residents and community activists; 2) Substitutes United for Better Schools (SUBS), working mainly through a monthly news organ *Substance* aimed at temporary and full-time teachers and educational reform activists; and 3) Citizens Panel on Public School Finances, a citywide watchdog agency composed of middle-class professionals and institutional elites with access to media, through which they criticized public schools mangement.

Women's Issues[77]

It might be recalled that Illinois NOW leadership endorsed Jane Byrne. While Byrne appealed to the independent, career-oriented feminists in the city, Daley and Washington attempted to tap the "abused women" and "women-as-workers" segment of the women's movement. Moreover, more than any other candidate, Washington took his campaign into the unemployment centers and CHA developments, where a disproportionate number of women were concentrated. Equally as important, many of the health issues that were undertones of the 1983 mayoral campaign were raised by women. Women constituted the organizational base of many of the coalitions around the issues of health, housing, education, crime, and community safety. Their special demands were focused within the umbrella organization, Women's Network for Harold Washington and in CBUC's Women's Auxiliary.

Senior Issues

Washington made several efforts to capture the seniors' vote in Chicago. In the primary, one of his initial issue papers targeted the conditions of the aged in Chicago's electorate. During the general election, he arranged for Claude Pepper (D-Florida), the leading seniors' spokesman in Congress, to tour Chicago neighborhoods on his behalf. Also, the Seniors for Harold Washington held a major press and public conference that focused on the mobilization of seniors against hunger, homelessness, and fear of violence.

Art and Culture

Jane Byrne had built a sizable constituency of influential "new culture" types on the basis of her "festivals." The social base for this constituency were the middle-class singles on the near North Side and the growing number of downtown residents who were attracted to Summerfest, Winterfest, Loopalive, Springfest, and the more notorious Chicago Fest. The problem with all these "fests" was their political errancy: the cutting edge was that Black artists were excluded from decision-making, denied equal access to special audiences, and given limited opportunities to make money. One of the more significant informal coalitions that contributed to the mobilization for Washington was the "Artists for Harold Washington," joined by small culture vendors and producers of cultural artifacts.

Energy

Since 1979, the basic cost of electricity and gas had increased by 89% in Chicago (Commonwealth Edison and Peoples Gas are the leading monopoly corporate utilities). Under Byrne, a city revenue-generating surcharge was affixed to the usage of energy. The city had no incentive to fight for lower rates before the Illinois State Commerce Commission. Com Ed continued to build generator plants and pass on the cost to consumers. Com Ed also bought hundreds of millions of dollars worth of coal, which consumers paid for, but which it never intends to use. The issue of affordable energy was one of the less ambiguous issues of the community/consumer economics: a broad constituency could be united against the interests of a few monopoly utilities and capitalist investors. Under the leadership of the Center for Neighborhood Technology, an Affordable Energy Commission was established, to fight for a cap on the energy surcharge and reinvestment of utility profits in neighborhood housing and residential energy conservation. Washington essentially endorsed these reforms. Most observers see the main obstacle to the implementation of these reforms as being in part the reactionary resistance and sabotage of the "old guard" who remain entrenched within the party, the City Council, and the bureaucracy on one hand, and the state of Chicago's fiscal economy on the other.

Fiscal Policy

The cornerstone of Washington's reform program is the elimination of patronage from Chicago government, along with sound fiscal policy. Despite his aggressive attacks on patronage, and his avowal of open government and redivision of decision-making, based upon the community-labor alliance as the cutting edge of his electoral coalition—all of which would type-cast Washington as a political progressive—Washington's fiscal policies are conservative (i.e., rigid fiscal controls, balanced budget, attention to bond ratings, positive relations with lending institutions). At the center of urban governance is the approach taken by the head of government to crisis management. In the Washington program, we see potential makings of an austerity program that, under a white mayor, Blacks might find untenable. But under a reform candidate like Harold Washington, an austerity program has the best chance of maintaining popular credibility—to win in 1987, Washington needs to remain credible and to extend his electoral coalition.

ELECTION DAY VOTER TURNOUT

Nearly 1.3 million people, 82% of the eligible electorate, voted for the Democratic and Republican candidates on April 12. Washington received 50.06% (668,176) of the votes while Epton received 46.4% (619,926) of all ballots cast.[78] The mobilization of the electorate along essentially racial and national lines (white ethnics included) made this one of the closest local elections in the history of machine politics in Chicago. Washington carried 23 wards, two more than he carried in the primary election. Epton carried 27 wards on the strength of the white ethnic backlash and a massive bolt of the 50-year tradition of Democratic hegemony at the polls.

Epton carried 86% of the vote in predominantly white wards, compared with 12% for Washington. Washington garnered 98% of the vote in predominantly Black wards, while Epton received less than 2% of the vote in these same wards.

In the traditionally liberal white Lake Front wards usually carried by Democratic candidates, Epton carried 72% of the vote, outpolling Washington (24%) nearly 3 to 1. When we consider that the Lake Front wards are more racially heterogeneous, and given the pattern of Black and Latino voting (9 to 1 and 3 to 1 respectively for Washington over Epton), it is not difficult to argue that Washington received a far lower percentage of the actual white vote than the percentage shown in Table 15.

Table 15 RESULTS OF MAYORAL GENERAL ELECTION, APRIL 1983

	Washington	*Epton*
Total vote	668,176	619,926
Percentage of total	50.06%	46.4%
Wards carried	46%	54%
Vote in Black wards	98%	2%
Vote in Latino wards	74%	25%
Vote in white wards	12%	86%
Vote in Lake Front wards	24%	72%

If the Latino vote (discussed below) is held constant, our data indicate that the general election was even more racially polarized than the vote in the primary. In the primary returns, the leading white candidates received an estimated 88% of the total white vote and 21% of the total Black vote. However, in the general election returns, the big difference is that Epton captured 85% of the total white vote but a virtually insignificant percentage of the Black vote (2%, given errors).

When Washington's electoral support is analyzed, the near-total Black support he received distorts the actual composition of his support base. Washington received 77% of his winning total from Black voters, 17% from Latinos, and 6% from white voters. By contrast, Epton received less than 2% of his support from Blacks, 3% from Latinos, and 95% from whites. This indicates that Epton's electoral coalition was more racially homogeneous than Washington's, although the latter had a main base of support (Blacks) that was more intensely supportive of his election than was Epton's main base of support.

This analysis would support the view that while racial polarization was extremely high in the general election—even more polarized than the primary election—racial polarization does not explain all the variance between the two elections. If racial bloc voting was the defining characteristic of the electorate in the primary, then voting along nationality lines was a characteristic feature of the general election vote. The single most important aspect of the nationality vote was the dramatic shift in support among Latinos for Harold Washington.[79]

Although Washington received 74% of the vote in wards numerically dominated by Latinos, the Latino vote varied markedly along subnationality lines. Puerto Ricans and Mexicans gave Washington a range of support from 79% to 68%, respectively, while the more conservative but smaller Cuban electorate gave Washington only 52% of their total voter turnout. Despite these differences, Latinos overall came close to voting as a bloc for Washington. One other point is significant with regards to the Latino vote. In November 1982 there were only 79,000 registered Latinos, and Latino-dominated wards tend to be less racially homogeneous than ethnic-white wards and the highly homogeneous Black wards on the South and West Sides of the city. Therefore, it is important to look more closely at the demographic distribution of the population comprising Latino wards. Table 16 focuses upon the five wards that have the highest percentage of Latino population. The percentage vote for Harold Washington is highly correlated with both the overall Latino percentage of the population and the combined plurality of Blacks and Latinos in the ward.

Table 16 THE HISPANIC VOTE IN THE 1983 CHICAGO MAYORAL ELECTION, BY WARD

Ward	Hispanic Voting-Age Population	% Hispanic of Total Voting-Age Population	% Hispanic and Black of Total Voting-Age Population	Primary Vote for Washington	General Vote for Washington	% Increase in Vote for Washington
22	25,676	69%	77%	1,780	4,674	163%
25	22,638	59%	75%	2,620	5,925	126%
26	20,032	50%	54%	1,488	7,449	401%
31	19,495	51%	59%	2,709	9,857	264%
City Total	252,077	12%	47%	424,107	668,176	58%

However, in each case, and for Latinos overall, the outstanding features of the Latino impact on the 1983 mayoral election are: 1) the almost 20% increase in Latino registrations (17,000) by March 15, bringing overall registrations close to 100,000; 2) the increase in Latino turnout as a percentage of registered voters; and 3) the dramatic increase in the percent vote received by Washington in the general election relative to the vote he captured in the primary election. For example, 69% of the registered Latinos went to the polls for the general election—a Chicago record. In the primary, Washington received an estimated 25% of the combined Hispanic vote (Puerto Rican, Mexican, and Cuban). However, in the general election, the exciting story is that in each ward, Washington received an increase in support of at least 126% over his performance in the primary. The most dramatic increase came in the 26th ward, where Chicanos and Mexicanos gave Washington an overwhelming 401% increase in support with 7,449 votes, compared to 1,488 votes he received in the primary. In the 31st ward, Washington received 2,709 votes during the primary, but 9,857 votes in the general election—a 264% increase in support. Over all, Washington received 17% of his support from Latinos as compared to 6% from whites and 77% from Blacks.

What explains this dramatic Latino turnabout? A study of campaign documents, including campaign schedules, internal memos, and budget reports shows that Washington made a major shift in his outreach to attract the Latino vote. In addition, the campaign made extensive efforts to bring Latinos into positions of visibility and responsibility within all levels of the campaign. Moreover, Washington targeted his campaign program to address the needs and aspirations of the Latino population, who express the same objective needs for jobs, housing, food, and protection from police misconduct and brutalization as do most Blacks and the majority of working people as a whole. Washington's major campaign literature was presented in Spanish. Also, the Washington campaign underwrote a major newspaper project, *El Independiente*, a "secret weapon" targeting the Spanish-speaking communities of Chicago. At least three issues were printed. In a racially polarized electorate, where the electoral capacity of Blacks slightly offset the number of whites who turned out as a percent of those registered, the dramatic turnabout in the Latino vote is the key aspect of the general election voter mobilization, which provided Washington's campaign with its margin of victory.

The interpenetration of race and nationality in the general election mobilization is also shown by the data in Table 15. While Washington received 74% of the vote in predominantly Latino wards, he received only 12% of the vote in white ethnic wards heavily populated by Irish, Poles, and Italians. However, most revealing is the low level of support given to Washington in the normally liberal and progressive Lake Front wards. There Washington received less than 25% of the vote compared with Republican Epton's 72%. It must be further noted that earlier attempts to analyze the Jewish vote—often thought to be progressive, at least by Chicago standards—have indicated that Jewish voters gave Epton (who was Jewish) 65% of their votes, while Washington received only 34.5% of the Jewish vote.

5.
Governance

I f there was a moment of apprehensive reflection by all political forces after Harold Washington won the primary, the post-election response—past the emotional ecstasy and psychological depression of the winners and losers—was more akin to the sober anticipation of war. Washington was a veteran of the machine; he knew them and their ways. Also, he knew the depths of ethnocentrism and racism mediated by machine favors that kept Blacks on the bottom. Washington had declared war on patronage, and he knew quite well this reform was a structural attack on the material basis of the machine party bosses—Vrdolyak, Burke, Marzullo, et al. The only other alternative was to make a deal, but while Washington is a Chicago politician, having made deals all the time, now he held the trump cards. Wilson Frost was prevented from becoming *acting* mayor in 1976; Washington *took* the office in 1983. This was not a time for deals with machine party bosses; it was a time for taking over City Hall and preparing to run the city.

Washington's major "peace" move was toward the political actors in the primary and general election. One ritual that reflects the institutional capacity of the U.S. political system to mediate conflict is the usual show of unity after an election by all candidates. Washington called a luncheon for this purpose. Byrne and Daley showed up, but Epton sent his brother, and Vrdolyak gave a lame excuse. The response seems perfectly rational: two Daley proteges united behind the party, at least while regrouping forces, to keep on good terms with the national party in a pre-presidential election period. Epton maintained his role as racism's standard-bearer and he failed to show up, although it seemed obvious that he would be forgotten as quickly as he had become a racist cause célèbre. Vrdolyak figured that as party chair he could rally white support behind his oppositional leadership in the City Council, and that Washington could be forced to come to him.

But Washington repudiated the old way, and publicly announced that the machine was on its way out. Patronage was to be cut, and City Hall records would be made open to the public. Perhaps no greater example of Washington's style makes this point better than the mayoral inauguration. He chose to have it in the open space at Navy Pier to accommodate thousands, whereas in the past it was held in the City Council chambers and witnessed by hundreds. All relevant city officials were in attendance. Byrne was seated next to the podium, and all newly elected City Council members were present. Washington pulled no punches, using his speech to restate his militant approach to reforming City Hall:

> My election was the result of the greatest grassroots effort in the history of the city of Chicago. [It] was made possible by thousands and thousands of people who demanded that the burdens of mismanagement, unfairness and inequality be lifted so that the city could be saved....In our ethnic and racial diversity, we are all brothers and sisters in a quest for greatness. Our creativity and energy are unequaled by any city anywhere in the world. We will not rest until the renewal of our city is done.[80]

While he openly attacked the past practices of the machine, he held out an olive branch of peace to the business community. This was not only or even mainly to Black businesses, which had supported Washington since the primary. The main target was the white corporate structure, the bosses of LaSalle Street. *Crain's Chicago Business* had earlier given Washington a mildly positive review.[81] Washington was keen on keeping this favorable image intact and building even more support.

The search for a rapprochement between business and Black politics is indicated by the social composition of Washington's Transition Team, a leadership group designed to sum up the state of the government and suggest a plan of action to implement the broad policies of the mayor's campaign platform. There was a proportional mix of Blacks and Latinos compared to whites on the overall Transition Team. This maintained a balanced approach, suggesting that the racist hysteria about a Black takeover was based on fear/guilt, not descriptive facts about who was making policy in Harold Washington's campaign.

The Transition Team was actually composed of two different committees, each of which reported directly to Washington: the Transition Oversight Committee, focused on administration of city departments, policy, and personnel practices; and the Financial Advisory Coordinating Task Force (FACT Force), focused almost exclusively on fiscal matters. The social characteristics of these two committees diverged, with fiscal matters virtually in the hands of a white elite group. The data in Table 9 present a contrast in sharp terms. The overall campaign steering committee was 71% Black; 33% were based in political, community, and labor occupations; 57% were professionals. Only 10% were from the business community. However, Table 17 shows that the FACT Force was 70% white, and virtually all were professionals or in business. There was no direct mass representation from politics, community, or labor. On the other hand, since until now every comparable transition committee had been virtually all white, it might be said that the FACT Force being 30% Black was a significant quantitative, if not qualitative change. Interestingly enough, the Blacks on the committee are comparable in that they are professionals who work in the Loop, and Black bankers from the South Side.

Of course, the main reason for a Black power vote is the existence of a "white power structure." This means that the corporate control of the economy is managed by and serves the interest of a predominantly white ruling class. There are few Blacks on corporate boards and in top administrative slots,

**Table 17 SOCIAL CHARACTERISTICS OF OFFICIALS
ON TRANSITION TEAM PREPARING FOR NEW MAYORAL
ADMINISTRATION OF HAROLD WASHINGTON**

Social Characteristics	Overall Transition Team (N = 82)	Transition Oversight Committee (N = 55)	Financial Advisory Coordinating Task Force (N = 27)
Race/Nationality			
Black	39.7%	41.8%	29.6%
Latino	7.5%	10.9%	-
White	54.8%	47.3%	70.4%
Occupations			
Professional	45.2%	41.8%	51.9%
Business	45.2%	43.6%	48.1%
Political	6.0%	9.1%	-
Community/Labor	3.6%	5.5%	-

and in no way do available data demonstrate the existence of a Black power bloc in corporate America. Also, a white power structure controls the government. This reflects disproportionate white control of political parties, elected and appointed offices, and government employment. Further, while Blacks are extremely overrepresented at the lowest job levels in government, the reverse—underrepresentation—is pervasive at the higher levels. White power at the top, and "equal opportunity" at the bottom.

Table 18 reports the relative proportional representation of Blacks in Chicago politics and government. If we generally assume that a figure below the Black percentage of the overall population shows an underrepresentation, we are pointing to white privilege and power. In every case, Blacks are underrepresented, and this has been more or less stable for the last decade and more. However, it is important to point out that the most equality is in City Council representation, which reflects the growing strength of the Black voter in numbers and effectiveness. Control of ward party organization lags behind, as does city employment.

Table 18 PROPORTIONAL REPRESENTATION (% BLACK) IN CHICAGO CITY POLITICS: PARTY, COUNCIL, BUREAUCRACY

	Overall Population	City Council (N = 50)	Ward Committeemen (N = 100)	City Employment
1970	34.4%	28.0%	15.0%	23.1%
1980	39.8%	32.0%	27.0%	26.4%

The struggle to govern has pitted the Black power vote against the white power structure. This is not Black power against the white corporate leadership, although one might well argue that it is at the heart of the struggle. The current fight is against white power control of the government and the Democratic Party. The fight has not been to radically change the system in a fundamental way—although many want to see such a qualitative transformation of the Black liberation movement—but to adjust the system for Blacks to get a proportionate share.[82] During the 1960s, an expanding economy made possible the reforms that opened the society to Blacks; therefore, Blacks got a higher percentage of new money, new jobs, etc. However, for a decade this country has been in crisis, with a contracting economy, and there is no new money. Blacks are fighting white power at a time when it is impossible even for all whites who had been beneficiaries of white power to be sustained. Blacks and whites appear to be in a zero-sum game in which for one to win the other must lose a corresponding amount. So the emergence of a movement for Black political power evokes fear in whites and a political response: the white power backlash.

Harold Washington faced this backlash in full form after he announced his Black power platform during his inaugural speech. The tense drama of the Chicago Black-white power struggle was on. Vrdolyak organized a majority block (29) of City Council members while Washington had the support of the rest (21).

Table 19 presents the relevant background data on the respective political constituencies of both blocs. The significant difference is racial—the Washington 21 are based in Black areas and the Vrdolyak 29 are in white areas. The apparent difference in higher education derives from the fact that the most educated wards in the city are also the white liberal areas with aldermen who unite with Washington wards; the percentage of their population with at least four years of college is higher than the predominantly "blue-collar" wards represented by the Vrdolyak 29.

Further, the difference on the mayoral vote is clear: the Vrdolyak 29 bloc is characterized by voters who bolted the Democratic Party and crossed over to vote for the Republican Epton. The racial hostility in the campaign was stronger than a 50-year solid political tradition.

Table 19 THE SOCIAL BASE OF WHITE POWER VS. BLACK POWER IN THE CHICAGO CITY COUNCIL: A COMPARISON OF FACTIONS

	Washington 21	Vrdolyak 29
Population of Wards		
Black	71.7%	10.8%
White	21.9%	68.8%
Hispanic	3.9%	16.9%
Blue-collar	55.7%	53.1%
Four years college	9.5%	7.3%
Mayoral Vote		
Washington	86.1%	25.9%
Epton	13.6%	73.7%

6.
Conclusion

O ur analysis of the Harold Washington mayoral victory in Chicago has been informed by the following historical developments. One basis for the election of Washington was the relative and absolute increase in the Black population of Chicago over the past 150 years, especially the past 50 years. The Black population increased from 109,000 in 1920 to over 1.2 million by 1982. Further, the relative growth of the Black population (Table 1) took place in the context of the overall development of the economic base of Chicago (Indian territory, commercial town, industrial city, and monopoly metropolis), and the resultant transformation of local politics. The last 50 years have been dominated by the Democratic Party machine. The development of Black politics and politicians fits into the overall pattern of Chicago mayoral types (Tables 2 and 3).

During the 1930s Blacks were differentially absorbed into the Democratic machine just as they had previously been absorbed into the Chicago industrial economy, *at the bottom*. Racism operated in the party to hold back Blacks from being incorporated equitably with anything approaching democratic representation. By the 1960s, and corresponding to the broader civil rights movement in the U.S., an independent Black political movement began to emerge and increasingly assert itself, pressing for welfare, status, and symbolic goals, usually within the framework of the Democratic Party. While systemic contradictions, manifested in various forms of the "urban crisis" (economic, fiscal, political, and social), continued to intensify into the 1980s, the system was able to contain political movements for change within the bounds of "acceptable" political behavior. Hence, the ruling elites have been able to manage the urban crisis, and to define the limited, reformist character of the movement for Black empowerment. The Washington campaign symbolized the mass response to growing systemic inequities within a limited electoral reformist framework.

The regime of Richard J. Daley (1955-1976) was based upon a Democratic coalition of white ethnics, State Street merchants, government employees, and Blacks. It had the outward appearance of stability, but was tenuous and transitory at best. For Daley presided over a city undergoing significant economic, demographic, and social transformation. These factors combined with a U.S. economy in contraction and federal domestic expenditure retrenchment to unleash political conflicts within his coalition, leading to fragmentation along racial and national lines after Daley's death.

His successors, Bilandic and Byrne, were unable to preserve the coalition or to unite the Democratic Party on a new basis. The disintegration of the machine into various warring factions (i.e., Daley the son, Pucinski, Vrdolyak-Byrne, and Black and white independents) grew increasingly sharp in City Council. Mayor-Council battles raged over the allocation and distribution of public resources. The fiscal crisis worsened as the political elites found it increasingly difficult to match declining revenues with expanding legitimate mass demands for public goods and services, and at the same time protect the old tradition of dispersing privilege, rewards, and jobs.

The pre-campaign period was marked by an increase of community-based protests around several concrete issues (private housing, jobs, health, education) and status-representational issues (appointments of officials to the School Board, Chicago Housing Authority Board, and other boards and City Council selection). Under the Byrne administration, welfare and status goals were pursued by various segments of the Black community, joined by popular elements among Latinos and whites.

These neighborhood forces targeted Jane Byrne as the symbol of both the machine and the conservative alignment of social and political forces (Reaganomics and Thompson welfare cuts) at the federal, state, and local levels. Policies had become increasingly racist in character. Thus, in order for there to be any new redistribution of resources for Blacks, the machine had to be dismantled. "Black power," Black electoral empowerment, became a tactic for reform, dictating the transformation of the economic goals of struggle among the masses into a political struggle for a Black mayor, a symbol of Black power in City Hall.

The selection of Harold Washington as the candidate of Blacks for mayor was unique in the respect that neither big business nor the machine wanted him to run. Harold Washington was a "reluctant" candidate who had been "drafted" by the Black community. Significant numbers of activist whites and Latinos were convinced to support Washington.

The most important development paving the way for his subsequent campaign was the transformation of spontaneous mass protest around specific issues into a political movement, the most extensive mass electoral mobilization in the history of Chicago politics. That mobilization was based upon the registration of nearly 240,000 voters, more than 160,000 of whom were Blacks, many previously alienated from electoral participation. This mobilization was sustained in a record turnout of the Black electorate in the February primary and the April general election. In 1979 only 34% of the approximately 490,000 eligible Black voters went to the polls. Only 72% of the Black voting age population was registered. In 1983, over 650,000 or nearly 90% of the potential Black electorate was registered. Harold Washington received about 80% of the Black vote in the primary and 98% in the general election (Tables 7, 15).

As overwhelming as the Black vote for Washington was in the primary election, racial bloc voting was most characteristic of the white electorate. Byrne and Daley, two viable white candidates, split 88% of the white vote, while Washington received some 80% of the Black vote. The Washington primary victory had been made possible by virtually total unity among Black community leadership, and the mass involvement of the electorate. The blue button was worn by hundreds of thousands of Washington supporters and became an important symbol, displayed in defiance of the machine.

There is common agreement that campaign organization was of secondary significance to the movement behind the campaign itself. The Washington campaign proceeded in stages. During the primary, it had two major elements: an informal organization under the leadership of the Task Force for Black Political Empowerment, and an extensive formal structure (Table 9).

The Task Force, composed essentially of activists from community organizations and labor, political, and some professional leaders, made major contributions to several tactical aspects of mobilizing the Black electorate and neutralizing opposition to the Washington campaign within the community. However, it contributed few resources to the formal structure of the campaign, or to the mass issue-based movement behind it. The formal organization of the Washington campaign, its steering committee, heads of citizens' groups and campaign staff were drawn mainly from middle-class Black professionals, with whites playing key roles in certain areas.

The campaign organization and leadership developed over time through stages: pre-campaign build-up, crisis, viability, and mobilization of the electorate. During the first two stages the campaign reflected a more broad-based input from the community. The viability stage was marked by the debates in late January that made it possible for Washington to capture the public eye, to take his program to the white electorate, and to acquire resources from among the national political elite. The fourth stage emphasized maximum turnout of the Black electorate on Election Day.

The general election more than ever was marked by racial bloc voting and the intensification of Black community unity. The development of a Black-white-Latino coalition was decisive because it led to a dramatic turnabout of the Latino electorate's support for Harold Washington. Washington increased his support among Latinos from under 25% during the primary to more than 74%. Latino support in the general election enabled Washington to snatch victory from the jaws of a racist backlash among the white electorate, who bolted a solid tradition of overwhelming support for Democratic primary nominees. Black empowerment and reform of the Democratic Party were the major political issues in the primary; the notion that a Black reform mayor would lead to a radical change in the distribution of goods and services along ethnic and racial lines fed a racist reaction that made racism the main feature of the general election (Table 13). Bernard Epton received 95% of his 620,000 votes from among white voters. Washington, while receiving 98% of the Black vote, only received 77% of his electoral support from Black voters. The outcome of the general election reflects the character of the Washington coalition and the relative success of the general election campaign strategy: to consolidate the Black base of support and expand the base among Latinos and whites (Tables 7, 15, 16).

To accomplish the general election strategy, Washington de-emphasized the role of the Task Force, upon which he had relied heavily during the primary period. A more significant feature of the general election was the role played by the national Democratic Party. Chicago witnessed presidential hopefuls and leading party officials invade the city in a steady procession to appeal for party unity and Democratic solidarity behind Washington's candidacy as the first step toward a Democratic defeat of Reagan in the 1984 presidential election. Also, Washington and other Black elected officials were able to gain support for his candidacy in Chicago in return for future help in mobilizing the Black electorate for Democratic candidates in the 1984 general elections. Locally, in extending an "olive branch" to corporate elites and white businesses, Washington moved aggressively (causing some consternation among Blacks) to bring more whites into his transition apparatus.

While the Washington Transition Team was on the whole well-balanced between whites, Blacks, and Latinos, there was a marked difference in the comparative composition of his primary campaign organization and the Transition Team as a whole (Tables 9, 17). There was a tendency toward middle-class professionals and business and corporate executives on the latter. Within the Transition Team there was a marked difference in the composition of its two major committees. The Financial Advisory Coordinating Task Force, which focused upon fiscal and budgetary matters, was smaller (27 members) and overwhelmingly white (70%), while the Transition Oversight Committee, which focused on government personnel and programs, was larger (55 members) and reflected a proportional representation of whites (47%), with Blacks and Latinos constituting a plurality (52%; see Table 17). Thus, while Washington was fighting against the intensely racist campaign of his Republican opponent, he was also preparing for governance. He assembled a Transition Team that in class if not racial terms was more characteristic of those in previous administrations than of the movement that fueled his victory (Tables 7, 15). Washington dispelled any notions that a "Black takeover" was imminent by appointing a nominal majority of whites to the Transition Team. And while more Blacks were appointed to a Transition Team than at any time in the city's history, the most significant aspect of the policymaking structure of the early Washington governance collective is its overwhelmingly high percentage of members drawn from business and professions.

The first 12 months of the Washington administration were akin to war. In typical fashion, Rudy Luzano, a Hispanic labor leader and staunch supporter of Washington, was murdered after the general election. In the previous two elections since Daley's death, the reconciliation of the Democratic Party had been marked by the negotiation of deals between Black and white party leaders that essentially blocked Blacks from attaining a greater semblance of power and privilege within the regular Democratic Party. Since party bosses had not supported Washington, and in many instances white ward bosses had actively opposed his election, many had supported Epton by withholding full support for Washington. Analysis of the period of governance focused upon several aspects of the tactical organization of Washington's forces. First, Washington called for a unity breakfast after his primary and general election victories, which many principals from the losing camps did not attend. Second, at the inaugural, Washington broke with the precedent of a City Council chamber ceremony that could only be attended by 300-400 and held an open ceremony at Navy Pier attended by several thousand. During Washington's inaugural speech he reasserted his stand upon the principles of unity that had propelled him to victory: reform government, elimination of machine patronage, and open government. Washington openly attacked the past practices of the machine while at the same time he promised fiscal restraint, stability in government, and sound business practices. Thus, an olive branch was extended to the corporate business community that had given him minimal support in his primary and general election bids.

The further working out of the economic (class) contradictions central to issues of urban governance has been overshadowed by the persistence, even intensification, of a virulent strain of racist reaction. A major theme in the early Washington administration was the confrontation of Black power marshaled in opposition to the existence and increasingly reactive character of the Chicago "white power structure." Historically, the material basis for a Black-power/white-power structure confrontation has been the underrepresentation of Blacks in Chicago politics and in government (Table 18). The immediate basis for the operation of Black power against the white power structure has been the result of Washington's struggle to govern. At the heart of the current City Council struggle between the Vrdolyak 29 and the Washington 21 is the continuation of the struggle of Black power vs. white corporate America. This scenario tells us as much about the limitations of reformist electoral Black power strategy as it reveals its inability to provide a fundamental redistribution of social resources. In Table 19, we pointed out that the essential differences between the Vrdolyak 29 and the Washington 21 had to do with the ethnic and demographic composition of their constituents. All of the 29 are white aldermen and tend to be ward committeemen; the Washington 21 either are Black or are white independents with liberal or predominantly Black constituencies. Beyond these distinctions, past all the hype surrounding the struggle to institute reforms that target the machine, there are few substantive bases for unity. Thus, on many class-based issues we can expect fragmentation within both camps.

We have attempted to base this analysis on the objective development of historical forces that led to the campaign, and the social character of the campaign itself. Indeed, it will be discussed as a permanent event in Black political history, and the history of Chicago. We believe this campaign should be studied to understand at least three major points: First, Black adults demonstrated that under specific conditions they will defy all expectations and mobilize at unprecedented levels. These conditions are unity of Black leadership, public attacks from white racism, and a legitimate form of mobilization such as voting. Second, Black movements to solve problems in society can be the basis for a multinational united front under certain conditions. These conditions are unity of a community-based multinational leadership, a build-up of community-based struggles around concrete economic and symbolic issues, and political ideology that is inclusive—not exclusive—of diverse communities and social groups. Third, when (reactionary) white power is confronted successfully by (progressive) Black power—especially if it is allied with a "rainbow coalition" in working-class and poor communities—the struggle will be of worldwide importance.

The promise of Harold Washington—what people are hoping for—may well exceed the realm of political reform. But when people dream so-called impossible dreams of a society free from class exploitation, racial oppression, and male supremacy, sometimes they search for new ways to make them come true. We have done this analysis to aid in this search.

The Washington campaign shows the vitality and viability of the Black liberation movement, specifically in an instance of struggle in the electoral arena. The election of Harold

Washington, a reformed machine politician, was the result of a crusade in the Black community. A network of militant organizations, developing from the late 1970s and early 1980s, led the spontaneous mass movement. The fundamental conditions for this electoral victory included successful mobilization of masses of people, a broad consensus of political focus, and a united leadership.

While these factors were internal to the movement, victory was also possible because of a change in the structure of political opportunity that began with Richard J. Daley's death and ended with a split white vote in the 1983 Democratic primary. These special conditions have led to the discussion of whether or not Washington will be a one-term mayor. The main swing factor is whether white liberals can get more whites to vote for political reform led by Black people. If white voters do not support Washington in increasing numbers, racial hostility is likely to be at unprecedented levels by the time of the next mayoral campaign.

There is also another issue of great importance: Can Jesse run like Harold? In states like South Carolina, Virginia, Mississippi, Alabama, and Georgia, and in cities like Chicago, New York, Detroit, and Los Angeles, the answer is likely to be yes. Here, the white candidates split the white vote, and Jesse pulled most of the Black vote. Racial issues are definitive in those areas: the structure of political opportunity in Southern states has been virtually closed, and it is reaching proportionate levels in the Black Northern cities, setting the stage for citywide and statewide Black electoral campaigns. The critical question is whether the long-term result will strengthen the Democratic Party *or* the movement. For the political efforts of Harold Washington and Jesse Jackson, the results should be in over the next three years. The big question is: How long will the cathartic ritual of voting "Black" satisfy the hunger of Black people for freedom, since the material benefits of Black elected officials are so limited?

NOTES

1. The importance of this election can be easily seen in the newspaper coverage in Chicago and other parts of the world. The primary and general election coverage has been collected in two documentary volumes published by Peoples College Press (P.O. Box 2696, Chicago, Ill., 60680), *Black Power in Chicago, Volume 1, A Documentary Survey of the 1983 Mayoral Democratic Primary*; and *Volume 2, The General Election*. Some headlines from the European press are as follows: *Le Monde* in Paris, "Un Noir a ete elu pour la premiere fois maire de Chicago"; *Die Zeit* in Berlin, "Ein Schwarzer Kandidat Schlagt die Burgermeisterin aus dem Feld"; and *The Times* of London, "Black Vote Wins Chicago: Mayor Tries to Heal Racial Rift."

2. The general historical development of the U.S. capitalist city can be traced in the following: David Gordon, "Capitalist Development and the History of American Cities," in William Tabb and Larry Sawyers (eds.), *Marxism and the Metropolis* (New York: Oxford University Press, 1978), pp. 25-63; Patrick O'Donnell, "Industrial Capitalism and the Rise of Modern American Cities," *Kapitalistate* 6 (Fall 1977), pp. 91-128.

3. Basic works on the history of Chicago include: Bessie Louise Pierce, *A History of Chicago, Volume 1, 1673-1848; Volume 2, 1848-1871;* and *Volume 3, 1871-1893* (New York: Alfred Knopf, 1957); Harold Mayer and Richard Wade, *Chicago: Growth of a Metropolis* (Chicago: University of Chicago Press, 1909); Milo Quaife, *Checagou: From Indiana Wigwam to Modern City, 1673-1835* (Chicago: University of Chicago Press, 1933).

4. Thomas Meehan, "Jean Baptiste Point du Sable, the First Chicagoan," *Journal of the Illinois State Historical Society* 56, 3 (Autumn 1963), pp. 439-53; Milo Quaife (ed.), "Property of Jean Baptiste Point du Sable," *Mississippi Valley Historical Review* 15 (June 1928), pp. 89-92; Eugene Feldman, *Jean Baptiste Point du Sable* (Chicago: DuSable Museum of African American History, 1973).

5. James B. Lane, *City of the Century: A History of Gary, Indiana* (Bloomington: Indiana University Press, 1978); Edward Greer, *Big Steel: Black Politics and Corporate Power* (New York: Monthly Review Press, 1979).

6. St. Claire Drake and Horace Cayton, *Black Metropolis* (New York: Harcourt Brace & Co., 1945); Chicago Commission on Race Relations, *The Negro in Chicago* (Chicago: University of Chicago Press, 1922); Allan Spear, *Black Chicago: The Making of A Negro Ghetto 1890-1920* (Chicago: University of Chicago Press, 1967); Dempsey Travis, *An Autobiography of Black Chicago* (Chicago: Urban Research Institute, 1981).

7. This rare mimeographed document is in the hands of the authors. We will be glad to send a photo copy to anyone interested for the cost of copying and postage.

8. Brian Berry et al., *Chicago: Transformations of an Urban System* (Cambridge, Mass.: Ballinger Publishing Company, 1976).

9. Chicago Planning Commission, *Chicago 1992 Comprehensive Plan* (Chicago: City of Chicago, 1982).

10. Eighty-eight of the "Fortune 1,000" leading corporations are head-quartered in the Chicago area. Six of the top 100 banks and insurance companies are located in Chicago; three major international transportation leaders are headquartered in Chicago, including United Airlines; three leading international industrial firms are based in Chicago, including Standard Oil of Indiana, Beatrice Foods, Inland Steel; two major diversified products companies, Esmark and IC Industries are based in Chicago. Three of the leading retail chain operations, Sears, Jewell Companies, and McDonald's, and one of the major utilities in the world, Commonwealth Edison, are based in Chicago. O'Hare International Airport is one of the most trafficked airports in the world. Chicago is a major electronic media outlet (NBC, *Chicago Tribune, Sun Times*). Further, 14 of the 100 largest multinational conglomerates in the U.S. are based in Chicago. The list of multinational corporations with direct investments in South Africa includes: First National Bank, Continental Bank, American Hospital Supply, Borg-Warner, Searle, International Harvester, Abbott Laboratories, and Motorola. Chicago has three major universities with over $15 million in investments in major corporations doing business in South Africa and/or with direct investments in the exploitation of South African workers: Northwestern University, $75 million; University of Chicago, $50 million; and Illinois Institute of Technology, $15 million. See *Fortune* 1982 and 1983 annual corporate surveys. *Forbes* (July 5, 1982); also Chicago Committee for a Free Africa, *Sell the Stock: The Divestiture Struggle at Northwestern University and Building the Anti-Imperialist Movement* (Chicago: Peoples College Press, 1978).

11. Donald S. Bradley, *The Historical Trends of the Political Elites in a Metropolitan Central City: The Chicago Mayors* (Working Paper No. 10, Center for Organizational Studies, Department of Sociology, University of Chicago, May 1963); Donald S. Bradley and Mayer Zald, "From Commercial Elite to Political Administrator: The Recruitment of Mayors in Chicago," *The American Journal of Sociology* 71 (September 1965), pp. 153-67.

12. Bradley, op. cit.

13. Harold Gosnell, *Negro Politicians: The Rise of Negro Politics in Chicago* (Chicago: University of Chicago Press, 1935, 1967); James Q. Wilson, *Negro Politics: The Search for Leadership* (Chicago: The Free Press, 1960); Charles Branham, "Black Chicago: Accommodationist Politics Before the Great Migration," in Peter Jones and Melvin Holli (eds.), *The Ethnic Frontier* (Grand Rapids, Mich.: Eerdmans, 1977), pp. 212-62; Dianne Pinterhughes, "Interpretations of Racial and Ethnic Participation in American Politics: The Case of the Black, Italian, and Polish Communities in Chicago, 1910-1940" (Ph.D. Dissertation, University of Chicago, 1977).

14. Wilson, op. cit.

15. The general development of Black politics in Chicago is discussed in the forthcoming proceedings of a major conference of academics and activists held during the primary campaign: *Black Mayors in American Cities* (Chicago: Peoples College Press, forthcoming).

16. Michael Preston, "Black Politics in the Post-Daley Era," in Sam Gove and Louis Masotti (eds.), *After Daley: Chicago Politics in Transition* (Urbana: University of Illinois Press, 1981), pp. 88-117; and Michael Preston, "Black Politics and Public Policy in Chicago: Self Interest Versus Constituent Representation," in M. Preston, L. Henderson, and P. Puryear (eds.), *The New Black Politics* (New York: Longman, 1982), pp. 159-86.

17. See the speech by that title delivered in Cleveland on April 3, 1964, reprinted in *Malcolm X Speaks* (New York: Merit Publishers, 1965), pp. 23-44. This is also the theme of panel presentations included in the proceedings, *Black Mayors in American Cities*, op. cit. Participants on this panel included Lu Palmer (Chicago Black United Communities), Mercedes Maulette (Citizens for Self-Determination), Conrad Worrill (Black United Front), Wylie Rogers (activist), and Locksley Edmondson (Cornell University).

18. Milton Rakove, *Don't Make No Waves, Don't Back No Losers: An Insider's Analysis of the Daley Machine* (Bloomington: Indiana University Press, 1975). Len O'Connor, *Clout: Mayor Daley and His City* (Chicago: Henry Regnery Company, 1975); Mike Royko, *Boss: Richard Daley of Chicago* (New York: New American Library, 1971).

19. Royko, ibid.

20. Scott Greer (ed.), *Ethnics, Machines, and the American Urban Future* (Cambridge, Mass.: Schenkman Publishing Co., 1981); Edward Banfield and James Q. Wilson, *City Politics* (Cambridge, Mass.: Harvard University Press, 1963). Thomas Guterbock, *Machine Politics in Transition: Party and Community in Chicago* (Chicago: University of Chicago Press, 1980).

21. M. Preston, R. Lineberry, and K. Kemp, "Last of the Great Urban Machines, Last of the Great Urban Mayors: Chicago Politics, 1955-77," in Gove and Masotti, *After Daley*, op. cit., pp. 1-26; also official mayoral election returns, 1971 to 1983, Cook County Board of Election Commissioners (Chicago: City Hall, 1971-1983).

22. Rakove, op. cit.

23. For empirical data on local health needs, see Chicago Regional Hospital Study: *Annual Reports*, 1973, 1974, 1975 (Chicago: College of Urban Sciences, University of Illinois-Chicago Circle); for a historical background see Chicago Board of Health, *Chicago Health Statistics Survey: Health Data for the 75 Local Community Areas* (Chicago: Chicago Board of Health, WPA, 1939). For an assessment of inequalities in hospital facilities and professional personnel, see Pierre DeVise, "Misused

and Misplaced Hospitals and Doctors: A Locational Analysis of the Urban Health Care Crisis" (Washington, D.C.: Commission on College Geography, Resource Paper No. 22, Association of American Geography, 1973).

Current health care conditions of Blacks in Chicago are documented in the proceedings from the Black Mayoral Politics Conference in *Black Mayors in American Cities*, op. cit. The most insightful accounts of the struggle to save Cook County Hospital, and the community unity and coalition-building dynamics around the issue, were provided by Lea Rogers and Quentin Young, health care activists and professionals directly involved in the work of the coalition. The most systematic documentation of the Cook County struggle in the public domain was printed in the pages of the *Chicago Defender*, April 1981 through September 1981. More general vital statistics on the health of the Chicago population are available through the Cook County Board of Health; its periodic reports can be found at the Municipal Reference Library at Chicago City Hall. For a view of health care issues in the primary, see "Health Care Urged as Key Primary Issue," *Chicago Tribune* (January 11, 1983). Also see "The State of Chicago's Health" by Harold Washington in *Black Power in Chicago, Vol. 1*, op. cit.

24. Paul Peterson, *School Politics Chicago Style* (Chicago: University of Chicago Press, 1982); Mary Herrick, *The Chicago Schools: A Social and Political History* (Beverly Hills: Sage Publications, 1971); George Counts, *School and Society in Chicago* (New York: Harcourt Brace and Company, 1928).

The critical issues of public education in Chicago were documented and published in the proceedings of the Black Mayoral Politics Conference, in *Black Mayors in American Cities*, op. cit. Principal participants in the workshop, Rev. Kenneth Smith (former School Board president), George Schmidt (Substitutes United for Better Schools), and Harold Rodgers (Black Faculty in Higher Education), are highlighted in the proceedings. The current status of the Chicago public school system is well documented in the "Annual Reports of the Chicago Public Schools," Chicago Municipal Reference Library, Chicago City Hall; also see the various reports of the Citizens' Panel on the Public School Finances (1982). For a critical assessment of the recurrent financial crises within the school system from the perspective of the business community, see the publication of Chicago United, *Agenda for Public Education in Chicago*, June 1983. For selected articles in public schools as a campaign issue, see *Black Power in Chicago, Vol. 1*, op. cit.

25. Devereaux Bowly, Jr., *The Poorhouse: Subsidized Housing in Chicago, 1895-1976* (Carbondale: Southern Illinois Press, 1978). The Chicago Housing Authority publishes bi-annually *CHA Facts*, as well as *Annual Reports*. The Cabrini-Green struggle is documented in the Chicago press of April-June 1981. The CHA Board struggle of April through

July 29, 1982 is also documented in the pages of the Chicago press. For a Black community perspective, see the *Chicago Defender*, April 1982 through July 25, 1982. For an insight into the organization of the struggle within CHA, see *Black Mayors in American Cities*, op. cit., on the Chicago Housing Tenants Organization; also available is a HUD publication, *Housing Crisis in Chicago* (Washington: U.S. Government Printing Office, 1983), which features an article focused upon CHA housing and the role of the Chicago Tenants Organization. The CHA housing struggle is also documented in the "Campaign Build-up" section of *Black Power in Chicago, Vol. 1*, op. cit.

26. The best sources for information about the Allan Streeter campaign are the pages of the *Chicago Defender*, April through July 1, 1982 and the *All Chicago City News*, a bi-weekly newspaper that has documented key-issue areas in the struggle for local political and social reform. Also see "Campaign Build-up" section of *Black Power in Chicago, Vol. 1*, op. cit.

27. The *Chicago Reporter*, a monthly publication of the Community Renewal Society, annually reviews the status of Black business relations within the public sector. The Chicago Urban League's *Current Economic Conditions of Blacks in Chicago* (Chicago Urban League, 1977), is an available source. The Chicago Fest boycott of 1982 was prominently covered in the *Chicago Defender* in August of 1982. Also see the "Campaign Build-up" section of *Black Power in Chicago, Vol. 1*, op. cit., for selected articles focused on Chicago Fest and the Black community boycott. Another source of coverage was *All Chicago City News*, from August to September 1982. For an overall account of the press coverage in the primary, see *Black Power in Chicago, Vol. 1*, ibid.

28. Rodney Coates, Ph.D. candidate at the University of Chicago, released findings of a study of the status of Blacks in municipal employment in the *Chicago Defender*, "Blacks Paid Less" (November 27, 1982). Coates's study is corroborated by previous *Chicago Reporter* investigations of minority employment and by the Chicago Urban League in 1977. It put a damper on Byrne's earlier claims that Black gains were made under her administration. See "Byrne Boasts of Black Gains," *Sun Times* (November 11, 1982).

29. The projected impacts of Reagan's domestic budget cuts were detailed in an assessment report published by the Legal Assistance Foundation: "The Reagan Budget Cuts: Impacts Upon the 'Truly Needy' in Chicago," edited by Doug Gills (1981). The origins, development, and activities of POWER are documented in the *All Chicago City News*, March 1982 through October 1982. POWER's role in the voter registration drive was documented in the Coalition Build-up Workshop of the Black Mayoral Politics Conference. See *Black Mayors in American Cities*, op. cit.

30. A major study of private housing in Chicago is Thomas L. Philpott's *The Slum and the Ghetto: Neighborhood Deterioration and Middle Class Reform* (New York: Oxford University Press, 1978); also see Metropolitan Housing and Planning Council, *Housing Chicago and the Region* (Chicago: MHP, May 1981); and Chicago Urban League, *The Black Housing Market in Chicago* (Chicago: Research and Planning Department, May 1977).

31. Chicago Urban League, "Why Blacks Do Not Register and Vote" (Chicago: Research and Planning Department, 1981).

32. Ibid.

33. Official voter registration records are available from the Cook County Board of Election Commissioners (Chicago: City Hall, 1982, 1983).

34. Ibid.

35. It was widely projected that this high turnout in the November 2 general election represented the orchestration of a resurgence of the Cook County regular Democratic Party by chairman Ed Vrdolyak rather than an independent upsurge based in the Black community. See "Huge Voter Turnout Enhances (Washington) Mayoral Bid," *Chicago Defender* (November 4, 1982); see also the summary analysis articles of the effects of the gubernatorial turnout on the mayoral race in the *Sun Times* and *Chicago Tribune* (November 3-4, 1982).

36. The Byrne record in opposition to the issues of immediate concern to Blacks is documented in the local Black press, the *Chicago Defender* and the *Chicago Metro News*. Also, Lu Palmer, the noted Black journalist, has retained the commentaries from his radio program, "Lu's Notebook," in *Lu's Notebook* (Chicago: Lu Palmer Foundation, Summer-Fall 1982); see "Jane Byrne: Displaying a New Maturity," *Sun Times* (November 7, 1982).

37. Lu Palmer, *Lu's Notebook*, op. cit.

38. See "Byrne vs. Daley: How They Compare," and "A Capsule Look at the Daley Campaign," *Sun Times* (November 7, 1982). Also, the "Daley Biographical Sketch" prepared by the Daley campaign, reprinted in *Black Power in Chicago*, Vol. 1, op. cit.

39. During the third debate, Byrne noted that Daley should be careful in attacking her source of campaign funds because Daley "hadn't done so badly" himself. This was taken as a signal to the party faithful that Daley was mounting an implicit critique of patronage—a source of privilege and jobs—even among his supporters. Byrne implied that Daley could not be trusted to preside over this system, also because of his alignment with "open government liberals in his campaign."

40. See *Sun Times* (September 9-10, 1983). The El Rukns were especially active in the South Side on election weekend, and during the primary they worked through the Independent Grass Roots Youth Organization registering and mobilizing Black youth in wards where they had a strong presence (3rd, 4th, 5th, 7th, and 20th wards). They received

some funds for these activities and for "poll working" during the primary election. Finally, they were seen frequently in attendance at meetings of the Task Force for Black Empowerment through December 1982. There they got names and phone numbers of people whom they called to intimidate during the latter stage of the primary.

41. See "Biographical Sketch" in *Black Power in Chicago, Vol. 1*, op. cit.; see also, press statement released by the Lawyers' Committee for Harold Washington, December 11, 1983, in authors' possession; and "Washington: 'My Life Is as Open as Anyone Else's,'" *Chicago Defender* (November 13, 1982).

42. *Crain's Chicago Business* is the leading news organ of fact and opinion of the business community, with a focus on the local and regional economy and public affairs affecting local and regional business. Weekly issues since 1976 are available. See "Washington Has Organization, Ability, Skills in Mayoral Bid" (December 24-31, 1982).

43. The factors were elaborated in a special conference newspaper circulated as a call to the Conference on Black Mayoral Politics, held at University of Illinois-Chicago Circle, January 28-29, 1983. The content of the *Black Mayoral Conference News* was developed by the Editorial Collective of Peoples College.

44. "Registration Totals," from Chicago Board of Election Commissioners.

45. Ibid.

46. A preliminary analysis of the correlation between racial distribution and vote for Harold Washington in the primary and general election has been undertaken by Ken Janda at Northwestern University. In the analysis of ward data, Janda found very high correlations (+.98) between percentage of Black ward population and percentage of vote for Harold Washington in both elections. The same analysis holds true (+.94) if the Latino vote is controlled. Janda found the most significant reversal was the dramatic shift in support for Washington among Latino wards in the general election. See K. Janda, "Notes on the Chicago Primary Vote," *Vox Pop* (APSA Newsletter Subfield Political Organizations/Parties) 2,1 (Winter 1983) and "More Notes on the 1983 Chicago Mayoral Election," *Vox Pop* 2,2 (Spring 1983). Also see Board of Election Commissioners, Official Canvas of the February 22, 1983 Primary Elections and various supplemental tallies, March 4, 1983.

47. Interview with Ken Glover, assistant campaign manager, held February 20, 1983. A similar proportion and total have been stated by various campaign officials (Al Raby, Bill Berry, Hope Mueller, et al.). However, the more definitive analysis remains. The data sources are the official campaign spending disclosure statements that candidates are required by law to file. See Committee to Elect Harold Washington Mayor of Chicago, Form D-2 Report of Campaign Contributions, or Annual Report of Campaign Contributions and

Expenditures (Chicago: Cook County Clerk, Nov. 10, 1982 to June 30, 1983).

48. *Black Mayoral Conference News*, op. cit.

49. See *Crain's Chicago Business*, "No Endorsement in Mayoral Primary" (February 14, 1983).

50. The authors have in their possession a listing of most organizations, individuals, and media endorsements for Harold Washington during the primary and the general elections. This material will be analyzed in detail in a future publication. The Black community leadership was virtually united in its support for Washington. However, Mike Scott with the Lawndale Peoples' Planning and Action Council supported Daley. Archie Hargreaves, former Shaw University president and leader of the West Side Organization, supported Jane Byrne, as did Oscar Brown, Jr., a well-known local Black artist.

51. The conclusions are based upon a recent study of the relations between ethnicity and religion and politics, sponsored by the American Jewish Committee, "Chicago Elects a Black Mayor: An Historical Analysis of the 1983 Election," a research report edited by Paul Kleppner, Office for Social Science Research, Northern Illinois University, for the American Jewish Committee (Chicago: 55 East Jackson Blvd., Chicago, Ill. 60604, July 1983).

52. Official Canvas of the Primary Elections, Board of Election Commissioners, op. cit. Also Kleppner, op. cit.; *Chicago Reporter*, op. cit.

53. *Black Power in Chicago, Vol. 1*, op. cit., Introduction. Each stage of the Washington campaign has not been fully elaborated in this analysis; however, the periodization scheme, first presented in *Black Power in Chicago*, provides a context for developing an analysis of the Washington campaign organization. This framework will be more fully articulated in subsequent publications, as products of research currently under way.

54. From *Black Mayoral Conference News*, op. cit.

55. Renault Robinson was appointed to the Chicago Housing Authority Board under Jane Byrne, becoming one of the most persistently vocal critics of CHA housing and management policy. Robinson had earlier earned popularity by leading the Afro-American Patrolmen's League, an organization of Black police officers organized in 1967 to fight against police brutality and misconduct against Blacks as well as against racial discrimination in employment, promotion, and assignment policies toward Blacks on the police force. The AAPL and Robinson were recently awarded a $350,000 settlement of an anti-discrimination suit filed in 1971. Since the election of Washington, Robinson, an avid supporter of increased Black representation on policymaking boards, has been appointed the Commissioner of the Chicago Housing Authority.

56. Al Raby became well known as the Convener of the Chicago Coalition of Community Organizations (CCCO) between 1964 and 1967. Organized in 1961, "Triple-CO" was the first citywide coalition of civil rights groups and activists. CCCO mainly targeted discrimination against Blacks in the public schools and in housing. With Chicago SNCC and CORE as its support base, CCCO sustained a three-year boycott of the Chicago School Board, which was headed by Superintendent Ben Willis. CCCO under Raby has been credited with bringing Dr. Martin Luther King, Jr., to Chicago in 1966 to dramatize the racist character of Northern cities. Raby was also a tenant union organizer and anti-Vietnam War activist in liberal Hyde Park. He began his political career as a delegate to the Illinois State Constitutional Convention, then served as an aide to Governor Walker through 1975. In 1976, he was appointed to the Peace Corps by President Carter and served as director of the Peace Corps mission to Ghana. After serving as campaign manager for Harold Washington (replacing Robinson), Raby ran unsuccessfully to fill the vacated seat of Washington in the First Congressional District. He placed a distant third behind Charles Hayes and Lu Palmer, Hayes's closest challenger. See Henry McCory's "The Activist: Al Raby," *Chicago Tribune Magazine* (April 17, 1983).

57. The Task Force for Black Political Empowerment represented the consolidation of institutional/organizational leadership and the mobilization of Black community resources solidly behind Washington's campaign bid. The extensiveness of Washington's Black community support base refutes the view of Milton Rakove, a machine apologist, that the Black community still lacked sufficient resources and institutional support mechanisms to make a successful Black mayoralty bid possible. Rakove, a frequent contributor to the *Sun Times* and *Chicago Tribune*, is the author of *Don't Make No Waves, Don't Back No Losers*, and *We Don't Want Nobody Sent*, two impressionistic histories focused upon the Chicago machine during the Daley years (see Note 18).

58. Warren Bacon is a vice president and manager of Community Relations and Manpower Planning for Inland Steel Company, one of the leading steel-producing corporations in the United States. Bacon is also a board member of Seaway National Bank (a major Black bank located in Chicago), a member of the Illinois Board of Higher Education, and chairman of the Business Research Advisory Concil to the U.S. Bureau of Labor Statistics. He holds a B.A. from Roosevelt University (1948) and a M.B.A. from the University of Chicago (1951). He serves on numerous civic boards, including the Metropolitan Housing and Planning Council; the Leadership Council for Metropolitan Open Communities; the NAACP Legal Defense Fund; and Chicago United. Bacon served on the Chicago Board of Education from 1963 to 1973.

Edwin C. "Bill" Berry, a longtime civil rights influential and community leader, was the director of the Chicago Urban League at the height of the 1963-66 school boycott. He led forces to prevent hostile confrontations with the white power structure by militant Black community leaders. Berry is a leader in Chicago United, along with representatives of the leading business and corporate firms of Black, Latino, and white elites in Chicago. In addition to serving as chair of the Washington campaign steering committee, Berry became chair of the Washington Transition Committee in March following the primary victory.

59. See James Q. Wilson, *Amateur Democrat: Club Politics in Three Cities* (Chicago: University of Chicago Press, 1962).

60. See the press statement by PUSH regarding major contributions made by PUSH and Jesse Jackson to the Washington campaign. While PUSH claims to have made direct financial contributions to the campaign, PUSH does not show up in the financial disclosures as a direct contributor.

61. "Brzeczek Resigns, Washington: 'I Won't Have to Fire Him'," *Chicago Defender* (April 6, 1983), p. 1.

62. See two articles by Marguerite Ross Barnett, "The Congressional Black Caucus," *Proceedings of the Academy of Political Science 32*, 1 (1975), pp. 34-50; and "The Congressional Black Caucus: Illusions and Realities of Power," in Preston, et al. (eds.), *The New Black Politics: The Search for Political Power* (New York: Longman, 1982), pp. 28-54

63. Given the policy of reciprocity, since his election, Washington has spent considerable time on the road campaigning for local Black electoral bids across the country as part of the "payoff" to the national Black political elite, first and foremost, and to the Democratic Party in its electoral push for the 1984 presidential election.

64. Official Canvas of the Primary Elections, Board of Election Commissioners, op. cit.

65. This is partially explained by the concept of "cross pressures": a person belongs to two or more groups pulling in different directions. See Berelson, et al., *Voting* (Chicago: University of Chicago Press, 1954).

66. See *Crain's Chicago Business* (March 7-13, 1983), "Viewpoint," p. 10; and " 'The Ball's in Your Court,' Washington Tells Business," pp. 1, 32. Also *Crain's Chicago Business* (March 14-20, 1983), "Four Cities with Black Mayors Show the Do's and Don'ts," p. 1.

67. See "National Demos to Byrne: 'Back Washington'," *Sun Times* (March 23, 1983).

68. "Leaders Reaffirm Support," *Chicago Defender* (March 14, 1983), pp. 3-4.

69. For background on Ed Vrdolyak, see the pamphlet "Stop Fast Eddie," available from Timbuktu Books (P.O. Box 7696, Chicago, Ill. 60680).

70. Between May and August 1983, the *All Chicago City News* published a feature highlighting what the newspaper's editors termed "Cabal-ocrats," Republicans who had been masquerading as Democrats within the Democratic Party. Of course, the root term has its origins in the 1979 campaign, when Jane Byrne charged that these same party leaders were a "cabal of evil men." After being elected mayor, Byrne made her peace with the "cabal," who continued to lord over the local Democratic Party organization.

71. See *Black Power in Chicago, Vol. 1* and *Vol. 2*, op. cit.

72. The firm of Bailey, Deardourff, and Associates of New York was hired by the Epton Campaign. This firm had a long record of playing upon the most backward racial sentiments among whites. It was retained by Charles Robb in the 1980 race for governor in Virginia. Bailey, Deardourff has become the major Republican consulting firm. See also, "The Case Against Harold Washington," a 600-page documentary detailing Washington's brushes with the legal system and public irresponsibilities, compiled by Epton researchers. Materials are in possession of the authors.

73. See Edward R. Kantowicz, *Polish-American Politics in Chicago 1888-1940* (Chicago: University of Chicago Press, 1975); John Allswang, *A House for All People: Ethnic Politics in Chicago, 1890-1936* (Lexington: University of Kentucky Press, 1971); Charles Emmons, "Economic and Political Leadership in Chicago Polonia" (unpublished Ph.D. dissertation, University of Illinois at Chicago, 1971), and Thaddeus Radzialowski, "The Competition for Jobs and Racial Stereotypes: Poles and Blacks in Chicago," *Polish American Studies* 33 (Autumn 1976), pp. 5-18.

74. In the possession of the authors is a set of records compiled by the Washington campaign on the legislative and public record of Bernard Epton. In addition, the reader should review the collection of policy papers generated by the Epton campaign and compare them with the "Washington Papers."

75. In Table 7, we presented election turnout data showing that 88% of the white electorate supported Byrne and Daley, while nearly 80% of the Black vote went to Washington. However, each campaign made attempts to recruit prominent community-respected leadership from across racial lines. On the other hand, during the general campaign period, Epton made little effort to recruit Blacks or Latinos to his campaign organization, and Washington, motivated by the reality of race as an issue in the campaign, redoubled his efforts to recruit prominent whites and Latinos into all levels of the campaign organization, including his Transition Team. See Tables 9 and 15; also Kleppner, op. cit.; Gove and Masotti, op. cit.

76. The authors have in their possession the campaign schedule of Harold Washington and the daily briefing notes and schedules

from February 1, 1983, through April 11, 1983; while in need of a much more thorough analysis, the preliminary analysis tends to confirm the claim that Washington campaigned in "all Chicago."

77. The Washington campaign issued a special paper on women's issues, as well as "street sheets" that targeted the concerns of women. The particular problems of Black women in Chicago must be assessed within the context of class exploitation, racism, and male supremacy. This has been highlighted by Peoples College in the 1979 *Black Liberation Month News* editorial, "The Triple Oppression of Black Women." A more historical treatment of Black women is found in the *Introduction to Afro-American Studies, Vol. 2* (4th edition) (Chicago: Peoples College Press, 1978), chapter on "Black Women and the Family."

78. These data are drawn from the official April 1983 returns, available at the Cook County Board of Election Commissioners. The Kleppner study, op. cit., represents the first published attempt to assess ethnicity as a factor in the election. Janda, op. cit., attempts to focus upon the comparative role of nationality (Latino) in the primary and the general election returns.

79. A starting point for an understanding of the historical role of the Latino community in Chicago politics is Joanne Belenchia's "Latinos in Chicago Politics," in Gove and Masotti, op. cit., pp. 118-45. See also John Walton and Luis Salces, "The Political Organization of Chicago's Latino Communities" (Evanston: Northwestern University Center for Urban Affairs, Red Cover Report, 1977).

80. From the 1983 Mayoral Inaugural Address of Harold Washington; the full text appears in the *Journal of the Proceedings of the City Council of the City of Chicago* (April 29, 1983, Chicago City Clerk's Office); *Sun Times* (April 29, 1983).

81. Ibid.; also see *Crain's Chicago Business* (March 7-13), "The Ball's in Your Court," op. cit.

82. See Stokely Carmichael and Charles V. Hamilton, *Black Power: The Politics of Liberation in America* (1967). In this book, the strategy of Black power, stripped of its militant rhetoric, reveals an essentially reformist content. Black leaders would be willing to limit the aspirations and interests of Blacks to a proportionate share of the action rather than a radical redistribution of social wealth based upon egalitarian or socialist principles.

DETROIT

Victory of a Black Radical

Interview with Ken Cockrel

Detroit: Victory of a Black Radical

An Interview with Ken Cockrel

K *en Cockrel, one of the most dynamic and eloquent black leaders of the 1970s, discusses his experiences as a maverick on the Detroit City Council. His multi-racial group DARE (Detroit Alliance for a Rational Economy) spearheaded a struggle against black Mayor Coleman Young's tax abatements for corporations. In the interview below done in August 1983, Cockrel addresses the contradictions inherent in the role of liberal politicians and lessons for building a more effective grassroots movement.*

Rod Bush: How did a Marxist get elected to the Detroit City Council?

Ken Cockrel: I wouldn't pretend for a second that my election constituted a referendum on Marxism; I believe I was elected in spite of being a Marxist, not because of it. In a city council race, the question of identity is important—when I ran, there were 81 candidates for 9 seats. I had long been associated with struggles around issues of material interest to the community, particularly the black community. I had been involved with a variety of organizations, among them the League of Revolutionary Black Workers, and a great deal of coalition work, much of it focused on the role of the police. I was involved in defending a number of cases, and had a long record of competent defenses in criminal and civil cases arising from allegations of police misconduct, that incorporated community organizing and community education. This kind of work made me sufficiently well known for people to say, "I trust Ken," or "He's paid some dues," and gave me enough credibility that the people in their wisdom felt I would be a satisfactory representative.

We conducted ourselves in a way that gave us credibility. Marxism hasn't permeated the general consciousness of the working class in this country or blacks, not by a long shot, although I think some of the central meanings of Marxism are *felt* almost intuitively by people who are objectively up against the forces arrayed against us in this society. So the work, not the label, is probably what got me elected.

Bush: Why wasn't the press able to use the label to discredit you?

Cockrel: Not to generalize unduly, the Midwest, specifically Detroit, has a unique history in its marriage or merger of circumstances that culminated in the kind of consciousness we have here—I think there's a higher level of working-class consciousness here, a greater ease and familiarity with heterodox political views. The notion of black people flirting with those perverse European communist ideas isn't that offensive in this area. The role of the United Auto Workers and the role of blacks in their organizing—there's been a lot of political struggle in this community by black people associated with leftist ideas. Rev. Charles Hill's Hartford Avenue Baptist Church, for instance, gave much comfort to the early struggles at the Ford plant, and was the kind of place where Paul Robeson could come. The pastor was one of the early candidates for City Council. There have been various black political personalities, in and out of electoral politics, associated with left ideas: Freedom Now Party, union organizing, the CP, even Master W. Fard Muhammad originating his program here.

So there's a long history of radical, quasi-, or neo-radical organizational activity in the black community, and of association in union organizing with whites of left political persuasion of various stripes. The purges of the communists in the UAW are an example. There's a history both of redbaiting and of giving support and comfort to leftist ideology. Indeed, the principal living repository of the collective black political coin in this community, Coleman Young (the mayor of Detroit), had socialist roots, so to speak—the National Negro Labor Congress and so on. He was revered as a black who almost literally told McCarthy to go fuck himself when he came here with his witch-hunt. Those are stories that are passed around in the black community, and proudly, proudly. George Crockett, who was a judge and is now a congressman, was involved in the Smith Act trials. So there's a long history of black personages connected with communists and leftists of all sorts, and it doesn't necessarily cause the kind of reactions it would in a community that didn't have this mixture of experiences.

Indeed, we regional chauvinists have a fair amount of pride about our contribution to the evolution of black left political thought and action, until recent times. There's not much happening now, which I think represents an objective contraction in the face of conditions that are about as onerous as one can imagine, short of a more overt military manifestation—everything else is being done.

So Cockrel gets called a rad, or a commie...this is my home, I've lived here 44 years—who cares? People know me, and labels don't mean that much. In some circles I'm talked about as the successor to the incumbent mayor. For some that's good, and some couldn't imagine anything worse. My having been associated with the term "socialist" doesn't impede that kind of thinking, and won't really be the ground on which the issue is fought out, if it gets fought out and that comes to pass.
Bush: A more mundane question—how did you win?
Cockrel: We had a very large campaign organization, since my campaign was not our first effort to win citywide office; we had elected Justin Ravitz as a recorder's court judge in 1972. I had run for office in 1966, when I was in law school and living in the projects: I ran for state representative in the Democratic primary and placed third. We brought all this experience to the 1977 campaign, and we had participated in a variety of community activities—marches, petitions, groups—so that a base had been built, in a sense.

A fair amount of work had been done by the black and white people who were the cadre of my campaign. We had the largest volunteer organization except for Coleman Young's re-election campaign, over 1,000 volunteers. It was a large organization, well organized, meticulously organized. This was primarily the responsibility of Sheila Murphy, who was my de facto campaign manager and is now my wife. She's a brilliant organizer, very good at motivating people to do things, breaking out tasks, and seeing that resources are married to requirements—and that's how we put it together.

So, there was meticulous attention to detail and organization, and we were able to raise money—we spent $70,000, which isn't a huge amount to have to raise, but it was huge to us. The amount of bookkeeping and business of a campaign is very demanding; you report in microscopic detail. Since I was a lawyer, I could contact professional types, black and white, who would give me some money, and I had sufficient popularity that we could organize mass events. We had picnics, runs, activities that people could come to and pay a small amount, in sufficient quantities to make a difference.

The fund-raising was key—although it's hard to ask for money for yourself instead of for something else. To be liberal about it for a second, there's a demeaning dimension to that requirement of politics in this country. To the extent that people are self-consciously political in this country, 99% of the time they think of themselves in relation to electoral politics and voting; that's the threshold at which political participation is conceptualized—voting or withholding their vote.

We published a lot of material, analyses, overviews, position papers, which had a wider mass circulation than people would think. There was the book *Detroit: I Do Mind Dying,* by Georgakas and Surkin, and a film that was widely circulated about our efforts in Detroit. In the campaign we did all the things you do—the phone trees, the door-to-door work—all the basic organizing you associate with mobilizing more than one person to realize an objective. We did all these things, successfully enough to run and be seventh (out of nine elected seats) both in the primary and in the general election.
Bush: Who supported your candidacy and who didn't?

Cockrel: As I say, we ran seventh despite the fact that my candidacy was not endorsed by the "key decision-making institutions of the black community," meaning I was not endorsed by the Building Trades Council of the AFL-CIO, except specified local unions of it, nor by the UAW, nor by either of the two black congressional district organizations—although [Congressman] John Conyers, who is a good friend of mine, did endorse me personally in the general election. I got endorsed by one of the major newspapers, the *Detroit News*, which has a reputation of being more conservative than the *Detroit Free Press*, but there wasn't any great mystery to it: As it often is, it was a case of "who you know." I had worked at the *News* as a jumper, loading trucks, and got to know some of the editorial guys. One of them was sort of the house socialist, boring from within. The *News* was changing publishers, there was a little hiatus there, and this guy did something for me.

The institutions that were important in the black community, something called the Black Slate, didn't support me. After the election, I imagine they got a little tired of hearing people ask why they didn't have Ken on their slate, but they didn't endorse me. I was thought of then among the orthodox as not being a team player—you know, "not in on the deal"—so I didn't get that kind of access, but I got elected anyway.

I was a known quantity, a proven element in the black community. We did a precinct-by-precinct analysis, as you might expect, since our campaign was very well organized technically, and 85% of the people voted for me. I was elected essentially over the opposition of Mayor Young, the UAW, and so on. This is a fact, it's not a question of thumbing our noses at the UAW or anything else. I went to them. I went through the charade with every organization when it was very clear they were going to follow the dictates of the mayor and the UAW.

They had agreed on a five-five split, five black and five white; the mayor's black, so that left four blacks for the Council. Ken Cockrel was the only person elected who wasn't on their slate. Their choice was a county commissioner, not particularly well-regarded. In fact, during the campaign he was revealed to have made some scurrilous racial remarks, and to be a landlord who had put some people out, but that was their choice. I upset the deal—the city of Detroit had a black majority City Council for the first time, but not because the people who now applaud themselves for it sought one. This kind of behind-the-scenes stuff is always there, and you have to go through the business of seeking endorsements just to make it impossible for them to say "you didn't ask."

The opposition of the UAW had a lot to do with my prior involvement with the League, with DRUM (Dodge Revolutionary Union Movement), the wildcat strikes, and so on. They didn't think much of DRUM, and the critique of the UAW and its complicity with racist elements of management didn't endear DRUM to persons seen as being part of that process. But the rank and file thought a lot of us, obviously, since the people who voted for me were rank-and-file working black people. So it was that kind of campaign. We basically had the support of black working people, with a small nucleus of white folks who worked in the campaign and some white votes— far fewer than should have been the case.

Ravitz got a different vote in 1972, including the UAW endorsement that I had requested for him. Let me say this very carefully—our lives have gone in different directions. He is a very good judge, a brilliant trial court judge. We have different backgrounds, and I think Ravitz might have been demographically more appealing to decision-makers in the UAW than someone like myself, for reasons that must be obvious. He was an attorney, as were many of the UAW influentials, and they knew him and thought highly of him. It doesn't surprise me that they embraced Justin Ravitz and didn't embrace me. Also, it was a different time from 1972—the black movement had moved a different way, and there was more estrangement among the elements of the old coalition.

I don't mean to disparage any of these people. They had a right to make a choice as they saw it. I thought I deserved the support people gave me and that it would have been in the interest of those organizations to affirm that support. I'm glad I was able to get elected in a citywide election with the label Marxist, which is supposed to be negative in the American political landscape, and over the opposition of some of the people who have been seen as the most progressive.

Bush: Did that opposition or lack of support from forces traditionally seen as progressive continue to manifest itself after you were elected?

Cockrel: If you think in terms of national program, these people have always been regarded as in the vanguard of progressive elements, but when you get into the local political scene and start breaking it down, you see an interesting kind of contradiction. I was seen as a pain in the ass during the four years I was on the Council because I raised questions about things like tax abatement. You would go to congressional hearings and hear international UAW representatives talking about how cannibalistic it was for jurisdictions to be raiding each other, and so forth; how the worker loses in this regional competition. But in Detroit on the City Council you'd be trying to combat the local application of these same concepts, and you would discover that these same officials were not on your side.

There were many examples of tax abatements for acquisition and demolition and construction, the use of publicly generated resources for essentially private gain, and many of these people who are seen as part of the progressive sector of the national political scene would act in ways that appeared to be diametrically opposed to the stand they took nationally. I saw quite a bit of that—it wasn't just a speech, it was "which plant will close, what will happen to these workers". . . .When it gets that specific, and you're facing representatives of a multinational corporation who are saying, essentially, "Do this or we'll move to Oklahoma," it breaks down a lot of the rhetorical cant that many people specialize in putting out.

Another thing, as a left political personality, you discover that you have a lot of enemies in the left, or half-hearted allies. There's a lot of personal insecurity, mistrust, petty personal shit, that plays a major role in what people who think of themselves as leftists are prepared to do in politics. It's a little sad, but it comes with the territory, and probably isn't different from any other walk of life. There are a lot of people with reputations as "flaming radicals," whatever that means, who are kind of closet Democrats. You never see any of those elements engaging in the debate when it focuses on the local political terrain—for example, the debate over city development policy, tax abatement, or preferential taxing strategy, the use of block grant funds inconsistent with the interests of low- and moderate-income people, a host of others. There are many ways not to be into things—you can assume a pristine ideological stance that disparages even attempting to manipulate those levers. It's another version of the brother who says, "I'm tired of talking, let's go kill somebody," and the guy's never seen a gun in his life, you know. There's another version of that kind of speech that gets made a lot: everything's incorrect, and so you do nothing but wait for a perfect set of circumstances.

You don't see much participation from the "unofficial" left elements, either, in these right-here, right-now kinds of matters. I think much of this has to do with a kind of timidity on the part of white leftists about race—and a patronizing predisposition to support anything that any black will do, or at least not to be critical when sometimes you need to be critical—for fear of being called a racist. And this can just be so sick—I've experienced the phenomenon of white progressive elements being more upset about approaches I might have taken to something Mayor Young might be trying to do than black people would ever be.

Coleman Young has gone through quite a lot of scrutiny over whether or not his administration has been on the up and up over things like a fuel oil contract. It got to the point where the City Council hired me, after I left, to represent them in an effort to compel Young to turn over papers to them. It's amazing—black people ride the buses and if anyone's being hurt by exorbitant bus fares inflated under improperly administered contracts to run the buses, it's black people—but people would be afraid to get near it. These are nice, careful people with Mercedes cars, who would be comfortable with the PLO representative coming over, but when it's right here and they may have to oppose somebody who's black, they can't deal with it.

Another really interesting thing abut these people is that they may present themselves as radical, but if you examine what they really do, where their money goes, they are the bulwarks of the Democratic Party. Coleman can throw a cocktail party and raise three or four or five hundred thousand at a crack—one event—and you'll see quite a turnout of the same people that you see periodically going through other exercises ritualistically in more left venues. But that's politics, I guess.

There have been critiques of our work in DARE (Detroit Alliance for a Rational Economy) by many of these people and others, but there are always those who are watchers and a few who want to take some affirmative responsibility. One aspect of how I feel about "the left" (which I distinguish from "the people") is that many of them take a therapy-group approach to organizing. While I don't disparage this, I never approached political action as therapy, though I don't at all deny the therapeutic benefit to be derived from doing something of consequence. The kind of people I worked with out in this other sector—real folks, that I always have had contact with—I worked with them, I represented them, I lived with them, and there were other sources of feedback and a sense of accomplishment. Those were very interesting years, positive and negative, very exhausting, very intense, rewarding, much betrayal, everything that's part of political interaction. But I didn't look for an assessment of my work to come from sitting around discussing how many pins will fit on the head of a needle.

Bush: What are some of the constraints or contradictions a progressive elected official may face in dealing with his constituency?

Cockrel: Well, things come up. For example, I experienced the opposition of some groups that I thought of as flaky, in regard to the Klan. I was on the Council and felt obliged to extend to the Klan their First Amendment rights. I'm an attorney. I represent people and I raise questions about their Constitutional rights being violated. I can't do it on the one hand and not on the other. You want to kill the Klan? Hey, be my guest, knock yourself out. But it's not for me to sit on the City Council where these elements have come for a parade permit, and deny their right. I was a protester, I come out of the whole tradition. We used to occupy the county building. But here's the Klan and don't give them a permit? No, I'm sorry, I'm not going to switch *that* hat. It's easy to be far-out when it doesn't cost you anything—you're not beating up on the Klan, you're sitting in a government building dumping on some politicians.

There's an aspect of being an elected official that takes a lot of strength, because it allows a lot of essentially sick people to get off on you, and you have to abide things you would never have abided. A public official kind of belongs to the people, and you have to let yourself be used as a rug. Someone threw a pie at Jerry Brown—you can't just grab the guy and cut his throat. Instead, you stick your finger in your eye and say ". . . mmm, lemon meringue." You have no humanity that can't be violated if your're a public official, and you have to become conscious of this. There is an aspect of being in public office that brings out the worst in people who are rather tenuously balanced psychologically, and who know that you're vulnerable because of your public role and identity, and are obliged to an extent to permit access. They'll try you . . . and it takes a ton of discipline. Sometimes it can require you to be almost masochistic, in order to abide so much of what comes with operating in that kind of fishbowl.

This is especially true of being on the City Council, as opposed to being the mayor. He goes out and does what he chooses to do when he chooses to do it, rather than meeting in public as the Council must, which is where people come with every imaginable grievance. You neither propose nor dispose, in a strong mayor-weak council situation. But you've got the sixth-largest city in America on your hands, here in Detroit, affected in incredible ways by the contraction of the economy, and with corresponding increases in every imaginable form of pathology that you associate with urban life. It's quite a thing to be on the Council, quite an education. Everybody should do it.

Bush: What was DARE and how did it come about?

Cockrel: One thing it represented was a commitment by leading elements from various coalition activities that had congealed into my campaign, who wanted ongoing organization of the huge number of people who wanted to work. We wanted an entity to last beyond the election. Also, the question of economic development was on the front burner. Jimmy Carter was President and Coleman Young was probably the most influential black political person in the country, bar none, through his access to Jimmy. This expressed itself in such phenomena as Coleman getting probably more discretionary grant funds than any other mayor, and things like special downtown development authorities and industrial development revenue bonds getting started, along with a host of other stratagems that basically are mechanisms for transferring public resources to the private sector.

DARE helped us critique this and propose alternatives. We had high-quality analysis and research, and program work, like the pamphlet "Rational Reindustrialization." We explored harnessing Detroit's metal-banging base to the need for alternative energy sources, talking about what are you going to *do* about those closing plants? We did a lot of education, took people on bus tours showing how the investment strategies had bad effects on working-class people's lives, organized a petition campaign against the tax abatements for developers. DARE did all of that: education, research, continuing to mobilize people's energy between elections. American parties usually solve the problem of what to do between elections by not doing much. If you don't stand for anything, at least you aren't going to offend anybody, so you're 50% ahead of the game in what passes for politics in this country.

One thing about all this was the Sisyphean nature of the task in sustaining organization, the erosion and wear-and-tear— the business of playing the opponent of this immensely popular black mayor. One danger in an organization having only a few people with limited visibility and connections is that the organization becomes prisoner of its own ambitions, real or imagined, and it becomes very hard to get things done if every move is susceptible to being blunted by an adversary who can turn it aside by saying "This is just another part of Ken's trying to take Coleman's job." A lot of DARE types wouldn't have the sophistication to deal with the elements that the real machine deployed to frustrate them, whatever the issue might be: the closing and selling of the city's last remaining hospital, the dismantling of the city's apparatus you've seen all over. DARE couldn't dig in because it needed more people with equivalent positions, equivalent clout, or media access or resources to open up more areas of struggle. There's a lot of grease there when you have a one-and-a-half-billion-dollar budget, and you'd be amazed at how far those tentacles can go. The professionals are getting a little bit, it goes on and on—and here's DARE talking about public investment. Nobody ever said we were wrong, or that we sold out, at least to our faces. They all said, "It ain't time." You're in trouble when you're messing with the black mayor.

Bush: These are hard times; there is a long-term contraction in the economy worldwide. Put yourself in the mayor's place. What do you do if you're the mayor?

Cockrel: Both aspects of this question interest me. The first is that the problems described as contraction, inflation, stagflation, whatever, are obviously global in their genesis: oil, the role of the International Monetary Fund, Mexico, everywhere we look, the decline in competitiveness of local industrial producers, transfers of investment capital all over the world. And you're talking about seeking to come to terms with them from the *least* significant level of government, even assuming that government at any level has the capacity to control the allocation of investment capital in the public interest—which is the essential question, OK? The city's powers are limited and specific, authorized by enabling legislation from the state level. What that means demographically about blacks in cities speculating on having political power—immediately you shaft the state legislators and state executive branch, and they don't have any power. Demographically the trend is away from the cities. You confront that reality and you're faced with the fact that you aren't in a position to do much of anything, other than offer a critical analysis of the city's experience and maybe pose alternatives for using the prerogatives that city government still has to strengthen and enhance the bargaining power of working people.

How will that express itself in city government? It expresses itself in how a city uses its powers of taxation, its regulatory powers, its powers of being a conduit for government funds designed to enhance private investment, urban development grants, and things of this type. That's where you have some room to speculate about economic development strategies. Another way is continuing to provide services when an inverse ratio exists between the demand for services and the capacity to provide them. That's all you can do instrumentally.

The other thing you can do is to use the prominence the position is invested with, the noninstrumental role—be a political figure who tries to coalesce nationally, and internationally for that matter, to develop a program that will have more national import. That might mean looking for more progressive manifestations of what you see in the U.S. Conference of Mayors, or the National League of Cities. There's no national party to which you can relate—if you don't come with Democratic Party connections, do you plug into that or what do you plug into? Is there a labor party on the national level? Obviously there isn't. I understand the constraints—they are considerable. I've met the Rohatyns just as you have. They've come in here already, and Coleman came up with the tripartite strategy of income tax increase, budget stabilization bonds, and concessions from municipal workers. This may be done on a national level—it may be the only alternative. I suspect it's within that arena that one is going to try to comprehend a national policy with a local adjunct. I would be a participant in that debate if I were a municipal executive, from a perspective of seeing more democracy in the process—who picks the winners and losers, who decides? I would be for a non-elitist approach, but what form that would take—who knows?

You're talking about the business of managing scarcity, in the strictest sense of the word. Harold Washington had to announce that he's fired 3,000. Koch has been able to get around it because he's turned over Manhattan to the developers, tearing down 20-year-old buildings and building ones twice as high, you know. But Coleman's bent over backwards and hasn't been able to interest developers. So it would be tricky. . . .You can't do much unless you're part of a whole lot more, which the left ain't. People say, well, could you do any better if you were elected? I don't know. But I don't have illusions about how great my options would be, because of the constraints imposed on a city. As I said, you're not really in the game.

But again, you can look from each end of the telescope. You look from the big end and say, "My, my, what a really small amount of power one has as the mayor of a city," and you look from the other end and say, "What other choices do you have? Aren't you better off trying to come to terms with whatever power is there and trying to use it, sensitized by the maximum democratic input that is possible, and used to enhance the strength, the stature, and the quality of life of the people who constitute that unit?" And there's where I'd be coming from. But, hey—make me President, it's a *little* easier. The options are very few, and you get whipsawed. If you're able to deliver an improved product, if you're actually able to materially enhance the quality of life, if you're feeding more people, or getting more people from point A to point B more rapidly and in greater comfort, then maybe you can get past all the symbolic arguments about whether you've surrendered control or all the rest of it.

These are the kinds of decisions that you're going to be permitted to play with, and the national historical backdrop against which that is perceived seems to be at an all-time low level. I follow the speeches of those seen as being national spokespersons very closely, and there's been a contraction in every center. Yet there is that impulse, that undefined impulse, which is racially comprehended, for *something*, that is expressed, you know, "Run, Jesse, Run." And there's Coleman Young saying, "It doesn't make any sense, Mondale's our guy." Others say, "Fuck 'em, whoever wins is a white male, they're all the same," and it goes on and on. It symbolizes the dilemma we're in. Coleman gets seen as a "what?" to black people. Is he stifling the aspirations of black people or is he trying to maximize the return on the black political investment? How in the hell will that debate ever take place in a meaningful context, since it doesn't have a programmatic image on either side that I'm able to see? If there is a programmatic dimension, probably Coleman has the better part of it. He would talk about Mondale and his commitment to industrial policy, whereas Jesse would talk about what? "They ain't done no good for us no way. Why not?" He has something to say, and it's really appealing, more appealing than what Coleman's got to say. Coleman's caught in a whipsaw: he's closer to being right, which is a pretty sad comment on our options today, wouldn't you say?

BOSTON

Blacks and Progressive Politics

James Jennings

1.
Introduction

The majority of black people in American cities have yet to achieve the standard of living enjoyed by most white people. Living conditions of blacks in the inner cities of this nation continue to be significantly worse than those for the majority of white citizens. The schools that most black children attend, the hospitals that most blacks use, and the kinds of housing in which most blacks live are usually inferior to those used by whites. Crime in many black communities is rampant. Depressed socioeconomic conditions have not only characterized life in black urban community life for at least three quarters of a century—they are actually worsening in the contemporary period.[1] As one observer pointed out:

> There has been in recent years an extreme racial polarization within U.S. civil society, accompanied with a pervading climate of fear and terrorism which has reached into virtually every black neighborhood. . . . Many black institutions which were either developed in the brutal crucible of Ante-bellum slavery or in the period of Jim Crow segregation are rapidly being destroyed. . . . A growing number of black workers have become irrelevant to the U.S. economy. The level of permanent unemployment for blacks under the age of 25 has reached staggering levels, and continues to climb. . . . An urban "ghetto class" or underclass has emerged since the recession of 1970, consisting largely of women and children, who survive almost totally on transfer payments and the illegal, subterranean economy of the inner city.[2]

Under these kinds of social conditions, it is important that we study the "tools" available to blacks for improving their socioeconomic status. Some people would argue that, as citizens, blacks do have the tools to determine—at least partially—the conditions of their communities. Blacks need to exercise their civil responsibilities, such as voting, to ensure that they are treated equitably. But this argument poses a fundamental question about American politics: Is it possible for citizens with little power, money, or status to use the political system as leverage to increase their relative share of the goods? Or is inequality destined to perpetuate itself indefinitely, even in a pluralistic, democratic political system?[3] In other words, can blacks effectively challenge the current distribution of wealth and public goods through electoral resources? "Pluralists," or those who believe that the American political and economic systems are flexible and open enough to provide relatively powerless groups—such as blacks—with opportunities to change the status quo in their favor, have not provided satisfactory responses.

This topic is especially urgent in the 1980s because many blacks are growing impatient with the status quo. As N. Johnson and P. Thompson explain, this question has "again come into focus, this time with a renewed urgency. The struggles that marked the past debates, particularly those in the 1960s over non-violent or armed self-defense tactics, over band-aid or revolutionary solutions—are with us again."[4] And we may heed C.V. Hamilton's ominous warning concerning the viability of American pluralism:

> The political system is no longer blessed with the economic abundance of an earlier time. . . . New political groups will make demands on the government to do more and for longer periods of time. . . . Again, pluralist politics are familiar with this, but it has usually had more resources. It would not be an exaggeration to say that the assumptions of pluralist politics in the United States will receive, in the next several years, their most serious challenge.[5]

These systemic demands will emanate primarily from the black community, because "Blacks are at the center of basic conflicts in most northern cities....They constitute the social group whose interests and activities have been most antagonistic to established institutions and better-off strata."[6] How blacks decide to use or not use electoral processes will determine the essence and form of these challenges; and these decisions will have long-ranging impact on the political and economic future of American cities.[7]

This is a study of the emerging black political challenges to organized and powerful groups entrenched in American cities, based on a case study approach to black politics in Boston. Recently there have been major contests in this city's electoral arena. One facet of these contests concerns the developing relationships between leadership in the black community and the political representatives of economic interests that maintain a status quo detrimental to black life. Taking place within a framework of what can be described as "traditional" local politics is the "old" but continuing thrust for black inclusion into the American city's patronage system. But emerging out of the turmoil of the 1960s, and in response to the retrenchment of public services in the 1970s, is a "new" kind of black political challenge.

This new challenge is founded upon a tension long present in black America. As Ronald Walters wrote over a decade ago, "There is a growing tension between the politics of 'man mobilization' and 'brokerage politics' in the Black community, and...the present and future course of Black politics must take this development into consideration."[8] Given this, some black leaders are not seeking mere inclusion into American politics, but are trying to significantly change the organization and structure of power in the public and private sectors. These black leaders are not interested in a "piece of the pie," but are concerned with altering the distribution of wealth in American society in ways that would benefit blacks. A difference between these emerging leaders and radical black leadership of recent periods is the insistence on electoral activism as a viable political tool.

In the evaluation of this new political landscape, progressive black leadership will challenge big-city mayors and their political machines. We will also witness an intensifying conflict between black leaders operating under "traditional" electoral activism and those seeking to use electoral processes for social change.

There are concrete examples of these contests in various parts of the country, where black communities are facing the choice of supporting the old kind of traditional politicians— black or white—or joining a movement to introduce progressive agendas into the electoral arenas of American cities. In an increasing number of cases blacks are opting for the progressive face. In Tacoma Park, Maryland, for example, the black community helped to elect a radical, Sam Abbot, as mayor in 1982. In Brooklyn, New York, independent politicians such as Assemblymen Al Vann and Roger Green and state Senator Major Owens are attempting to build a power base capable of challenging City Hall and the private interests that support public policies detrimental to the black and poor people of Brooklyn. In Tchula, Mississippi, Eddie Carthan, the black mayor, went a bit too far in trying to introduce a progressive city agenda and consequently had to fight numerous criminal charges trumped up by powerful political and banking interests in Mississippi. And in Boston, perhaps for the first time in 1979 and 1983, voters were given an opportunity to support a black mayoral candidate who developed progressive, people-oriented alternatives to housing and jobs.

In the 1979 preliminary mayoral election, Mel King finished third; while an important achievement, this did not get him into the general election. In 1983 Mel King finished second, a few hundred votes behind the first-place winner, and thereby won a spot in the general election for the mayoralty of Boston. This was historic not only because Mel King had become the first black person to qualify for the general election, but also because it was the first time a *progressive* candidate—who happens to be black—won a runoff position in Boston, one of America's most important major cities.

The outcome of clashes between "traditional" local politics and the "progressive" face of local politics will influence the direction of American society as far as justice, equality, and political stability are concerned. Boston represents a bellwether by which to understand the meaning of recent black political developments for this nation's future. The political successes and failures of blacks in Boston will be paralleled in other American cities.

There are other reasons Boston is interesting in this kind of study. It is significant historically for those interested in black politics. One might argue that historically Massachusetts—at least compared to other states—has been more considerate of its black citizens. It was the first state to outlaw slavery. Furthermore, the only black U.S. senator since the Post-Reconstruction period was elected here. Booker T. Washington founded the National Negro Business League in Boston; W.E.B. Du Bois was born in Barrington, Massachusetts, and attended Harvard University in Cambridge; William Monroe Trotter lived and founded the *Guardian* in Boston. This is Minister Louis Farrahkan's home city and young Malcolm X's adopted city. Indeed, Boston has had a prominent place in the political struggles of blacks.

Boston is a medium-sized city, with about 540,000 persons in 1980, which is an advantage for this case study approach. It is small enough to allow the researcher to understand the social, political, and even personal dynamics of Boston politics. But it is large enough to allow the formulation of ideas relevant to blacks in the larger cities of America. This city provides an important microcosm by which to assess factors influencing the directions of black political power in urban America.

Surprisingly, information about black politics in Boston is scarce; one would tend to expect otherwise, considering the place of Massachusetts in the history of black people.* It is

---

*A few materials have touched upon some of the discussion presented in this study, although not extensively. *In Freedom's Birthplace* was published in 1914 by John Daniels; it discussed black political developments in 18th-century Boston and also the early 1900s. "The Political Status of the Negro in Boston" by Oswald Jordan is an unpublished master's essay that reports black political activities between the 1920s and the late 1930s. Stephen Fox also gives us

hoped that this study may fill a gap of basic analysis of black political struggles in Boston. The present study represents an investigation and documentation of contemporary black politics in Boston; but it is also an attempt to develop an effective political blueprint for the improvement of black life in urban America.

This study first discusses a conceptual framework by which to understand black politics today. Chapter Two describes the "two faces" of black electoral activism: the differences between

---

a glimpse of black politics from the early 1900s to the 1920s in his biography of William Monroe Trotter, *The Guardian of Boston* (1970). In *The Other Bostonians* Stephen Thernstrom collected and analyzed demographic and socioeconomic data on the black community between 1880 and 1970; this work supplements much earlier information on West Indians in Boston reported by Ira Reid in *The Negro Immigrant* (1939).

An article that discusses trade unionism within the political context of Boston and its consequences for blacks in the labor movement was published in *Social Forces* in 1936; Seaton Wesley Manning's "Negro Trade Unionists in Boston" was perhaps the only published material available to the public on this topic for many years. A more recent work, James R. Green and Hugh D. Donahue's *Boston Workers: A Labor History*, while enlightening in many ways, did not add much information beyond that already provided by Manning. This particular study also relies extensively on Charles Trout's work, *Boston, the Great Depression and the New Deal* (1973) for some of the information on black workers before World War II.

Adelaide Hill's "The Negro Upper Class in Boston" was completed as a doctoral dissertation at Harvard Univrsity in 1952; she did not, however, treat black politics as a major focus of her investigation. Ralph Otwell wrote an informative article, "The Negro in Boston," published in *A Report on the Politics of Boston, Massachusetts*, edited by Edward C. Banfield and Martha Derthick for the Joint Center for Urban Studies of MIT-Harvard University in 1960. Banfield provides some information on various political characteristics of blacks in Boston in his *Big City Politics*, published in 1965. A recent account of black political developments in Boston is provided by an individual who participated extensively in electoral and community activities during this period; in *Chains of Change* (1980), Mel King focuses on various stages of black politics between 1950 and the 1970s. Other important works on politics in Boston and Massachusetts have ignored or only slightly discussed black politics. An example of this is J. Joseph Huthmacher's *Massachusetts People and Politics* (1959), which offers information about the black community but is episodic and incomplete. The best that the author does here is to provide a few facts on the political activities of black activist Julian Rainey. Other examples are Edgar Litt's *The Political Cultures of Massachusetts* (1965), and Murray Levin's *The Compleat Politician* (1962); the former, a discussion of gubernatorial politics in Massachusetts, did not look at all at the small—but electorally significant—black community in Boston.

"traditional" and "progressive" politics in the black urban community. Chapter Three describes recent demographic developments and electoral characteristics of the black community in Boston, to dispel electoral "myths" about blacks in this city—myths that have discouraged black political mobilization. Chapter Four examines political obstacles that black voters have attempted to overcome in order to participate effectively in Boston politics. These include structural characteristics of city government, the roles of City Hall-supported black leadership, and other resources that have been used by City Hall to control and manipulate the direction and level of black political mobilization.

To illustrate how the obstacles presented in Chapter Four impinge upon progressive black political mobilization, Chapter Five discusses the mayoral campaigns of Mel King in 1979 and 1983, the roadblocks that had to be overcome in the electoral arena, and the issues developed by King for the two campaigns. Chapter Six concludes this study by exploring more fully the ideas raised in this Introduction within the context of Boston and other major cities. It also outlines the emergence of the next stage of black protest in America.

2.
Black Power and
Electoral Activism

Throughout American history black people have debated various strategies in response to the continuing depressed socioeconomic status of their communities. A prominent component of this debate has been the nature of black participation in the American political system. Historically, two general responses have been proffered, both based on what W.E.B. Du Bois once described as "two difficult sets of facts." While one set of black political experiences pointed towards integration, the other pointed towards separatist possibilities, or what some have erroneously dismissed as black nationalism. In the 1960s, the "Black Power" movement reflected this dichotomy. The call for Black Power also took two forms. One thrust sought opportunities for full black political participation in the traditional American pluralist order. The other sought opportunities for separatist black political development. But both versions were basically reformist in that the integrationist and nationalist (i.e., separatist) strands challenged the structure and distribution of American wealth only so far as to incorporate black participation in the standard political and economic parameters of American society. A redistribution of wealth and power in American society was not a major goal of either the integrationist or nationalist strands of this version of Black Power.

But there was, and continues to be, yet another kind of black political thrust; it is progressive in that it calls for a qualitative change in the structure of wealth and power.[9]

Consequently, it seeks to replace a model of pluralistic politics with a participatory model, posing masses of people against established elites as a challenge to the particular structure and arrangements of wealth. Unlike the "integrationist" or "separatist" versions of Black Power, this type of progressive black political orientation focuses on national and international issues, as well as local ones; it approaches "local" politics as an integral part of a national and international framework of interrelated economic and political issues.

Black nationalism, or what E.V. Essiem-Udom has described as the conglomeration of efforts of blacks to resolve problems of cultural identity and sociopolitical weakness as blacks, is approached differently in the two versions of Black Power.[10] Under the integrationist strand, or "conservative" Black Power, black nationalism is used as a justification to argue for equal participation in American pluralism; blacks are but another ethnic group that should have opportunities to rely on group resources to climb the socioeconomic ladder. In the electoral arena this is basically reflected in attempts to replace white politicians with black politicians. This strategy is similar to that of the "separatist" strand under Black Power; the differences here are in the particular emphasis on black culture and the long-range goals of both kinds of Black Power. The integrationists ultimately seek acculturation and assimilation into American society, while the separatists for the most part see a continuing viability in a society organized by culturally distinctive and land-based racial groups. The Black Power integrationists envision a society where there are few significant social and economic differences between blacks and whites; the Black Power separatists hope for an American society made up of semi- or fully independent racial enclaves, each based on its own cultural definitions.

It is possible to borrow elements from these schools of thought in order to develop a fresh political outlook for the 1980s and 1990s. Manning Marable refers to this as a "new black common sense":

> The groundings for [a] unified black common sense have always
> been a merger of both the integrationist and nationalist tradi-
> tions, with strong historical emphasis upon the autonomous
> racial and nationalist tendencies. . . . In the pursuit of an
> ideological consensus, a new black common sense of libera-
> tion, it is crucial that the positive elements of integration be
> merged with the activist tradition of black nationalism. . . . We
> must begin building our political agendas upon a comprehensive
> understanding of our historical and ideological experiences,
> both nationalist and integrationist.[11]

A new understanding of black political power can be built upon
these principles; differences between this new model and Black
Power as it is usually understood may be subtle, but they are
very important for understanding black political mobilization
in the electoral arena today.

Black political power within a progressive framework
approaches black nationalism dialectically; this suggests that
black nationalism is useful for mobilizing masses of blacks—
especially those characterized by lower socioeconomic life conditions. But progressive black nationalism is not an end; ultimately it is a means by which to encourage people to question the distribution of wealth and power in American society.
Because of this, black nationalism becomes—albeit indirectly—a
useful tool by which to discourage racism among white working-
class sectors; in the long run, black nationalism can help to
raise the political and social consciousness of white ethnics
in American cities. Black nationalism as "integrationist" or
"separatist" may begin as a healthy reaction to the history of
black oppression in this country, but eventually it becomes
decisive and "exploitable" by wealthy and powerful interests.
Black nationalism under a progressive understanding can become
a bridge between blacks and whites in American cities by
challenging the political and economic status quo.

Integrationist and separatist approaches to Black Power raise
a tactical question: how useful are electoral processes in improving
black life in urban America? The integrationists generally have
argued that black political participation ultimately can be effective
in raising black living standards; the separatists have described

electoral processes as useless for the masses of black people in the United States. H.V. Savitch summarized these two orientations towards black electoral participation:

> Traditionalists and liberals have concentrated on the "disadvantages" and liabilities under which black Americans labored for so many centuries. Racial prejudice, poll taxes, school segregation, and other bars to decent housing and employment have been foremost in the minds of liberals when analyzing the problems of race. Given this point of view, their conclusions point in the direction of eliminating these bars to opportunity so that blacks can make it on their own, in what is presumed to be a free and mobile society. . . . In the more radical literature which followed in the 1960's the writers scoffed at the liberals' naivete and pointed out that American politics was dominated by elites who were set on keeping their power and status. . . . Formalistic and legal methods to make opportunities available were seen as a sham which benefited only a few black bourgeoisie and kept the masses down.[12]

Yet a third alternative emerges from the progressive tendencies of black political mobilization. Here electoral activism is not perceived as an end in itself, but as a tool to mobilize not only blacks in American cities, but also poor and working-class people of all races and nationalities. This orientation utilizes electoral activism as a dialectical and educational process. It is a means by which to confront the particular lopsided arrangements of wealth and power in American society.[13]

The black community has yet to develop clear strategies and tactics that use electoral processes to challenge their position in this country's social structure. Despite the impassioned exhortations of some local and national leaders, and evidence that in certain limited ways the political system has become more accessible to blacks, much black resistance to electoral participation remains intact.[14] Significant numbers of blacks have decided that participation in electoral politics is basically a waste of time because, "Despite significant gains in the election of blacks to public office since 1965, the policy goals of the new black politics have not been realized. Social and economic conditions in the black community have not been dramatically transformed. Black politicians have encountered enormous difficulty in their efforts to use the authority of their public office to deliver meaningful benefits to their black constituents."[15]

From an economic perspective, there is relatively very little that even a sympathetic big-city mayor can accomplish for black and poor people. A mayor's office simply does not have the control over the economic resources necessary to improve life conditions for the powerless; there are too many powerful financial interests converging in the mayor's office to allow the occupant a free hand in introducing ideas and policies that are beneficial to the poor but threatening to powerful economic interests. This is why, from a strictly economic point of view, black communities in large cities with black mayors are not better off today than when the black mayors were first elected in the late 1960s and early 1970s.

Those who reject black electoral participation as a way to confront America's power structures may agree that certain limited benefits are possible to obtain; but they argue that electoral processes in American cities cannot deliver the kinds of benefits that would require a redistribution of wealth and power, and that, until this takes place, blacks will remain on the social bottom of American society. Many have refused to register as voters, join political parties, support candidates, or become involved with any traditional electoral processes. This refusal, however, comes from a misunderstanding of the role that electoral activities within a "progressive" framework can play in improving black living conditions in urban America. It is also a response to private and public institutional discouragement of the kind of black political participation that could produce meaningful change in the lives of blacks and the poor.

A serious challenge to the distribution of wealth and influence cannot take place until blacks increase qualitatively their level of local electoral activism—within a progressive framework. Economic or social development schemes will not be successful until black communities are controlled politically and progressively by the people who live in them. Despite numerous historical and contemporary efforts, for example, black economic development on a meaningful level has failed; generally business ventures in the black community remain weak and disorganized. "Black capitalism," community development corporations, appointments to powerful corporate boards and partnerships with the private sector—all have received major attention. When specific projects associated with these schemes fail, the blame is usually placed on lack of business experience and know-how, lack of access to credit, or the intensity of poverty and crime in black communities. These excuses have validity in some situations; but the crucial explanation is the inability to develop the political strength of the black community within a progressive framework. Until this occurs it will be difficult for any kind of economic or social development schemes to succeed.

The improvement of present social and economic conditions today demands the mobilization of black voters to obtain electoral control of their communities. Blacks must organize themselves as voters in order to capture governmental positions that will place them closer to those responsible for present black living conditions.

In many ways, societal institutions have discouraged blacks from pursuing electoral activism that might produce meaningful change; they have not done this by intention necessarily, but by supporting governmental processes, and implementing public policies in ways that ignore or discourage participation from the black community. Social and educational institutions (operating for, but not controlled by, blacks) have failed to respond to the political needs of blacks; instead, these institutions are threatened by uncontrolled or unsanctioned black political mobilization. Electoral activism is encouraged only in the most conservative sense; it merely means voting for one media-manipulated personality or another. As William Nelson has concluded:

> The concentration on electoral politics also exaggerates the importance of the vote as an instrument of black liberation. Voting is rarely a revolutionary act....To the extent that a new politics for the black community genuinely seeks a social transformation of American society, a search for strategies, beyond the act of voting or electoral mobilization, is required.[16]

Progressive electoral activism could have a positive and revolutionary impact on the nature of American society. Political participation may be either directed at substantively changing the distribution of wealth and power, or at maintaining that system of distribution. This distinguishes "progressive" from "traditional" electoral activism: the former emphasizes the well-being and political strengthening of poor and working-class people, while the latter emphasizes social continuity and political stability.

There are a number of "rules" or "rituals" that have to be followed in order to play the game of traditional politics; in the contest for elective seats, the successful politician may not have to follow these rules as long as he or she pays homage to the rules and participates in the rituals. As Robert Dahl points out: "Although a certain amount of legal chicanery is tolerable, legality and constitutionality are highly prized," and "the American creed of democracy and equality must always be given vigorous and vociferous support."[17] However, he writes, "Adherence to the creed as a general goal and a set of criteria for a good government and a good society does not mean that the creed is, or as a practical matter can be, fully applied in practice."[18] Thus, political leaders need not implement values suggested by terms like "legality," "constitutionality," or "equality"—they need only to pay lip service to these ideals. This is politics under traditional electoral activism.

Under a progressive orientation, certain values guide politics and the pursuit of various public policies. Ideals such as sharing, compassion, creativity, respect, and community are used as a basis for organizing people at a grassroots level.[19] Specific activities under both kinds of electoral activism may be similar: both call for the registration of potential voters, the exercise of the franchise as a means of pressuring governmental officials, or the mobilization of voter support for candidates of choice. But while the thrust of traditional electoral activism is to secure benefits from those having wealth and power in this country, the progressive alternative is to dislodge the holders and controllers of wealth, to force a more equitable distribution of wealth. Traditional electoral politics represents a "buffer" process. It keeps the populace, the poor, the working class, and particularly blacks, from being able to confront powerful "private" decision-makers. Progressive electoral activism seeks to transform these "buffer" processes into arenas of conflict between the poor and the working class and those who control the distribution of wealth. Traditional electoral activism seeks merely to manage the natural conflict between the have-nots and those with wealth and power; leadership operating under this framework perceives itself as a controller, rather than a representative, of those on the bottom of America's socioeconomic ladder. These leaders use minor material inducements to satisfy the wants of the populace at various levels of society. Traditional electoral leadership behaves as a broker between institutional elites and the general citizenry.

Progressive electoral leadership does not accept the accumulation or protection of capital as a greater priority than the needs of poor and working-class citizens. While economic development is vital for any modern society, the purpose of development must be the improvement of living conditions in the American city—not greater profits. This idea can serve to differentiate both kinds of leadership in all communities.

There are other ways traditional and progressive leadership can be distinguished in black communities. Black leaders operating under a framework of progressive electoral activism actively pursue massive black voter registration. Of course, all politicians in black communities will agree that this is important. But some are in fact threatened by the possibilities of increased black voter registration and do not pursue this avowed goal. For a politician who does not wish to "rock the boat," and who has not cultivated widespread support in the black community, more registered voters may be inimical to his or her own career interests.

Traditional and progressive black leadership can also be evaluated on the issue of youth nonparticipation in the electoral arena. In the inner cities of America, black youth have said "no" to electoral participation. From a progressive point of view, youth represent not only a wasted economic resource but an important political weapon. The idealism of youth and their potential for activism may represent organizational dangers to established politicians. Unemployed youth, for example, who are also active in the electoral arena may expect more aggressive leadership from elected officials than the latter may be able to give within the traditional context of local politics. Again, traditional politics pays homage to voter registration and youth participation, but will not sponsor or support meaningful activities to bring significant numbers of nonregistered black and youth participants into the electoral arena.

Another difference between the two kinds of electoral activism concerns the pursuit of institutionalized power and influence. Traditionally oriented black politicians are content to seek "influence" rather than "power," because they accept as a given the present system of wealth distribution in the U.S. To this group of politicians, appointments of blacks by white officials are significant; presumably, these black appointees will be able to convince those in power, via suasion, that they should pursue policies advantageous to the black community. Invariably, however, "soft" influence cannot compete with "hard" power. If blacks seek solutions to the systemic problems resulting in depressed black living conditions, then it is power that must be sought—power that under normal circumstances cannot be withdrawn by white officials. The black community must capture "institutionalized" positions, rather than those dependent upon the benevolence of various power structures. In effect, blacks must be heard through those who are not concerned about offending their employers.

The approach toward City Hall-controlled patronage is still another yardstick by which to differentiate traditional and progressive political behavior in the black community. Patronage is especially important for poor and working-class communities. But progressive black politicians recognize that the relatively few jobs under City Hall control today cannot satisfy the needs of the black community; it cannot dent the massive extent of black unemployment and crime. The purpose of the progressive assault on City Hall is not to capture the few patronage slots still available to political machines, but rather to confront a system of wealth distribution built partially upon high black unemployment rates.

Political educational activities are an important and vital concern of progressive leadership in black communities. The goal of political education is to help the citizenry at a grassroots level to understand what is in their best economic, political, and social interests, and how to pursue these interests as effectively as possible. Progressive leadership continually attempts to develop "conceptual tools" necessary for this task. These tools not only help voters to evaluate their elected officials but encourage greater political sophistication.

Black politicians operating within a progressive framework seek public policies that respond to the needs of white working-class as well as black communities. They recognize the possibility and the necessity of political alliances between blacks and working-class whites. This kind of leadership, for example, understands that racial violence and ethnic hostility between blacks and whites benefits various powerful interests. A political front of black and working-class whites could pose serious threats to the control usually exerted by powerful groups in the electoral arena.

Political participation within a progressive framework can provide elected representatives of black communities with platforms by which to confront public and private decisions favoring those in control of wealth. Issues can be pursued in ways that benefit the poor and the working class, to enhance the quality of life at the neighborhood level. For example: parks and recreational facilities for the young are more important than luxury hotels. Transportation is oriented toward the need of the working-class and elderly residents of the city rather than those who merely use the city. Tax benefits and housing policies do not disadvantage those who must work hard for a living. Economic policies that would minimize crime and social alienation are pursued. The issues that should be part of a city's agenda are developed by citizens at a grassroots level—from the bottom to the top, not the other way around.

Some have argued that traditional electoral activism has been effective in resolving the social and economic problems characteristic of black urban communities. But even when leaders are well-intentioned and seek to represent the powerless, their effectiveness, within the traditional modes and values of American politics, is quite limited. As Harrington argues,

> When the government intervenes into an economy dominated by private corporations to promote the common good, those corporations will normally be the prime beneficiaries of that intervention. The planners may be liberals, or even socialists, but they will not be able to carry out the policies that run counter to the crucial institutions of the society.[20]

He adds that leaders will be ineffective in challenging the status quo "unless they have the support of a determined mass movement willing to fight for structural change."[21] Under traditional electoral activism, "Even though the ruling powers can (thus) be driven and cajoled into a modicum of decency, they refuse to allow the welfare state to change the relative shares of wealth."[22] This kind of activism does not allow the poor to shape it, a crucial requirement under progressive electoral activism. Piven and Cloward claim "that governmental action has not worked for the unorganized poor and is not likely to work for them in the future unless they become a political force in initiating and shaping it."[23] Traditionally organized political participation, as a matter of fact, impedes mass-based movements in the electoral arena.

Today, progressive electoral politics offer a primary channel for blacks to question the status quo and seek entry into American society on an equal basis with whites. The electoral arena is becoming ever more crucial for the future of America's diverse peoples. It is here that American democracy will be tested. By examining current developments in the electoral processes of this nation's cities, we may arrive at some understanding of the political and economic forces directed against black America, and also determine how these forces can be defeated for the benefit of all those without wealth and power.

3.
The Black Voter in Boston, 1967-1983: Myths and Realities

Despite the historical significance of Boston in the political struggles of black people and the importance of the black vote in the establishment and maintenance of one of America's most powerful urban political machines, blacks in Boston face massive problems of impoverishment and economic malaise. Interestingly, by the 1970s the black community was the most stable in Boston in terms of residents. Only 16% of all blacks in 1980 had less than one year's residency in the city, but 21% of all whites had lived in Boston less than one year; 41% of all black residents in Boston have lived here for a period of three to nine years, but only 27% of all whites could claim this length of residential tenure.* Yet, for the most part, the black

---

*The demographic information provided in this section is based on the following documents pertaining to Boston: U.S. Bureau of the Census 1970 General Population Characteristics, PC (1)-B23 1970 Census Tract, Final Reports, PHC-1-29; 1980 Advance Report, Final Population and Housing Unit Counts, PHC 80-V-23; and 1980 Census Tracts P.L. 94-171 Counts. In addition, this study used two surveys conducted by the Boston Redevelopment Authority (BRA): *Characteristics of Boston's Housing and Population, 1980* (1981), and *Boston Population Trends and Shifts by Neighborhood, Ward and Precinct, Census Tract District and Census Tract, 1980, 1975 and 1970* (1982). There are a number of ways in which one might find information about the black voter in Boston from "Annual Election Reports" published by the city's Election Department. We used two methods. First, wards 9, 12, and 14 were used as representative of the black community in Boston. These three wards encompass Roxbury, Mattapan, Dorchester, and parts of the South End, which are predominantly black and have been so since the mid-1960s. Furthermore, close to two thirds of Boston's black population reside in these three wards. One can, therefore, use wards 9, 12, and 14 as a general yardstick of the black community's electoral characteristics and behavior. For more specific information about the black voter, however, another method

community in Boston remains impoverished, and this condition can be characterized as worsening compared to whites.

Census data from 1970 to 1980 and various other primary data sources not only suggest that the problem of segregation is increasing, but also show that the black community has realized little social and economic progress during this period. By 1980 the proportion of blacks in Boston's labor force had grown to 26% of the total, but 43% of all unemployed persons in 1980 were black. In certain age categories, black unemployment in 1980 reached levels two and three times those of white unemployment. Among white teenagers (16 to 19 years) the unemployment rate was 9%; for blacks in this age category it was 17%. Among those 20 to 24 years old, whites were unemployed at a rate of 7%, compared to 27% for blacks.

Unlike the case for whites in Boston, the proportion of service workers among all black workers is still much greater than the proportion of professional, managerial, and technical workers. Only 15% of all black workers hold the latter kinds of positions, compared to 35% of all white workers. This represents a 13% increase since 1970 (22%) for whites, and a mere 2% increase for black workers (13%) since 1970. The percentage of all white workers employed as service workers was 16%, compared to 25% for blacks.

Blacks live in the worst housing in Boston. In 1980 20% of the total black population lived in subsidized housing, compared to 6% of the white population. Black families in Boston have yet to reach the level of income attained by white families. In 1979 the median family income of whites stood at $15,700, while for black families it was but 68.4% of this, or $10,750. Roxbury, a predominantly black neighborhood, registered the lowest median income level of any neighborhood in the city. In Boston, 39% of all black families live below the poverty level,

---

had to be used. With census tract data for 1970 and 1980, one can try to pinpoint electoral precincts in Boston. By selecting those precincts that are at least 70 to 75% black, and aggregating the electoral characteristics of these units, a close approximation of various black electoral characteristics can be obtained.

compared to 17% for all white families. As in many black communities across urban America, it seems that things are not
getting better in Boston.

Some community activists in Boston believe that, at least
until the mayoral election of 1983, politically the black community had not reacted as would have been expected, given
these kinds of socioeconomic conditions. And this is not a
new complaint. In the early 1960s, Otwell reported that in Boston,
"The colored vote is regarded with contempt by many white
politicians. Despite their increasing number, they are of little
importance in public affairs."[24] In his study of politics in Boston,
Banfield arrived at a similar conclusion:

> By the standards of other big cities, the Boston Negro com-
> munity is still passive. Some think this is because it is still
> too small to provide enough highly motivated young people
> to constitute a "critical mass." Others think it is because Yankees
> and Jews have done the talking for the Negroes for so long
> that they have never grown accustomed to talking for themselves.
> Still others think it is because the "upper crust" of the Negro
> community is separated from the rest of it by a distance even
> greater than in other cities.[25]

Byron Rushing, president of the Museum of Afro-American
History, reported that blacks are held in political contempt.[26]
Pearl Shelton, a former president of the Black Political Task
Force, described City Hall's traditional posture towards blacks
as "paternalistic and racist."[27]

One usually hears three conventional explanations for the
way in which the black community has evolved politically in
recent years; these explanations serve as rationalizations for
the passivity ascribed to blacks under the Kevin White administration in Boston between 1967 and 1983. They are:

1. The black community is too small to provide a numerical
base by which to influence political processes and decisions.

2. Because of the small size of the black community, the
ballot is an unrealistic resource for blacks.

3. The black community does not have to become politically

aggressive because the city's power brokers have been responsive to the needs of blacks.

These rationalizations are similar in that each overlooks the role of white power structures as a major influence on the development of black politics. But contrary to these "blame the victim" explanations, under Kevin White's leadership, City Hall represented a political front for powerful and wealthy interests; as such, it discouraged the development of progressively oriented politics in both black and white communities, but especially in the former.

The black community in Boston is capable of developing a power base by which to confront public and private decision-making processes that subvert the interests of the poor and the working class in favor of those who own and manage wealth in the metropolis. One major function of the mayor's office— especially since World War II—has been to prevent this development. Before proceeding with the task of illustrating this (which is the goal of the next chapter), the conventional "blame the victim" explanations of black politics in Boston must be evaluated; so long as these myths are accepted as reality, it will be difficult for blacks to believe that organized political pressure— within a progressive framework—can make a difference in how public decisions are made and implemented. The first two explanations can be challenged by a demographic and electoral overview of the black community in Boston. The third claim will be evaluated by examining the distribution of benefits to the black community during Mayor Kevin White's 16-year tenure in office.

EXPLANATION NUMBER ONE:
THE BLACK COMMUNITY IS TOO SMALL

"The black community is too small to have any influence on Boston politics."* A few observers have offered size as a major factor to explain what they perceive to be a relatively powerless black community in Boston. One researcher has reported that until World War II, "The small size and scattered

---

*Interview with a black civic leader in 1979.

location of Negroes here limited the opportunities for the routine political or patronage job opportunities which soon were afforded Negroes in other northern communities where they could and did exercise their use of the ballot in a strategic fashion."[28] Although the present study is concerned primarily with the black community after World War II, it should be pointed out that in terms of the rate of growth, rather than merely absolute numbers, the black community was not as insignificant as this statement suggests. For example, Thernstrom found that, "Throughout the entire period from the Civil War to World War I, Boston had as large a population of Negro residents as New York, Chicago, Detroit or Cleveland; only Philadelphia, among the leading eastern and mid-western cities, had a substantially higher fraction of black inhabitants."[29] In another study, Trout found that the same could be said of Boston's black community in the 1930s:

> Although the folk migration out of the South during the 1930s touched Boston less than New York and Indianapolis, and while the proportion of blacks living in Boston remained smaller than in other cities, the 13.5 percent increase of the black population in the Hub approximated that of most urban areas.[30]

The rate of growth in the black community in Boston during this period was similar to those in Chicago, Pittsburgh, and Philadelphia.

During the 1940s, the black community continued to increase significantly; Thernstrom reports:

> The next great wave of Negro migration affected Boston in much the same way as other major cities. The proportion of Negro residents in the city nearly tripled between 1940 and 1960, a rate of increase exceeded only by Detroit and Cleveland, and continued to grow very rapidly in the 1960s. There were proportionately more blacks in Boston in 1970 than in New York in 1960 or in Chicago and Cleveland in 1950 (though fewer in absolute numbers, of course).[31]

Between 1940 and 1950 the black community in Boston grew by 70%; between 1950 and 1960 it grew by 57%; and between 1960 and 1970 its growth increased by 66%.

Table 1 THE GROWTH OF THE BLACK POPULATION IN BOSTON, 1940-1970

Year	No. of Blacks	% Increase	% of City Population
1940	23,679	15.0%	3.1%
1950	40,157	70.0%	5.0%
1960	63,165	57.0%	9.1%
1970	104,596	66.0%	16.3%

Source: Stephen Thernstrom, "Growth of the Black Population of Boston, 1865-1970" (Table 8.1) in *The Other Bostonians* (Cambridge, Mass: Harvard University Press, 1973).

Between 1970 and 1980 the number of blacks continued to increase, although at a slower rate than in the previous 10 years. The total population of Boston continued to decline during these years; the rate of decline was 12.2%; in 1970 approximately 641,071 persons resided in this city and 10 years later the figure was 562,994 persons. The number of whites declined by 25% while the black population increased by 21%.

Table 2 POPULATION OF BOSTON BY RACE, 1970-1980

Race	Number of Persons 1970	1980	% Change (1970-1980)
Whites	524,709	393,937	– 25%
Blacks	104,707	126,229	+ 21%
Other*	11,655	42,828	
Total Population	641,071	562,994	

Source: U.S. Bureau of the Census, Census of Population: 1970 General Population Characteristics, Final Report PC (1)-B23 (Massachusetts), and Census of Population and Housing: 1980 Advance Report, Final Population and Housing Unit Counts, PHC 80-V-23 (Massachusetts).
*Includes Latino, Asian-descent, and Aleutian; Latinos may be counted among blacks and whites.

During this same period, the number of Latinos grew explosively; in 1970 there were approximately 17,984 Latinos residing in Boston and 10 years later this number increased by more than 100% to 36,068 persons. The Asian-descent population grew even faster than did Latinos. From 7,831 persons in 1970, this group increased by 127.3% to 17,789 persons in 1980.

Complementing continual growth since World War II is increasing concentration of blacks in the geographic center of Boston. In 1970 the black community was located in the "core"

Table 3 POPULATION OF BOSTON BY RACE AND ETHNICITY, 1970-1980

	Number of Persons 1970	1980	% Change (1970-1980)	Proportion of Total Population in 1980
Blacks	104,707	126,229	+21.0%	22.0%
*Latinos**	17,984	36,068	+101.0%	6.0%
Asian-descent	7,831	17,789	+127.3%	3.0%
Whites	524,709	393,937	−25.0%	70.0%
Total Population	641,071	562,994		

Source: Compiled from U.S. Bureau of the Census, Census of Population: 1970 General Population Characteristics, Final Report PC (1)-B23 (Massachusetts), and Census of Population and Housing: 1980 Advance Report, Final Population and Housing Unit Counts, PHC 80-V-23 (Massachusetts). *Latinos also may have been counted under "Blacks" and "Whites" categories as a result of U.S. Bureau of the Census enumeration techniques.

of the city; the growth of the black population between 1970 and 1980 occurred through increases in already predominantly black areas, and expansion into the fringes of these areas. The overall residential pattern in 1980 is basically similar to that of 1970: a core of blacks, surrounded by a ring of whites. The difference is that the black core is larger and more concentrated in 1980 than 10 years earlier; the black community in Boston is still best described as segregated and confined to the central core of the city.[32]

This brief demographic overview of Boston's black community illustrates two points; first, it can no longer be argued that this community is too small to be considered politically significant. Blacks and other minorities presently make up close to one third of the total population and are concentrated in the core of the city, both characteristics that tend to support heightened political activism. Second, it cannot be strongly argued that there were too few blacks in the past to be able to exert themselves politically. This is supported by surveying a few significant black political developments in other parts of the country. Black Chicagoans, for example, began to make impressive electoral gains in the 1950s and early 1960s, when they were no more than 15 or 16% of that city's total population. More recently, we witnessed the election of a black person as mayor of Los Angeles in the early 1970s, although blacks constituted no more than 12% of the total population. In Raleigh, North Carolina, where the black community, although quite small in absolute numbers, was about 23% of the total population in 1970, a black man won the mayoralty in the mid-1970s. And in Grand Rapids, Michigan, where blacks comprised only 12% of the total population, a black person was elected as the city's mayor during this same period.

When Boston is compared to other cities with black populations of similar size, however, we find that this city does lag in terms of black electoral accomplishments. Welch and Karnig found, for instance, that of all big cities with black populations less than 35% of the total population and with electoral structures similar to those of Boston, this city scored among the lowest in terms of black representation on a school board or school committee.[33] This all suggests that in order to understand black politics in Boston we cannot rely too strongly on the size of the black community as an explanation.

EXPLANATION NUMBER TWO: THE BALLOT IS UNREALISTIC FOR BLACKS

"The black vote is insignificant."* Related to the argument that the black community in Boston is too small to be taken seriously in the electoral arena is the claim that the black vote can have only a negligible influence on the city's leaders. The decision to change Boston from a totally at-large to a combined district/at-large system of voting has done much to destroy this myth, as did Mel King's preliminary election victory in September 1983. But the myth persists among some. To be able to discuss this fully we must describe various electoral characteristics of the black community in Boston. These include voter registration patterns, the size of the potential and actual black electorate, the black voting turnout, and the "impact" of the black vote on various city elections.

The white middle-class and working-class neighborhoods in Boston are characterized by higher voter registration rates

---

*Interview with a black nonvoter in 1980.

than those of the black community. While voter registration among blacks has usually not exceeded 50-55%, voter registration levels in white neighborhoods have hovered between 65 and 75% in recent years. As Table 4 shows, there are a few predominantly white neighborhoods with relatively low voter registration rates; these include parts of wards 21, 5, and 4. But these sectors of the city have tended to attract highly mobile professional residents. Such individuals will have a more "cosmopolitan" than "local" outlook on politics and will not generally gravitate toward the city's electoral arena. Therefore, they will not register or vote in city or state elections to the same degree as Boston's more permanent residents.

Table 4 VOTER REGISTRATION RATES IN BOSTON BY NEIGHBORHOODS, 1977-1980*

Ward/Neighborhood	1977 (%)	1978 (%)	1980 (%)
Ward 20, West Roxbury, Roslindale	76.7%	79.9%	74.7%
Ward 2, Charlestown	72.9	77.3	70.7
Ward 7, South Boston, Dorchester	72.3	77.3	67.0
Ward 6, South Boston	70.9	76.0	67.3
Ward 16, Dorchester, Neponset, Cedar Grove	70.8	75.3	68.8
Ward 18, Hyde Park, Mattapan	69.1	73.1	64.2
Ward 1, East Boston	62.2	66.3	65.2
Ward 19, Roslindale	62.1	67.2	62.6
Ward 17, Dorchester	60.8	66.8	52.7
Ward 13, Savin Hill	59.6	63.9	53.8
Ward 12, Roxbury*	59.2	65.5	50.1
Ward 15, Dorchester	57.3	61.3	46.8
Ward 22, Brighton	55.0	57.9	53.1
Ward 11, Jamaica Plain, Roxbury*	52.2	56.0	49.4
Ward 3, North End, West End, South End	51.7	56.6	49.5
Ward 10, Jamaica Plain	51.2	55.6	47.1
Ward 9, Roxbury, South End*	50.2	50.2	51.0
Ward 14, Dorchester, Mattapan*	48.6	54.1	41.3
Ward 8, Roxbury, South End*	44.5	52.1	41.7
Ward 21, Allston	38.1	40.7	31.9
Ward 5, Beacon Hill, Back Bay	37.3	42.9	38.8
Ward 4, Back Bay, South End	30.9	35.1	27.9
Boston	60.0	61.0	62.0

Source: "Annual Report of the Election Department," Boston, Massachusetts (1977-1981).
*Wards 8, 9, 11, 12, and 14 represent the bulk of the black community in Boston.

As reported earlier, the black population of Boston reached 126,229 persons in 1980. The median age of this population is 24 (23.9) years,[34] with about 13,000 blacks between the ages of 18 and 24 years.[35] This means that in Boston between 76,000 and 80,000 blacks are eligible to vote, which represents 25-30% of all registered voters in the city. Before the Mel King campaign in 1983 there were 41,000 registered black voters in Boston, close to half of whom lived in wards 9, 12, and 14; this number represented slightly more than 16% of all voters registered on the city voting lists by the end of 1982.[36]

The weight carried by this number of voters can be appreciated when one realizes that Kevin White, mayor of Boston between 1967 and 1983, won his first mayoral preliminary election with slightly more than 30,000 votes; he won the 1971 preliminary election with 46,913 votes, the 1975 preliminary election with 49,248 votes, and the 1979 preliminary election with 49,528 votes. Thus, a black electorate of 41,000 registered voters is anything but insignificant in Boston.

Studies of black and white voter turnout rates further show the importance of the black vote; although black voter registration lags behind the registration of whites generally, black voter turnout is similar to white voter turnout in various kinds of elections. Seven preliminary city elections were held in Boston between 1967 and 1979; as Table 5 shows, in only two instances

Table 5 PERCENT VOTER TURNOUT IN CITY PRELIMINARY ELECTIONS BY WARDS 9, 12, AND 14, 1967-1979

Ward	1967* (%)	1969 (%)	1971* (%)	1973 (%)	1975* (%)	1977 (%)	1979* (%)
Ward 9	47.8	18.9	49.6	11.4	39.1	22.9	48.8
Ward 12	55.4	20.5	52.9	10.4	41.3	28.0	49.7
Ward 14	48.2	16.4	46.2	8.0	34.6	23.8	40.9
Average Turnout Rate for Wards 9, 12, and 14	50.5	18.6	49.6	10.0	38.3	24.9	46.5
City Turnout Rate	56.4	27.6	51.7	18.3	38.8	24.6	51.3

Source: "Annual Report of the Election Department," Boston, Massachusetts (1967-1980).
*Mayoral election years.

was the average turnout in the black wards significantly lower than the turnout rate for the entire city. Based on information for wards 9, 12, and 14, the black voter turnout in the 1969 preliminary city election was 18.6% while the citywide turnout rate was 27.6%. In 1973 10% of all black voters cast a ballot; but the city's turnout rate in this same election was 18.3%. In the other five preliminary city elections during this period, however, registered blacks turned out to vote at rates similar to the rest of the city. Blacks voted at a higher rate than whites in the 1983 preliminary election. The overall city turnout rate for this election was 63%, but for blacks the turnout rate was closer to 65%.

During general elections in non-mayoral years, the black community has also voted at rates similar to those for the entire city. Of interest, in 1977, a non-mayoral general election year, voting turnout in the black wards slightly surpassed the rest of the city. This may have been primarily because of the presence of John O'Bryant, a black candidate, on the ballot for the School Committee race. The gap between black voter turnout and the city's turnout rate was greatest during the mayoral general elections of 1975 and 1979; the gap in other years is relatively small.

For a long time, the black vote has had a crucial impact on Boston mayoralty elections. In particular, the black vote helped Kevin White to win mayoral runoff positions in the

Table 6 PERCENT VOTER TURNOUT IN CITY GENERAL ELECTIONS BY WARDS 9, 12, AND 14, 1967-1979

Ward	1967* (%)	1969 (%)	1971* (%)	1973 (%)	1975* (%)	1977 (%)	1979* (%)
Ward 9	65.9	41.4	64.2	30.1	57.5	36.8	53.0
Ward 12	73.7	46.4	67.2	31.4	58.7	42.0	57.1
Ward 14	64.0	31.1	57.8	25.4	50.0	35.4	49.0
Average Turnout Rate for Wards 9, 12, and 14	67.9	39.6	63.0	29.0	55.4	38.0	53.0
City Turnout Rate	68.1	43.8	64.3	30.2	62.0	34.9	60.9

Source: "Annual Report of the Election Department," Boston, Massachusetts (1967-1980).
*Mayoral election years.

preliminary elections of 1967 and 1971 (see Table 7). In 1967 White "lost" to Louise Day Hicks outside of the three black wards. It was the black vote that carried him into the mayoral general election that year. In 1971 it was again the black vote that made White victorious in the mayoral preliminary election—although a black candidate, Thomas Atkins, was in the race. In the 1975 mayoral preliminary election, the vote in the black wards provided White with a comfortable cushion over his major opponent, state Senator Joseph Timilty. If Mel King had not carried the black vote in 1979, White's lead over Joseph Timilty would have increased by at least 6,000 to 8,000 additional black votes. And it was the black vote in 1983 that made history by propelling the Mel King candidacy into the general election for mayor.

Table 7 VOTE RETURNS FOR PRELIMINARY MAYORAL ELECTIONS IN BOSTON AND WARDS 9, 12, AND 14, 1967-1979

Candidate and Year	Votes Cast in All Boston Wards Except Wards 9, 12, and 14	Votes Cast in Wards 9, 12, and 14	Total Vote
September 1967			
Kevin White	27,500	3,289	30,789
Louise Day Hicks	42,020	1,702	43,722
September 1971			
Kevin White	42,593	4,320	46,913
Louise Day Hicks	41,803	490	42,293
September 1975			
Kevin White	43,131	6,117	49,248
Joseph Timilty	37,931	1,066	38,997
September 1979			
Kevin White	47,291	3,053	50,272
Joseph Timilty	32,501	525	33,026
Melvin King	12,679	4,811	17,490

Source: "Annual Report of the Election Department," Boston, Massachusetts (1967-1980).

The importance of the black vote can also be seen in the mayoral general elections between 1967 and 1979 (see Table 8). In this first year White beat Hicks by 5,000 votes, or by less than 3% of the total vote cast for these two candidates.

Table 8 VOTE RETURNS FOR MAYORAL GENERAL ELECTIONS IN BOSTON AND WARDS 9, 12, AND 14, 1967-1979

Candidate and Year	Votes Cast in All Boston Wards Except Wards 9, 12, and 14	Votes Cast in Wards 9, 12, and 14	Total Vote
November 1967			
Kevin White	79,470	15,569	95,039
Louise Day Hicks	86,879	3,202	90,081
November 1971			
Kevin White	98,581	14,556	113,137
Louise Day Hicks	69,482	849	70,331
November 1975			
Kevin White	71,307	9,751	81,058
Joseph Timilty	71,716	1,906	73,622
November 1979			
Kevin White	70,638	7,410	78,048
Joseph Timilty	61,374	2,895	64,269

Source: "Annual Report of the Election Department," Boston, Massachusetts (1967-1980).

But White received more than 15,000 votes in the three black wards. In 1971 the black vote was not as important to White's victory as in the three other mayoral general elections. That year he won with a margin of over 40,000 votes, but close to 40% of this margin was provided by loyal black voters. In 1975 White would not have won the election without the support of black voters. He beat Joseph Timilty by only 7,436 votes; this was a result of the 9,751 black voters who supported the mayor.

Based on this electoral overview since 1967, the second explanation of black politics in Boston must be rejected; indeed, by supporting Kevin White, the black vote has been crucial in the emergence, development, and survival of what came to be recognized as one of the nation's most powerful political machines.

EXPLANATION NUMBER THREE: THE CITY HAS RESPONDED TO THE NEEDS OF BLACKS

"Under the mayor's [Kevin White's] leadership blacks have realized much progress."* There are a variety of ways to measure

---

*Interview with a black minister.

Table 9 RACIAL PROFILE OF CITY HALL'S WORK FORCE BY DEPARTMENTS AND COMMISSIONS, 1981

Department/Commission	Total No. of Employees	Total No. of Black Employees (% Black)	
City Departments and Commissions Not Receiving HUD Funding			
Assessing	95	13	14.0%
City Clerk	14		1.0%
Community Schools	83	19	23.0%
Consumer Affairs	11	2	18.0%
Data Processing	51	3	6.0%
Drug Abuse	6	0	0.0%
EDIC	17	3	2.0%
Elderly	108	23	21.0%
Elections	28	2	7.0%
Fire (Civilian)	165	7	4.0%
Fire (Non-Civilian)	1,868	201	11.0%
Health and Hospitals	4,249	1,033	24.0%
Hynes Auditorium	9	1	11.0%
Law	51	6	12.0%
Licensing Board	13	3	23.0%
Manpower (EEPA)	345	102	29.6%
Office of Criminal Justice	12	3	25.0%
Penal	155	23	14.8%
Police (Non-Civilian)	2,020	158	8.0%
Printing	48	2	4.0%
Public Library	505	44	9.0%
Purchasing	23	0	0.0%
Registry	34	1	3.0%
Rent Control	38	1	3.0%
Retirement Board	34	2	6.0%
Traffic and Parking	170	10	6.0%
Veteran Services	44	7	16.0%
Treasury Division	27	2	7.0%
Total	10,223	1,672	16.4%

Department/Commission	Total No. of Employees	Total No. of Black Employees (% Black)	
City Departments and Commissions Receiving HUD Funding			
Administrative Services	46	4	9.0%
Auditing	54	2	4.0%
Accounting and Auditing	15	4	27.0%
Boston Housing Authority	648	171	26.0%
Boston Real Property	171	3	2.0%
Boston Redevelopment Authority	226	24	11.0%
Buildings	122	3	2.0%
Buildings	9	1	11.0%
Development and Construction	8	1	12.0%
Fair Housing	16	4	25.0%
Housing Improvement Program	124	22	18.0%
Housing Inspection	88	12	14.0%
Human Rights Commission	29	26	90.0%
Management and Budget	20	2	10.0%
Neighborhood Business	30	6	20.0%
Federal Relations/Compliance	23	2	9.0%
Office of Public Services	104	21	20.1%
Parks and Recreation	509	39	8.0%
Police Department (Civilian)	294	6	2.0%
Program Development	57	13	23.0%
Public Facilities	107	11	10.0%
Public Works	702	59	8.0%
Treasury Collections	51	4	8.0%
Total	3,470	450	13.0%
Total (All Departments and Commissions)	13,693	2,122	15.5%

Source: Utilization Report submitted by the mayor's Office of Human Rights to Massachusetts Commission Against Discrimination, February 25, 1981, and Utilization Report submitted by the director of Affirmative Action to Commission of Human Rights, February 17, 1981.

the progress, or lack of it, for blacks in Boston. One could begin by comparing the following kinds of "benefits" with the number of black people in the city, and the importance of the black vote in city elections:[37] the number of black municipal heads; the size of the black non-civilian, uniformed work force; the number of black workers on the city's payroll, and the positions they hold; the amount of public dollars distributed to black contractors; and the quantity and quality of municipal services delivered to the black community. Lack of progress would be indicated by a lesser amount of benefits distributed to blacks than would be suggested by their numbers.[38]

Kevin White claimed that under his administration the proportion of black firemen and policemen had increased significantly. In 1967, for example, less than 2% of all firemen and policemen were black, but by 1980, 8% of all policemen, and 2% of all firemen were black. A weakness of this evidence, however, was that the proportion of black firemen and policemen was still not comparable to the proportion of black people in the entire city. A second weakness was that the mayor's office could not take responsibility for increases in the number of black firemen and policemen, which had resulted from minority and federal government pressures on Boston to meet required affirmative action guidelines. As a matter of fact, the city has a poor record in this area. Among civilian, non-uniformed personnel in these city departments, where minority and federal government pressure had not been as intense, black employment had been almost non-existent. In 1981 only 7 out of 165 civilian employees in the Fire Department were black; in this same year, only 6 out of 294 civilian employees in the Police Department were black.

White's 16-year record in hiring black employees was as dismal in other areas. In 1981 only 4 of 34 department heads were black; approximately 17% of the entire city's work force was minority, but most of these workers were segregated into a few of the lowest-paid city departments. For example, there were a total of 2,122 black employees on the city's payroll, but 56.7% of these employees, or 1,204 persons, were found in the Health and Hospitals Administration and the Boston Housing Authority. If we exclude these workers, less than 7% of all city workers were black in 1981. According to reports submitted by the mayor's office to the Massachusetts Commission Against Discrimination, and the Housing and Urban Development Department (HUD), only 12 out of 54 city departments and commissions had a black work force comparable to the proportion of blacks in the city's total population. In many city agencies the proportion of black employees did not even surpass 3%.

Table 10 BLACK CITY WORKERS EARNING MORE THAN $12,500 IN DEPARTMENTS HAVING A BLACK WORK FORCE GREATER THAN 20%, 1981

Department/Commission	Total No. of Black Employees Earning Less Than $12,500	Earning More Than $12,500
Accounting and Auditing	3	1
Boston Housing Authority	104	67
Fair Housing	1	3
Human Rights	10	16
Neighborhood Business	0	6
Office of Public Services	7	14
Program Development	3	10
Community Schools	16	3
Elderly	23	0
Health and Hospitals	848	185
Licensing Board	2	1
Manpower	51	51
Office of Criminal Justice	3	0
Total	1,074 (75%)	357 (25%)

Source: Utilization Report submitted by the mayor's Office of Human Rights to Massachusetts Commission Against Discrimination, February 25, 1981, and Utilization Report submitted by the director of Affirmative Action to Commission of Human Rights, February 17, 1981.

The black community was vastly underrepresented on the city's payroll, considering that, in 1980, 21% of the total population in Boston was black, and that this group has been important to the survival of White and his machine. Blacks on the city's payroll were concentrated in the lowest-paying positions. In the 12 departments and commissions with a black employment force greater than 20%, three quarters of these workers earned less than $12,500 per year, while only 46% of the white employees in these same agencies earned less than $12,500 per year.

The black community was also short-changed in the expenditure of public construction funds. Blacks received a minuscule amount of construction patronage under White's control. For example, between January 1979 and June 1979, City Hall spent $7,363,418 in funds for various kinds of construction projects through the Public Facilities Department. These funds were spent among approximately 49 private construction and contracting firms. An unreleased investigative report found that 29 (or 60%) of these firms had been cited for "no or poor minority utilization and/or no minority business participation."* These particular firms accounted for almost 90% of the $7,363,418 spent by the Public Facilities Department during a six-month period. Mayor White's office had been lax in enforcing its own affirmative action policies in this area. The contract compliance officers were encouraged not "to pressure" construction and contracting firms about their affirmative action practices; in a few cases, aggressive contract compliance officers were threatened with bodily harm and termination of employment.**

Even public dollars intended for poor and working-class people were distributed in ways that discriminated against the black community. The summer job youth programs sponsored throughout the 1970s were an example of this. These summer jobs were to be distributed to the neediest according to federal and state guidelines, but instead were used as patronage to to reward White's political friends; a newspaper exposé reported that during the summer of 1977,

> The administration of Mayor Kevin White has used Boston's $1.5 million summer job programs as part of a concerted effort

---

*Interview with Equal Opportunity Contract compliance officer, December 10, 1979.

**Interview with Equal Opportunity Contract compliance officer, August 22, 1982.

to reward pro-administration City Council members and political allies, mayoral aides and city councilmen said yesterday. The bulk of the 1,700 jobs, according to the well-placed White aides, were used as political leverage to ensure the council's support of administration programs...and to reward and placate the mayor's political laborers throughout the city.[39]

But the black community was not equally treated for its overwhelming political loyalty to the mayor between 1967 and 1979. On the basis of size and the weight of the black vote in various city elections, blacks have been severely short-changed in terms of City Hall-controlled benefits. Blacks have been treated as an unwanted stepchild by City Hall; ironically, as has been pointed out, Kevin White would have stumbled out of office long ago if not for the black vote.

Despite the dismal record of minority employment by City Hall, White claimed that under his leadership blacks made much political progress. For instance, in a welcoming speech at the 1982 NAACP convention, the mayor stated that blacks had been able to capture 20% of the citywide electoral seats, although they are only 22% of the city's total population; presumably this was a sign of political progress. A close examination of this claim reveals a different conclusion. By approaching the School Committee separately from the City Council, we find that in the School Committee two out of five members were black, while the rest were white. But at least two thirds of the public school population in Boston are black and Latino; one could argue therefore that two black members out of a total of five is, in fact, underrepresentation. Further, White adopted a hostile posture toward the public school system. By denying the public schools sorely needed financial support, he was responsible for squeezing vitality out of the school system. By not making public schools a priority, he contributed to white flight, social polarization within the school system, and deteriorating educational services.

Just as the mayor tried to starve the public school system, he took a similar position on public housing. Despite the fact that 17% of all housing in this city is publicly subsidized, White

expressed no compunction about simply dropping the concerns of the people living in public housing.[40] Instead of representing the interests of public housing tenants, White continually shifted the blame for deteriorated living conditions onto
the courts and federal government. By not confronting public
housing problems, White contributed to racial segregation and
increasing rates of housing abandonment. This parallels an
earlier finding of the Massachusetts Commission Against
Discrimination, which accused White of using $58 million in
federal funds to "maintain a pattern of racial segregation in
housing."[41] The mayor ignored a number of approaches to housing that could have benefited black and poor people, including:
homesteading policies, rehabilitation tax credits for tenants and
small homeowners, low-interest loans, and prioritizing the needs
of public housing tenants.[42] In his 16 years in office, White
did not consider these alternatives because he did not ever
represent the interests of those who cannot afford luxury housing
in the most choice spots in Boston.

Black leaders have criticized various municipal services under
City Hall management, including police and fire services, education, public housing, and the maintenance of public property
in black neighborhoods.[43] Mel King's study on Boston black
politics provides a wealth of detail about black dissatisfaction
with municipal services.[44] Perhaps the greatest concern of blacks
has been continuing racial harassment and violence. Many blacks
believed that White's failure to take forthright action as mayor
was partially responsible for the degree of racial violence in
this city. This was a major reason why the Black Political Task
Force (BPTF) did not endorse White for re-election in the fall
of 1979; the BPTF stated that their course of action was based
on "inequities of property tax abatements, lack of commitment
to a comprehensive economic development program for our
community, and a general lack of respect, indicated by poor
services to our community, and particularly due to the lack
of leadership around the issue of racism in Boston."[45]

The Police Department's Community Disorders Unit (CDU),
which investigates racially motivated crime, reported that in

1975 there were 490 such crimes, compared to 293 incidents in 1980. But a representative of the CDU stated that this decline was not because of a lessening of racism, or the effectiveness of the CDU. Instead, "two unhealthy reasons" probably explained most of the decline: 1) school busing had declined, and 2) blacks had come to realize that they should just avoid various parts of Boston.* This is why in 1981 the *Boston Globe* referred to its own city as the nation's most unlivable city for blacks. Numerous and continuing racial incidents keep most of Boston "off limits" to black people.

The charge of racism is a serious one for any mayor of a city like Boston; it poses an electoral threat from growing numbers of minority and progressive voters; it could be detrimental to higher-level political aspirations the mayor may entertain. But most importantly, it can tear a city apart; it can make life dangerous for its citizens. However, instead of responding to this problem, White decided to deflect the issue as other city mayors have done, by claiming: 1) that incidents of racial harassment and violence were "isolated phenomena"; 2) that despite isolated incidents of racial violence blacks in this city had realized much economic and political progress; and 3) that racial violence was "not any worse here than in other cities." These three arguments were the basis for the mayor's response to racial violence.

CONCLUSION

According to Edwin Lewinson, "Political activity is of continued and increasing importance to the black community because it provides potentially the most effective vehicle for the expression of grievances and the most effective form of pressure to bring about their remedy.[46] He writes that political participation for others has resulted in jobs and better government services:

> With increased political power (come) the pay-off in jobs—political jobs, civil service jobs, jobs with firms doing business with government. These opportunities ranged from unskilled jobs to positions requiring several college degrees. Most important, political

---

*Interview with an executive official of the Community Disorders Unit, June 29, 1982.

power means greater access to government and ultimately better government services.[47]

It is not clear that in major American cities blacks will realize
the benefits described here by merely increasing their level of
political participation. It seems that political participation, under
our traditional understanding of local politics, has been tried
by blacks—and it has failed.

Blacks and other minorities comprise almost one third of
the total population in Boston today. Blacks have participated
actively in the electoral arena; the black vote has been a crucial
commodity for white politicians—especially the mayor. Yet, what
has this meant for blacks? They have been short-changed in
terms of the traditional kinds of benefits usually accruing to
a mayor's loyal followers; for 16 years, and with the complicity
of the mayor during that period, public housing and education declined in quality, and racial violence remains rampant
in Boston. Traditional electoral activism has not provided meaningful answers to Boston's black community. If increased political
participation is to become an effective vehicle for the socioeconomic
improvement of the black community, it must take place within
a context that challenges the structural positions of powerful
and wealthy interests. And the mayor's role in representing and
protecting the structure of wealth and privilege must be critically
examined.

The black community is ready for change in Boston; the
masses of black people do not feel that City Hall has represented their interests. If blacks have not participated fully in
the electoral arena, it is not because they have been satisfied
with City Hall leadership, but as we have discussed, neither
has it been because of "small size" or insignificant voting power.
Blacks are ready to make a political move challenging the power
brokers of Boston. This was evident in the large numbers of
blacks who registered as voters to support Mel King in 1983,
and the high level of voter turnout in the black community
that same year. They may have not done so earlier largely because
of City Hall machinations with voter registration procedures,

the political use of public dollars, the nurturing of "cooperative" black leadership, racial "divide-and-conquer" practices, and public relations gimmickry. We will now discuss these "political resources" in greater detail.

4.
Urban Machinism
and the Black Voter

O ne of the major functions of America's big-city mayors is to provide "political managerialism" beneficial to powerful economic interests. An unstated responsibility of political leadership of cities is to maintain a stable environment in which banking, real estate, academic, commercial, and media conglomerates can realize their political and economic goals. This becomes especially evident during periods of fiscal crisis, when big-city mayors sacrifice the interests of the poor and the powerless to the well-being of organizations that own and manage wealth.

Although political managerialism has increasingly replaced "political leadership" as the major function of big-city mayors since World War II, City Halls in earlier periods of American history also provided this important service. But it was the political machine and its influential bosses, rather than strictly the mayor's office, that provided it.

The difference between earlier periods and the post-World War II era lies in the fact that it was easier to provide political managerialism in the 19th century and the first 30 years or so of the 20th century. The political machine before World War II provided a "network that connected the 'boss' to both the upper and lower class of urban society. To the upper class, the boss supplied utility and street car franchises, construction contracts, and other juicy patronage plums. To the [lower class] immigrants whose votes kept the machine in power, the boss 'ward heelers' provided petty jobs, turkeys at Christmas, and other minor favors."⁴⁸ Today, big-city mayors and their political organizations must perform similar duties. They must create and maintain a healthy environment for the economic interests of powerful groups. But to do so is far more complex today. The mayor's office must be able to manage the demands of labor upon industry, including the demands of public-sector workers; it must be able to maintain the allegiance of volatile white working-class groups, using either City Hall patronage or the subtle threat of black and Latino "invasions"; and, increasingly since the 1960s, in most larger American cities, mayors must contain the growing black and Latino groups whose social and economic interests cannot be responded to within the traditional political framework of urban America.

The big-city mayor, in effect, is the hired manager of the "metropolitan establishment":

> This is a multi-level network of power centers (including institutional hierarchies) that are held together less by formal control than by mutual interests, shared ideologies, and accepted procedures for mediating their endless conflicts. It is both public government and private government, permanent but constantly changing, and seen in various degrees of visibility and invisibility. It is a network of government officials, corporate managers, law firms, accounting firms, wealthy individuals, professional associations, chambers of commerce, union leaders, dependable academics, think tanks, media executives, and, last and occasionally least, the leaders of some of the many political machines in the metropolitan area.⁴⁹

This metropolitan establishment exercises considerable influence over the daily lives of powerless poor and working-class people. The control exercised by the metropolitan establishment over public policy "is invisible and unelected...the power of this interlocking network of elites is based on the control of institutions, money, property, and the law-making process." It endures "no matter who the voters elect as mayor, governor, or president. Its collective power, when organized, is greater than the elected, representative government."⁵⁰

These are powerful forces, indeed; and to be sure, a mayor

cannot make much of a difference in the poor quality of life in the nation's cities. As Greer writes, "The political and economic priorities of our society make it likely that these difficulties will continue. Moreover, there is currently no political coalition with any prospect of changing these priorities to the extent necessary to compel a sharp alteration of the existing urban plight."[51] Further, "The difference in the daily life of the average city dwellers made by a change in the occupant of the mayor's office is too small to be noticeable."[52] He also maintains, "The leaders of contemporary political machines have been quite unwilling to share power with the black community. Blacks are rarely given important parts within the machines themselves, and even more rarely appointed beyond the token level to key positions in city government."[53]

But the *structural* position of the mayor's office can give the occupant opportunities to initiate political decisions that begin to favor the interests of the powerless. Before this can happen, however, blacks must be organized around an agenda of progressive issues. And black leaders must be aware of all the political resources that big-city mayors will use to obstruct the growth of a black progressive politics.

The office of the big-city mayor represents the "dominant force in the formal governance structure, . . . the central figure in the visible policy network."[54] But just as significant,

> The mayors also have ample linkages to the less visible parts of the establishment. These linkages, especially those with corporative management and the super rich, are often forged through fund raising drives for election campaigns. Other links are developed through "lend-an-executive" technical-assistance programs, where management skills and other forms of technology are transferred from the private to the public needs.[55]

On the top layer of this metropolitan establishment sit the "super rich" and their corporate managers. At the middle level are those "who provide the material, intellectual, and leadership resources that keep the establishment functioning." And "on the junior ring sit most party machines, bureaucrats, and union leaders." Finally, "There are also those outside the establishment network—the unemployed, the poor, the minorities, and others who are unable to influence, or receive tangible benefits from, the transactions of the metropolitan establishment."[56] Thus while the mayor is expected to represent the electorate, he or she must also be responsive to organized interests. The former encourages a mantle of leadership, the latter an opportunity to be a good manager.

Because of the growing influence of the big institutional networks, the political-managerial function of big-city mayors has become more pronounced in recent years. Perhaps one of the most prominent examples of this is the role of New York City's former mayor, Abraham Beame, during that city's fiscal crisis in the early 1970s. Mayor Beame was reduced to acting as a messenger boy between the corporate representatives on the Emergency Financial Control Board (EFCB), the Municipal Assistance Corporation (MAC), and Governor Hugh Carey. The one individual who was elected by the voters of New York City had very little influence in deciding the political and economic future of the city—his leadership role was transformed completely into a managerial one.[57]

This kind of leadership transformation has been resisted in a few cities. A handful of populist-oriented mayors have tried to adopt advocacy roles in favor of poor and working-class citizens; they have sought to avoid the managerial role imposed upon mayors all over the country. In most cases these mayors have not been successful up to this point in American urban history. Either they have not been allowed to be effective, or have been defeated when facing re-election. And in more than one case, progressive mayors have been exposed to physical attack and various forms of legal harassment.[58]

Despite these defeats, an increasing number of groups are willing to take on the metropolitan establishment. They are increasingly turning towards the electoral arena as the place to challenge the powerful and wealthy. The first major step in confronting these interests is the capture of the mayor's office by progressive forces. As traditional mayors increasingly face progressive challenges, they will find themselves doing battle with groups seeking not merely to replace them, but also to introduce a new kind of politics in urban government. In Boston, such a battle has already emerged.

Mayor Kevin White and his personal political machine came to be recognized as one of the most powerful in America.[59] In 1979, black, white, and Latino progressive groups attempted to dislodge White from power. While two of the major challenges to White sought merely to replace him with other alternative "personalities," groups representing state Representative Mel King spearheaded a progressive challenge to politics-as-usual. These efforts are continuing in local and citywide elections.

The significance of this incipient, popularly based electoral uprising is that it will be repeated in other major cities. Underlying the new challenge to entrenched power in the electoral arena is the feeling that "change for the better comes only when movements of common people rally around an idea and create new leaders from the bottom up," and that "movements of ordinary people, acting out of self-interest, can write law. The moral authority of exemplary action can change lives."[60] But these ideas will be resisted by big-city mayors and their political machines.

Such resistance can be witnessed in Boston. During his tenure, Mayor White performed his political-managerial responsibilities superbly; he adopted and implemented policies that favored the powerful and wealthy and hurt the poor. His major accomplishment was the development of an atmosphere that was considered positive by big business interests; most of the mayor's more important actions were taken at the expense of those at the lower end of the socioeconomic ladder. Under his leadership, various electoral practices and processes were used to discourage and circumscribe any significant level of progressive black political activism.

A few community activists have argued that the black community in Boston has not been aggressive politically; that blacks have not participated in the electoral arena as much as they should; and that therefore it is understandable that white politicians have not been as responsive as they should be to black voters. Furthermore,

> Until black voters begin to demand more jobs and appoint-
> ments for their support, politicians will continue to seek the
> black vote only as a necessary balance of power to guarantee
> the margin of victory. . . .Until black voters are secure enough
> and militant enough to demand that white politicians take a
> strong liberal stand on the racial issue, even at the risk of defeat,
> the white politicians will continue to compromise and postpone
> the inevitable day of full black participation in the administration
> of American democracy.[61]

But the black community of Boston has a long history of demand-
ing equal treatment by City Hall. The fact that blacks have
not been as organized and mobilized as they should be is not
an attitudinal problem; rather, it is a consequence of the depress-
ing effects of various political decisions made by Kevin White
between 1967 and 1983. Under his leadership, City Hall utilized
four general approaches to prevent the development of a progressively oriented black politics in Boston. These included:
1) the selective use of City Hall patronage and public dollars
for purposes of reward and punishment; 2) manipulation of
public relations techniques to preserve the "liberal" image of
the mayor; 3) manipulation of various electoral processes, such
as voter registration procedures and city elections; and 4) the
nurturing of "cooperative" black political leadership. Each of
these approaches has been used to discourage black political
activism that City Hall found threatening.

Numerous instances in Boston politics show how City Hall
patronage and public dollars were used to strengthen the White
regime, by rewarding a loyalist or punishing an enemy. The
mayor's use of summer youth funds to reward his political
friends and workers is one example; another was his threat
to cut off city funds to the programs of uncooperative Latino
human service leaders during the mayoral campaign of 1979.
That same year White also provided financial grants to a few
black ministers who agreed to support his re-election effort.
Cooperative black leaders were appointed to prestigious boards
and commissions while the more independent ones were banish-
ed from City Hall-controlled processes.

Political fear prevented some blacks from becoming identified
with issues in ways not sanctioned by City Hall under Kevin

White. The *Boston Globe* and the *Boston Herald* stated in various articles that the mayor had control over money and jobs that he used to punish those not loyal to him. Another paper, the *Boston Phoenix*, commented that this affected all sectors in Boston politics and influenced the endorsements White received in his 1979 mayoral bid: "The power blocs who have no votes but who carry a great deal of influence—the banks, the utilities, the insurance companies, the major real estate houses are with White out of fear more than anything else."[62] So it was with some elements in the black community.

The fear of political reprisals may be a real obstacle to increased black political participation in Boston. Fear was described as one of White's most important political resources by every black elected official in Boston—one stated that fear of political and economic reprisals is what helped to maintain the paternalistic relationship between some black leaders and City Hall. He explained that since the economic foundation of blacks in Boston is so dependent on white power structures, black leaders were not willing to participate in political activities that might be viewed as threatening by the White machine.

Black former state Senator Bill Owens offered an example of the mayor's style in dealing with those not loyal to him. Owens was personally assured by White that he would have a large amount of influence with the economic development of the Blue Hill Commission in Roxbury in the mid-1970s, but when the two were involved in a conflict over the Commission's priorities, White ignored his promise and turned to the now-deceased Robert Forst, believed by Owens to be more cooperative with the mayor. Another black elected official, state Representative Doris Bunte, had a similar experience upon her appointment as a board member to the Boston Housing Authority. After Bunte refused to follow White's dictates, he attempted to punish her by removing her and making it clear that she was to be regarded as persona non grata in City Hall.

The threat of reprisal for not supporting the mayor or his policies may have been subtle, but the message was always quite clear. (Some who wanted to volunteer assistance to Mel

King's 1979 mayoral campaign stated that they had to maintain a low profile; a few prominent individuals who worked with King did so surreptitiously.) There was an understanding in Boston that if you worked for City Hall or desired any governmental assistance, you were expected to support the mayor; if you didn't follow this rule, then your job or grant would be given to more cooperative individuals. This is why in 1979 some members of the Vulcan Society (an association of black firemen in Boston) told a Mel King campaign worker seeking their support that while as an organization they would not openly defy the mayor, they would individually and "quietly" work and vote for Mel King. In Boston, political fear was not completely based on violence, as it might be in other cities, but rather on the professional and economic dependence of black citizens on City Hall. The political vulnerability of blacks working for City Hall produced the same effect: independent black political behavior was discouraged and punished.

The other approaches that were available to the White machine may not have been as obvious during certain periods as the one just discussed, but they were important in helping to establish the environment under which black politics has developed. They may even have been more important, because their utility was not merely in keeping a manager like White in power, but also in maintaining a political environment that did not encourage black-led challenges to the overall workings and interests of the metropolitan establishment.

Bachrach and Baratz argue that a public image can be manipulated by those who enjoy power so that the powerless do not question the arrangements supporting the powerful.[63] This means that political imagery or symbolism can be used to prevent blacks from raising these questions, and at the same time keep blacks from realizing their potential for political power. In urban politics a "set of predominant values, beliefs, rituals, and procedures...operate systematically and consistently to the benefit of certain persons and groups at the expense of others."[64] Those groups with power seek to maintain their positions by discouraging public discussion of issues that might threaten the structures and processes supporting their base of power. An important "resource" used to maintain conditions for keeping intact a particular arrangement is "non-decision-making": any issues that do emerge must not question the structures underlying certain processes of interaction between the powerless and the powerful:

> The primary method for maintaining a given mobilization of bias is non-decision making. A non-decision, as we define it, is a decision that results in suppression or thwarting of a latent or manifest challenge to the values or interest of decision makers. To be more nearly explicit, non-decision making is a means by which demands for change in the existing allocation of benefits and privileges in the community can be suffocated before they gain access to the relevant decision-making arena or failing all these things, maimed or destroyed in the decision implementing stage of the policy process.[65]

This "non-decision-making" approach to public policy in Boston was partially dependent upon the mayor's liberal reputation. White's liberal image was used to suffocate issues that might question the paternalistic political relationship between the black community and City Hall. Even in his dealing with the problem of racial violence, White used his liberal reputation to dilute black efforts to create greater degrees of racial harmony in Boston. According to Reverend William Alberts of Boston, the mayor accomplished this by "redefining problems" in ways that rendered them innocuous to his political position. This is another form of non-decision-making. Alberts writes, "A key dynamic of systemic racism is the ability of its leaders to *redefine the problem* in terms acceptable and favorable to them and their constituents."[66] In this way, City Hall under White manipulated the black community and some of its leaders so that they did not consider political options that would threaten the mayor's power. An example of this is the way racial violence was continually approached by the mayor's office; such incidents were handled as isolated occurrences. According to Micho Spring, one of White's confidants and a deputy mayor, this was the most effective way to deal with racial violence.[67] This approach kept the public from seeing both the relationship between racial harassment and broader public policies of the mayor's office, and the connection between racial violence and the necessity of political mobilization with a progressive agenda.

"Political symbolism" was indeed an important resource for White's machine; it was vital in attempting to discourage black political activism within a progressive framework. Through subtle manipulation of media exposure and public relations events, White portrayed himself as a relatively liberal mayor who could be responsive to the needs of black people. Unfortunately, some black voters allowed themselves to be fooled by the mayor's liberal image. During the mayoral general election in 1979, for example, some black supporters of White voiced the opinion that he "tries hard." Other blacks, while agreeing that the black community had been short-changed in terms of city services and that racial violence was increasing in Boston, supported White because "he has done the most that he can do."

When blacks criticized White's affirmative action performance in the 1979 mayoral race, he cleverly suggested that his opponent, state Senator Joseph Timilty, had not hired any blacks to his staff. Of course he did not mention that Timilty was not under the same obligation for affirmative action as was the mayor of Boston. White's—and indeed Boston's—historical liberal image slowed the politicization of blacks in Boston. Mayoral races that pitted White against Louise Day Hicks, or Joseph Timilty—who have either been openly antagonistic to black interests or, in the latter case, ignored black Bostonians—served to emphasize to black voters White's liberal image. This explains some of the previous attachments of the black community to City Hall—attachments that hindered the politicization of the black community.

The "political climate" in Boston since 1967 allowed Kevin White to use his liberal credentials to depress black political participation. Danigelis explains how the political milieu of a city affects the actualization of black political power:

> The political climate theory of black political behavior maintains that different areas and time periods in this country's history can be characterized by political climates intolerant or

supportive of or indifferent to black political participation and that, as a consequence, blacks have faced differing levels of political climate. This type of political climate, therefore, is the key to understanding the political profile of black Americans.[68]

Different kinds of political climates have elicited various black political patterns:

> Where laws and feelings are highly hostile toward black participation in politics, an intolerant political climate should be found. A supportive political climate involves at worst incomplete white resistance to black participation and at best active white support. A neutral or ambiguous political climate, where discriminatory barriers are absent or basically irrelevant to black political participation, probably is found throughout much of the North during the period between 1959 and 1972.[69]

Boston can be described as a city in the third category. This political climate effectively depresses black political aspirations and maintains black political noninvolvement. An ambiguous political climate allows ineffective mayoral leadership in the area of race relations to seem more important than it actually is. When the climate is not openly hostile toward black political participation, insignificant instances of leadership are perceived as important, because these actions are contrasted to a hostile or neutral political climate.

Other kinds of political resources were used by the mayor's office to discourage black political participation from threatening the metropolitan establishment. From 1950 to 1982, Boston was organized under an at-large electoral system, which effectively prevented black candidates from winning seats on the City Council and School Committee. Two exceptions were John O'Bryant, the first black to sit on Boston's School Committee in the 20th century (elected in 1977), and Tom Atkins, who sat on the City Council between 1967 and 1971. The discriminatory effect of at-large elections was illustrated vividly in the 1979 city elections, when three black candidates won runoff positions but lost in the general election because they did not have enough resources to appeal to the general electorate.

In 1980 the mayor of Boston stated in his inaugural address that he would attempt to change the at-large system of voting so that neglected neighborhoods and minorities could begin to enjoy access to their government.[70] But he did virtually nothing to encourage the adoption of this kind of reform. In November 1982, the voters of Boston narrowly approved a referendum to change the at-large system to one based on nine district seats and four at-large seats in City Council and School Committee elections. The mayor and his machine took a hands-off position toward adoption of this reform. The advertising campaigns and vote-pulling had been done by the Committee for District Representation (CDR), an organization composed of black, Latino, and white community activists from various parts of Boston. CDR collected the 22,000 signatures to place the question on the ballot and coordinated the effort to pull out favorable voters. While an earlier 1977 reform effort was directed in part by the mayor and his machine, the 1982 reform effort was spearheaded by progressive organizations having no connection with the mayor's office.

Although Boston instituted a district-based system of voting to take effect in the 1983 City Council and School Committee elections, the district lines that were finally adopted and approved by the mayor discriminated against the black and Latino community. The Black Political Task Force, an organization of black and Latino community activists, and the CDR objected to the final district boundaries for two reasons.* First, the district map relied on the state census of population published in 1975, rather than the federal population census taken in 1980. The former not only overestimated the total population of Boston by more than 100,000 persons, but also underestimated the size and growth of the black and Latino population in Boston. In addition, some predominantly black and Latino areas were placed in districts with a history of racial hostility and violence towards these groups; thus, even under a district-based system of voting, thousands of blacks and Latinos in locations like the South End and North Dorchester were in effect disenfranchised because they were placed in virtually all-white, hostile districts in neighborhoods like South Boston, South Dorchester,

Latino Political Action Committee, et al. v. City of Boston, et al., 1982.

Savin Hill, and Neponset. The mayor approved the final map, although the only black city councilor raised these concerns as did a number of black, Latino, and progressive white community groups.

Another electoral process under the mayor's control and leadership that has been used to discourage black political mobilization is voter registration procedures. In Boston, this process is so cumbersome that effective voter registration drives in the black community require herculean efforts and extensive resources. If these resources are not available, voter registration will not be given the attention it requires—unless it is to the advantage of City Hall to do so. Voter registration should be an "easy" process for potential black voters to become actual voters. This is crucial for the development of black political power. But voter registration procedures make it very difficult to increase the number of black voters in Boston.* During nonelection periods, for instance, potential voters must register in person at City Hall or the various neighborhood "Little City Halls" under the Office of Public Services, and only on weekdays between the hours of nine and five o'clock. These hours are extended only two weeks before an upcoming election.[71]

As suggested by the information in Table 4, these arrangements work to disadvantage potential black voters. Note that the voter registration rates in all of the white working-class areas, as well as in most of the white middle-class areas, are located in the upper ranges. All areas with significant numbers of black or Latino residents are located in the lower range. The only white areas in the city located in the lower range are Allston, Beacon Hill, and the Back Bay. The latter two areas, however, have a greater number of black and Latino residents than do any of the white areas with a voter registration rate greater than 60%.[72] These areas also have been traditionally characterized by low rates of voter registration. This arrangement may change as a result of the massive voter registration effort conducted by Operation Big Vote and the Mel King for

*Campaign for District Representation, Boston Tenant Organization, District 40 Community Education and Social Agency Employees, and Boston People's Organization v. Kevin White, 1982.

Mayor campaign in 1983; but again, the change is not through the efforts of City Hall—it is in spite of the efforts of City Hall.

When one notes that in New York City, with a population more than 11 times that of Boston, a voter registration system by mail has been implemented effectively, the procedures in Boston can be viewed as conveniently anachronistic.[73] Voter registration in Boston could be made relatively easy. This is not the case, in our view, because the mayor's machine has used voter registration procedures to control the number of blacks who are allowed to participate in the electoral arena. Encouraging this perception is the fact that very few blacks work in the Elections Department. In 1981 this city department employed 28 people, of whom only 2 were black.

Kimball has pointed out how voter registration procedures can create legal and psychological obstacles for minority potential voters when it is not in the interest of the entrenched to have new voters registered:

> It is imperative to focus on the institutional barriers that prevent increase in registration. . . .The staffing of registration points is usually under the control of local organizations who sometimes have special interest in excluding potential new voters who might threaten the distribution of power. In areas where residents speak a language other than English, the absence of bilingual materials and bilingual registration workers can be keenly felt by timid applicants. The frequency of registration dates, the hours when the public is accommodated, the availability of registration opportunities in locations other than central government offices—all have differential effects on the ability of some to register, particularly those with limited time off from work or limited access to transportation.[74]

Psychological obstacles are also created when unregistered potential voters are not encouraged actively to become participants in the electoral processes. Kimball argues that individuals must be made to feel that their participation is not only welcomed, but important. In his study of Newark he discovered, for example that given

> . . .two persons with similar disadvantages as to education, income, or race, the one who would register and vote displayed no self-evident differences from the neighbor who failed to

participate. Although recency of arrival was sometimes a factor, mobility as such was not especially significant. Family
backgrounds of participants or non-participants more or less
washed out in the sample of unregistered surveyed in Newark.
The key difference between voters and non-voters seemed to
be their own opinion of themselves, whether or not they felt
they possessed the aptitudes for politics, whether or not they
felt that the participation of one individual like themselves
would make any difference.[75]

Those in power therefore have the capability of encouraging
or discouraging voter registration and, generally, participation
in a city's political processes.

Boston is a city where voter registration in the black
community has been difficult or easy depending on the political
needs of the mayor and his machine. In 1967, for instance,
Kevin White squeaked by Louise Day Hicks in the mayoral
general election. As shown in Chapter Three, if not for the
black vote in wards 9, 12, and 14, White would have lost to
Hicks by 426 votes. In the black community White swamped
Hicks 15,569 to 3,202, thus beating her citywide 97,340 to 85,399.
Because of this close election in 1967, as well as his poor showing
among black voters in his 1970 gubernatorial bid, White aggressively wooed the black vote in 1971. In this year Robert A.
Jordan, a black political columnist for the *Boston Globe*, reported
that White's re-election campaign was intensively seeking a
major portion of the more than 35,000 potential voters in the
black community through black-oriented radio and newspaper
advertisements, including some that suggested, "A vote for
Atkins [a black mayoral candidate] is a vote for Hicks."[76]

Not coincidentally, a total of 8,000 new black voters were
registered. Frieda Garcia, a longtime human service worker
and community activist in Boston, explained how easy it was
to register blacks and Latinos to vote during this period. The
mayor made it possible for potential voters to be registered
in their homes! Workers were allowed to carry official registration
rosters to various sectors in the black community. In fact, some
even felt that White paid too much attention to the black community during this period. One observer wrote of an unspoken

issue in the 1971 preliminary mayoral election: "There is the issue that no candidate talks about—the 'Mayor Black Phenomenon.' People in many areas of the city have felt, ever since he defeated Mrs. Hicks for mayor in 1967, that White funnels city resources into the black community at the expense of other neighborhoods."[77]

In the general election of 1971, White beat Hicks in the black community by 13,707 votes, but won the election by 40,873 votes. At this point he began to build a base in white working-class areas, forsaking the black community because during general elections, when he was challenged by candidates perceived to be anti-black, that community did not have to be wooed. Under these circumstances, the registration of new black voters was no longer a priority of the city's political machine. When high voter registration in the black community has been advantageous to City Hall, obstacles have been overcome in registering blacks; however, when it has been a disadvantage, blacks have received less encouragement to register.[78]

We have discussed a few institutional factors that have inhibited black people in Boston from greater levels of political participation in the electoral arena. Another major factor is the type of black political leadership that emerged in this city under Kevin White. Though black community leadership is diverse, the political machine in Boston attempted to prevent the emergence of a broad leadership group that might challenge the mayor's influence. The machine successfully established and legitimized its own black leadership by appointing "liaisons" to the black community. These liaisons were of two types, described in an earlier study of black politics by Wilson: the "prestige" leader and the "token" leader. The former included those individuals who "invariably represent high—for the Negro community—personal achievement, achievement that usually flows from success in business or professional life."[79] These "prestige leaders are cited most often by other Negro leaders as having the 'best' or the most 'extensive' contacts with influential white leaders."[80] The other kind of liaison was the token leader,

> ...the Negro selected most often by whites, to "represent"
> the Negro community in civic activities and on public agen-
> cies where it is felt such representation is required. He lacks
> the status of the prestige leader, and the scope of his contacts
> with the white community tends to be narrower and more
> focused.[81]

These highly visible individuals were recruited by the political
machine of Boston to positions lacking in substantive or institutionalized power. Part of this strategy was to make available
to the black community a certain amount of patronage, controlled by City Hall via these liaisons. This patronage was
characterized not only by its relatively small amount, but also
by its very nature. It was patronage that would not arouse
concern on the part of white neighborhood groups. It might
be a small grant from a public agency or a job for a loyal worker;
it would not include, for instance, a reduction in property assessment for blacks in Roxbury, where rates are the highest in Boston.
This latter type of patronage would require an equitable distribution of the property tax burden, which would mean that
assessments of white homeowners would have to be increased.
The relatively small amount of patronage made available to
the black community was accepted as a given by the black
liaisons.

This liaison system short-changed blacks even in terms of
petty patronage by inhibiting the effectiveness of independent
black leaders, who tended to demand greater amounts of
patronage and systematic benefits. But by the creation of an
artificial leadership for the black community and the appearance
of access and influence through the careful use of limited
patronage, City Hall ensured that segments of the black
community remained quiet and loyal. In this way, the machine
attempted to convince blacks that independent political mobilization was not even necessary. This allowed City Hall to maintain the political and economic arrangements that it had
established with the white working class, as well as with more
powerful groups in Boston.

The role of leadership is crucial for the political development of any black community in the American city; how leader-

ship defines itself and is defined by external forces determines what issues will be generated and also affects the self-image of the black community. Without denying the importance of environmental factors, or the education and skills of black leaders, we would argue that the particular type of leadership is a crucial influence on the development and the level of political power. The significance of leadership for black political power is confined neither to Boston nor to the contemporary period.

In a study of blacks in Massachusetts at the turn of the century, Daniels claimed that the quality of leadership provided by prominent Negroes determined the racial progress of the group.[82] And even earlier, black leaders in the ante-bellum period had developed extensive political and organizational expertise as a result of abolition committees, convention politics, and race-issues agitation; this experience, however, did not necessarily result in greater political sophistication—partly because of the role that leadership played:

> Negroes gained considerable experience in methods akin to those of politics, which subsequently gave them greater confidence in advancing their claims. After the war they of course expected to be of more political consequence. But whatever effort they exerted on their own behalf was of secondary importance and effect, for they were immediately made the proteges of white friends and enthusiasts, at whose hands they forthwith became recipients of bountiful patronage. During a period of twenty years at least, the outflowing favor of the other race was the factor in the appointment of Negroes to many respectable posts and in their election to the City Council and the State Legislature.[83]

Daniels describes specific instances illustrating this pattern and its consequences in the early 1900s: "Though four of the nine members of the Republican ward committee have usually been Negroes, they have obediently taken their orders from the white boss and have probably done more to injure their race in a political way than to help it." The author continues,

> The Negroes have failed dismally in this ward to realize their political opportunities. By 1905, the Negro males of voting age formed over 25%, and today they form close to 35%, of all the males of voting age in the ward. The white Republican

males of voting age constitute a proportion of about 20% of
the total. By enterprising registration of their own and the white
Republican vote, and by taking advantage of factional quar-
rels among the Democrats, the Negroes could probably have
obtained control of the ward and have elected members of
their race to the Common Council and to the Legislature. But
whenever the better element have nominated a ward committee, as a first step in this direction, the Negro members of
the regular "machine" committee have forthwith sown seeds
of dissension. . .with the result that the "machine" has always
won.[84]

A contemporary observer has also detected weaknesses in
Boston's black leadership that have hurt the political advancement of black people:

The dynamics of the black community have been enigmatic
and unpredictable and often hard to see. Largely, the black
sub-culture dynamics, particularly with regard to political
behavior, have operated in a reactive manner; these dynamics
have seldom been asserted through a political logic of their
own but have been more inclined to respond to movements—
shifts of power—within wider (white) societal structures. This
has had the predictable but nonetheless detrimental effect of
advancing a few—those closest to the centers of power—beyond
the confines of the sub-culture at the expense of the rest.[85]

The patterns outlined here are still prevalent today. Sectors
within the black leadership spectrum have not developed inde-
pendently, but as scions of white power structures. The consequences of this type of leadership for the black community
are remarkably similar to those observed in the early 1900s.

In Boston the black leadership established by the mayor's
office between 1967 and 1983 inhibited the political growth
of the black community and discouraged the development of
progressive electoral activism. Until the black community in
Boston asserts its independence and challenges the distribution of wealth and the particular arrangement of power, it will
not enjoy political power. A significant step in this direction
occurred in the September 1983 mayoral preliminary election,
when Mel King received close to 95% of the black vote.

The appointed black officials who act as if they are in fact leaders in the traditional sense slow this potential development. One prominent educator in the black community described the following scenario when asked how the interests of the black community are expressed under a system of appointed black leaders: "A group of blacks will come together to discuss an important problem and then seek out someone who may have a personal contact with someone in the mayor's office; this person will then be asked to petition the mayor or some public bureaucrat for the favor of satisfying the request." This type of relationship is not based on power or the threat of power but on the benevolence of City Hall's machine. This is an accurate description of the traditional "gate-keeper" role assigned to some black leaders by white power structures in cities throughout American history.

In discussing early black leadership in New York City, Katznelson described the relationship between City Hall and the black community: "A black leader, handpicked by the white-controlled machine, delivered votes while avoiding contact with white voters in the area. In return, the leader achieved prestige because of his influence with his white patrons, and personal privilege....The black voters which the leader mobilized were awarded a few menial patronage jobs to create an illusion of progress."[86] These black leaders, argues Katznelson, were not "representative in that territorial community procedures for leadership selection were absent. The black leaders were chosen by the white party elites, not by the community—territorial or racial—they claimed to represent."[87] These leaders were not "of" the black community, and therefore their positions were dependent on the good will of those whites on the top:

> These liaison or buffer leaders were given a taste of honey, the illusion of political access and some visible patronage. But these political rewards, they knew, came not as the product of independently organized territorial control, but from the white party leadership. The result, of course, was to detach the recognized black leaders from the mass of the black population. If position, for the black leadership, rested not on a mass base from below but was conferred from above, then what was conferred could always be retracted.[88]

Various sociological studies of black communities in the 1950s also help to describe the weaknesses of "non-institutionalized" leadership:

> Although there is an identifiable structure of leadership in the sub-community of Pacific City at the present time, the leaders themselves are not "power wielders" or "decision makers" in the sense in which the terms are used by Hunter and Mills; they hold positions of little importance to the community's institutional structures; their decisions have no serious ramifications for the larger community.[89]

These same weaknesses are evident today with part of the black leadership stratum in Boston. Black leadership supported by City Hall and white power structures was used effectively to slow the momentum that Mel King was developing in the black community during the mayoral preliminary campaign in 1979. Appointed black leaders have also been used to provide electoral support for white candidates such as Louise Day Hicks, recognized as being an "anti-black" politician by the black community.[90]

In addition, this artificial leadership has presented obstacles to the development of genuine black leadership. Former state Senator Bill Owens has said that he first decided to run for office because this type of leadership was hurting the black community by not allowing potential black leaders to exercise options for growth. He stated that a few political families in the black community have been nurtured as "gate-keepers" in order to maintain the political, economic, and social status quo. Representatives of these families have established political and economic structures that are specifically used to dampen the growth of black political independence. Owens explained, "If you look at organizations with positive intentions that have failed to get off the ground since the early sixties you will find the same names associated with them; the same people over and over again have been responsible for black political failures."[91] At times "organizations" without any structure are established to discourage independent action. In return for their services to the various white power structures, black "influentials" remain in what they consider to be prestigious positions, and accrue some minimal individual economic benefits. Remaining aloof from various efforts to mobilize the black community politically, these appointed black leaders have not addressed public issues in ways that might be disfavored by City Hall. Liaison leaders are used as "lightning rods" to "cool out" angry blacks,[92] serving as buffers between the black community and City Hall. They have been noticeably absent in electoral activities discouraged by City Hall. An example was the lack of active involvement by liaison leaders in voter registration efforts during the 1979 preliminary election, when black voter registration would have been detrimental to Kevin White because of the presence of a black mayoral candidate.

Black liaison leaders have been used by white power structures to dampen the political aggressiveness of the black community. These anointed black leaders do not have institutionalized access to City Hall or to the powerful interests operating in Boston; they serve not at the pleasure of their constituents, but at the pleasure of the mayor. Black leaders who are sanctioned by City Hall are allowed to distribute small amounts of patronage in order to maintain the loyalty of black voters, but they cannot represent the interests of the black community. Their function is rather to explain or rationalize City Hall's political behavior and policy to the black community. Black political mobilization is thus redirected from targeting City Hall onto these individual leaders who are powerless to respond to the needs of the black community.

Black communities in American cities are beginning to reflect an electoral activism that rejects leadership by the mere appointees of the powerful—whether black or white. Blacks are realizing that change can only be a result of direct challenges to power; for this to occur, "propped-up" black leaders, such as those supported by the liaison system in Boston, must be replaced with leaders who are progressive and independent.

Another segment of black leadership in Boston includes individuals associated with the human services bureaucracies, specifically the "anti-poverty" structures. The relationship between this sector and the mayor's machine has been complex. Unlike other major cities, where anti-poverty structures have made an impact on the political development of black and Latino communities by providing resources to emerging political leaders of color, the impact of these structures in Boston has been limited.[93] Action for Boston Community Development, Inc. (ABCD), the city's umbrella anti-poverty structure, has had a stormy relationship with City Hall but has not attempted to exercise power or influence in the local electoral arena. This organization has restricted its major role to that of a pressure group, periodically becoming activated around issues that directly affect the organization's delivery of services and its clients. This has led the organization to be more state- than city-oriented in the electoral arena, a posture not consistent with ABCD's history in Boston. Thernstrom reported that the agency's structure "was carefully designed to mirror the leadership structure of the community itself."[94] Initially this meant control of the agency by the business elite, but by the late 1960s the elite was replaced by City Hall.[95] A third phase, during which City Hall's influence declined, was only possible with the tacit understanding that ABCD would not seek to politically mobilize the black or poor citizens of Boston.

ABCD's apparently neutral role in city electoral activities has had a cost—discouraging the politicization of blacks in Boston. It has dampened the thrust for black political mobilization and inhibited the development of black leadership. Many neighborhood activists, recruited into ABCD, are in effect discouraged from participation in the city's political processes. This is similar to Hamilton's findings concerning the effect of anti-poverty structures on the institutionalization of political power in New York City's black and Puerto Rican communities. He found that while "participation in poverty-programs politics has increased in black communities, the level of political influence in the electoral arena has decreased."[96] In New York, Hamilton writes,

> The black constituency has lost, not gained, political influence, if one measures this in terms of the capacity to elect and influence people who will likely have control over the way programs

are run. The black constituency has evidenced a marked decline in participation in the process (electoral politics) aimed at capturing and controlling not funded programs, but positions of governmental (institutional) power. This is the function of a politicization process gone awry.[97]

Hamilton focuses on the development of "recipients" as contrasted to "clients" as the key to an understanding of how anti-poverty programs have discouraged the institutionalization of black political power. As he argues, "A patron-recipient relationship is a political benefit structure that does not require the recipient to reciprocate in any sustained political way in order to receive benefits."[98] This discourages an electorally focused political socialization.

ABCD presents an additional "discouraging" dimension not discussed fully by Hamilton. This organization also minimizes the development of institutionalized power by depleting the number and energy of individuals who would tend to be attracted to electoral politics. Here we refer to those who are aware of the importance of local electoral activity but have been burdened with professional responsibilities associated with social services distribution. Their work orientation diverts political interests to human service and bureaucratic matters. For example, a number of individuals in ABCD, previously active in local politics, were co-opted into the delivery of human services and excluded themselves from electoral politics. But as Hamilton writes, "The leaders and spokepersons of such a constituency are at a distinct disadvantage in the pluralist bargaining process. They must attempt to function in the competitive political industry with less than adequate resources. They are rendered weak by the nature of their own benefit support system."[99] Potentially influential community leaders are rendered harmless in the electoral arena by ABCD.

In addition to ABCD, there is another layer of programs, either linked to ABCD as local neighborhood offices or supported by private funds. In contrast to ABCD personnel, leaders in this sector have been more active electorally. For example, some supported and actively campaigned for Mel King in the preliminary mayoral elections of 1979 and 1983. These leaders are issue-conscious and sensitive to the linkage between the services their clients receive, various kinds of community problems, and the electoral development of the black community.

Generally, however, City Hall used its influence to discourage political independence based on black-managed anti-poverty structures. This was done by allowing some blacks a relatively free hand in administering local poverty funds. An understanding was reached between City Hall and these administrators that those who were not a threat to the political machine would be rewarded, in part, by being allowed to use poverty monies as they saw fit—as long as it was done within the legal guidelines of specific programs.

One writer commented that this system of electoral control is similar to that used by Mayor Joseph Alioto in San Francisco: "Both White and Alioto employed Model Cities, OEO, job programs, and similar federal patronage resources to sustain minority community support while acting tough on disorder and boosting growth. They employed their federal resources all the more shrewdly by allowing 'community control,' rather than exercising tight oversight over funds and employees. But they knew when to call in their debts."[100]

Even in Chicago, a powerful political machine had to allow a "certain semblance of participation" in controlling anti-poverty funds. Greenstone and Peterson found that:

> However efficiently the Neighborhood Service Center (NSC) was operated, among the purposes which it studiously avoided fulfilling was the political activation of low income groups. The Daley Administration was uninterested in spawning political competitors, and it had the political resources and bureaucratic apparatus sufficient to prevent CAP encouragement of such developments. A certain semblance of participation was a necessary concession to OEO, but the clear preference and actual accomplishment of Chicago's CAA was to keep it at the minimum feasible level.[101]

Mayor White influenced the direction of Boston anti-poverty funds in this same way. In contrast, the mayor of Philadelphia encouraged the politicization of the anti-poverty programs to fight established interests. Here, Bailey found, "Politics is very much a part of the city's war on poverty. . . .The mayor has used the anti-poverty program to gain political support in his fight with the city's Democratic Party chairman. Anti-poverty workers were perceived to work for the mayor's re-election to office."[102] In Boston, White controlled the political machine thoroughly. He did not necessarily need anti-poverty programs to keep him in control of his machine. The White strategy was based on neutralizing this potential political resource.

When this strategy was not effective, the White machine directly challenged uncooperative anti-poverty program leaders. For example, in 1972, the Model Cities Program—under the mayor's control—was used against uncooperative individuals in one anti-poverty program, the Roxbury Action Program (RAP). Paul Parks, the Model Cities administrator appointed by White, was directed by City Hall to challenge public funding to RAP for the development of a housing project in Kittredge Square in Roxbury, an area virtually ignored by City Hall until RAP expressed an interest in it. In a related development, White also used Parks in his position as Housing Commissioner to hold up approval of Boston Housing Authority's sale of its property to RAP. State Representative Doris Bunte, who was aligned with RAP and a member of the Boston Housing Authority, was dismissed by White. In a study of this incident, Perry writes, "Part of this campaign included foot-dragging by White administration officials in other city departments on actions necessary to the work of the BHA Board."[103] In response to these attempts to control and coerce RAP, the organization attempted (though unsuccessfully) to run a slate on the Boston Model Neighborhood Board in 1969 and 1970. By co-opting some black anti-poverty program leaders and forcing others onto the defensive, the White machine used the anti-poverty funds to help maintain the arrangement of power relationships in the city or, at the minimum, to neutralize these programs as potential sources of political challenge to his regime.

White and his personal machine used the political resources described here to depress the level of black participation in the electoral arena, and to discourage a progressive politics that would seriously threaten business as usual in Boston. The political obstacles that big-city mayors place before growing and aware black communities will become more obvious as blacks grope for power. As independent black leaders seek to challenge the political and economic status quo, City Hall impediments will have to be removed or eliminated. We will next show how the Mel King campaigns in 1979 and 1983 sought to do this.

5.
The Mel King for Mayor Campaigns

The Mel King for Mayor campaigns in 1979 and 1983 were attempts to introduce a progressive public agenda in Boston. These campaigns were in fact extensions of many earlier efforts for justice and equality in Boston—the culmination of numerous broader struggles for access, better housing, and better public schools. They were important because they directly challenged the political status quo founded upon racism, economic exploitation, and sexism. Mel King introduced into these mayoral campaigns discussion of issues that no other candidate could ignore. He set not only the tone, but the substance of Boston politics in 1979 and 1983. Many found this threatening, and reacted accordingly.

This section examines how the King mayoral efforts sought to overcome the obstacles placed before them by Boston urban machinism. Although King did not win a runoff position in the general election of 1979 and was defeated in the general election of 1983, his campaigns provided a model for subsequent progressive electoral efforts in Boston and other cities. What actually was achieved by the Mel King organization during these elections? What were the consequences for the development of black political power in Boston? What lessons about political organizing in the black community can be learned from the campaigns of 1979 and 1983? And how did King help to mold the issues that would serve as the basis for political confrontation with the "metropolitan establishment"? We begin to answer these questions by first describing the kind of electoral organization that emerged from the effort to elect Mel King as mayor of Boston in 1979.

THE 1979 PRELIMINARY ELECTION

Undertaken with the idea that the present distribution of wealth and its subsequent benefits in America must be challenged as unjust and inequitable at the local level, the Mel King for Mayor campaign of 1979 had four broad organizational goals. These organizational elements are vital to any progressive electoral thrust on a citywide basis: 1) intense mobilization of black voters, 2) an issue-oriented campaign, 3) a grassroots-dominated campaign leadership, and 4) black and white working-class coalitions. The 1979 campaign experienced varying degrees of success with each of these goals. The most important organizational goal for the development of a progressive politics in Boston was the mobilization of black voters. This was a difficult but essential task.

In a study of black mayoral campaigns in different cities in the United States, Nelson and Meranto attempted to compose a profile of the successful electoral contests.[104] They identified four major requirements for effective black political mobilization:

1. Group cohesion: "a feeling among people that they are in a common situation and face a common fate."

2. Leadership: "individuals from the group who gain support for their suggestions as to how the group may improve its fate."

3. Political Consciousness: "the realization by the group and its leadership that their common fate can be influenced by group political action."

4. Organization: "the building of political organization to achieve group goals."

These conditions, in conjunction with relatively large numbers and a concentration of blacks, are necessary for blacks to realize political power at the local level. The authors write,

> Political power (the ability to influence the allocation of governmental resources), insofar as it flows from electoral action, is

achieved only if numbers are augmented by group cohesion, leadership, political consciousness and organization. Within this context the political mobilization process means the utilization of these resources to achieve group political goals. The fundamental point to be noted is that when a group manifests potential strength in numbers and high concentration, it does not automatically manifest the latter four resources. These supporting resources develop only after the group has surmounted certain barriers to its effective emergence in the political process. Political mobilization only results when all of the mentioned resources converge at a particular point in time.[105]

Nelson and Meranto should have specified two other important requirements: time and money. Other than these two factors, the above conditions, including the necessary numbers, were available during the Mel King mayoral campaigns in 1979 and 1983.

But these are conditions necessary to win local elections within our traditional understanding of American politics. These are conditions necessary to merely replace white politicians with black politicians. If we move toward a progressively oriented politics, these conditions will not suffice. Victory under traditional electoral activism does not represent change for blacks or whites; political power under this context, as Nelson and Meranto admit, is but the "ability to influence the allocation of governmental resources." This goal is important, of course, but exclusive reliance on this as a single objective politically entraps citizens. It prevents working-class people from breaking a vicious cycle of service deterioration, racial and social tension, and increasing profits for those who are already well-off.

As a progressive candidate, Mel King had to not only meet the requirements described by Nelson and Meranto, but also develop a broad strategy for challenging the wealthy in Boston. Organizationally, this meant that he had to develop ways to bring blacks, whites, and Latinos together; he had to remind the voters constantly that as mayor he would confront certain issues differently than had previous mayors; and he had to sacrifice certain principles of "good" organization in order to allow a democratically based campaign to flower. These two campaigns illustrate that, as difficult as it is for blacks to achieve electoral office under traditional politics, it is much more difficult for blacks to win electoral office as progressive leaders.

Conceivably, with a better-financed campaign Mel King could have won a runoff position in the general election—the first time he ran for mayor—even with black votes alone. As cited earlier, Timilty won the second spot in the general election with 32,456 votes. If King had been able to mobilize half of the total black electorate in Boston in 1979 (80,000 voters), he could have beaten Timilty. However, King ran not merely as a black candidate, but as a progressive one. This differentiated his candidacy not only from other mayoral candidates in 1979 and 1983, but also from the 1971 mayoral campaign of Thomas Atkins. Although Atkins received considerable white voter support, his campaign was not generally seen as a coalition of black, white, and Latino citizens crusading against racial and economic injustice. Atkins's campaign more represented an attempt for "a piece of the pie" than a questioning of the size of the pie. The basis of black and white electoral alignment under Atkins was an attempt to attract white middle-class taxpayers back to Boston; but the electoral glue between blacks and whites in the King candidacy was a concern for the needs of poor and working-class people living in the city.

Atkins emphasized the importance of keeping a strong middle-class tax base in Boston. King used social issues, such a crime, gay and women's rights, gentrification, and even international issues to attract segments of the white community. Unlike Atkins, King did not express major concern for issues usually associated with the white middle class; as an editorial in the *Boston Globe* correctly pointed out, he was more interested in the problems of Boston's poor. In the summer of 1971, Atkins stated, "If we can't solve the problems that send the middle class in exodus, then our society's going to crumble, and our cities will crumble."[106] King attracted those white voters who saw the problems of poverty and racism as being of greater concern than the flight of the middle class.

Also, unlike Atkins, one of King's electoral priorities—which went beyond the mayor's race—was the development and persistence of a broad issue-oriented coalition between black, Latino, and white voters. The coalition created by King was not merely a response to the 1979 mayoral preliminary election; it was an attempt to bring blacks, whites, and Latinos together to work on a wide variety of issues in a coalition that would continue even after this race. The support that Atkins garnered was not transferable to activism beyond the mayor's race in 1971. In the 1979 Mel King campaign, this was the first time in Boston's political history that such an ethnically diverse progressive coalition emerged so powerfully. This development may have many consequences and implications for Boston politics in the years to come. Indeed, it laid the groundwork for victory in the 1983 preliminary election.

The Mel King for Mayor campaign of 1979 helped to create and propel various political coalitions in Boston. After the mayoral contest, a multi-ethnic network of various groups continued to work on common concerns. The "Boston People's Organization" was a by-product of the 1979 mayoral campaign; this citywide group has attempted to continue electoral efforts started during that campaign. Another citywide organization partially originating from the mayoral campaign was the Committee for District Representation (CDR). Composed of branches in black and white neighborhoods, the CDR was responsible—in large part—for the adoption of a combined district/at-large system of representation for the City Council and the School Committee in 1981. Other examples of the effects of the King campaign were the "Community Action" slates, composed of black, Latino, white, and French-speaking residents, organized in the neighborhoods of Jamaica Plain and Dorchester to campaign for seats on the Democratic Ward Committees in 1980.

One of the requirements of any progressive electoral campaign is a focus on issues; this means that voters are sought by appealing to their intelligence rather than by media manipulation of a candidate's personality. The issues pursued by King in the 1979 campaign not only set him apart from Atkins's 1971 campaign; they also differentiated him from the three other major candidates in 1979. Kevin White, Joseph Timilty, and

David Finnegan sought to win office by emphasizing personalities, which encouraged issue-evasion and also inhibited
discussions of public policy alternatives that might lead to
challenges to the powerful and wealthy interests operating in
Boston.

A city like Boston, dominated by a strong political machine,
discourages the widespread discussion of issues and public
policy alternatives in its mayoral campaigns. As Nordlinger
pointed out,

> Issues and issue-problems are rarely accorded more than a
> passing attention, which also means that incumbents are rarely
> "held responsible" for their behavior when standing for
> re-election. . . .The politics of personality, featuring small follow-
> ings, narrowly circumscribed support from particular ethnic
> groups, and the absence of any sizeable political organizations
> also detract from responsiveness by reducing the extent of
> information about citizen concerns available to both candidate
> and elected officials.[107]

In 1979, the King campaign began to change this. The issues
that King emphasized were a result of input from all levels
of the campaign organization; issue positions were consistent
regardless of the neighborhood or the racial or economic
background of the audience. The impact that emphasis on particular issue positions might have on King's public image or
the number of votes he would attract was virtually ignored.
Based on a series of interviews, a Boston University graduate
student who researched the campaign styles of the different
candidates concluded that Timilty, Finnegan, and White were
indeed more concerned with their image in the media than
they were about the various issues that were discussed in the
mayoral campaign.[108]

Although Mel King and his staff developed a set of issues
specific to Boston, the parameters that he used to define these
issues are relevant for other American cities. Five general principles were reflected in this progressive campaign: 1) the
"empowerment" of black and Latino people; 2) racial and ethnic
cooperation on common socioeconomic problems; 3) conser-

vation and improvement of neighborhoods, and community-based institutions; 4) economic development that balances the interests of poor and working-class people with those of the middle-class citizenry; and 5) redefinition of the values citizens act upon in the electoral arena. These general principles helped to mold the issues of major importance to the people of Boston. From this conceptual format, positions on issues such as education, health, crime, and employment could be developed for a citywide constituency.

We have outlined the political boundaries of the King mayoral campaign of 1979. Now we will discuss some of the specific organizational problems facing this campaign, and then examine what might be some of the general do's and don'ts for other progressive campaigns based in black communities across urban America. In his study of black mayoral elections in six cities (Cleveland, Gary, Memphis, Philadelphia, Chicago, and Youngstown), Stone found that the following factors are necessary for victory:

> The black candidate must be regarded seriously by the black community....The black community must believe the black candidates honestly have a chance to win....The black candidate must have a strong organization and sufficient finances or develop imaginative techniques for unearthing them....The black community must unite as a solid bloc vote....The black candidate must campaign for the white vote as assiduously as he campaigns for the black vote....The black candidate must be a member of the political party which controls the community which has the highest number of registered voters....There must be no other black candidate of significance or popularity in the race....There must be a minimum of one third registered black voters in the city, and the city's principal newspapers, radio and television stations must either endorse the candidacy of the black candidate or remain neutral.[109]

Some of these requirements did present serious difficulties for the King campaign in 1979. Organizational problems concerned money, the image of "seriousness," black political efficacy, voter registration activities, and race.

A major difficulty was the shortage of funds, a problem

common to any effort seeking to represent impoverished groups. But for progressive black candidacies it is still a greater problem because large campaign contributions from the corporate sector are not likely. Although Mel King was able to generate almost three times the money in 1983 that he did in 1979, he was outspent by all of his mayoral opponents. Black candidates are at a clear disadvantage compared to others because of the economic state of the black community in Boston. Studying Atkins's race for city councilman in 1967, one observer noted,

> [A] consequence of the Negro's precarious economic status in Boston is seen in the severe handicap which this fact imposes upon any would-be candidate for public office—or anyone, for that matter, who engages in political activity (which does not necessarily take place exclusively in the "civic" arena) that requires an economic base in the black community makes politics a tough business, especially in a city where such a strong personality-orientation dominates the political scheme of things.[110]

And another observer reported,

> For the Negro who would engage actively in politics, the absence of an economic base is a severe handicap. In the Boston scheme of personally-oriented politics, it is peculiarly harsh.... By passing the hat in Roxbury, a promising Negro candidate might raise $500 to $600, principally from two or three persons.[111]

This actually happened in the house parties for King in black parts of the city. Fundraising in these areas netted relatively small amounts of money, whereas such events in white communities resulted in much more money.

Mel King's 1979 campaign was run on a small budget of $60-70,000. Atkins's 1971 mayoral campaign also had problems with fundraising, raising only $50,000, according to his campaign manager, Herbert A. Hershfang.[112] Considering inflation, Atkins's $50,000 probably went further than King's. But because of the commitment of individual campaign workers for King, this problem was not as critical as it could have been; for King this meager budget produced 17,401 votes! His supporters were "hard-core": they were people who were attracted to the issues King was expressing. Had more money been available, King could have carried his message and proposal further to various parts of the city.

Another major problem that had to be overcome by King's organization in 1979 was the perception held in some sectors of black and white communities that his candidacy was not a serious one. This was not as great a problem for Atkins in 1971. The *Boston Globe* conceded, as a matter of fact, that Atkins had a good chance to gain a runoff spot in the November 1971 general election.[113] This especially seemed possible in light of the large number of black voters added to the electorate during Kevin White's gubernatorial effort in 1970. But in 1979 the *Boston Globe* virtually laughed at King's candidacy, treating it as a "media event" rather than a serious bid for power. Contributing to the image of "non-seriousness" was King's unorthodox style—he did not look or act like a politician. It was rumored, for example, that King lost support in the 1979 preliminary election because he refused to wear a tie.

Another contributing factor to this "non-serious" image was King's endorsement of state Senator Joseph Timilty in the 1975 mayoralty campaign. In the early and middle phases of the 1979 race, the two major newspapers questioned whether King, was performing a "stalking horse" role in the mayoral campaign. Since Timilty was viewed as the major challenger to Kevin White in the 1979 race, some felt that King's participation in the preliminary campaign was a ploy to dilute the mayor's black support. As it turned out, King's candidacy proved to be a fatal blow to Timilty's efforts.

Newspaper polls also tended to emphasize King's apparent lack of standing among white and black voters. Late into the preliminary phase of the mayoral election, a few polls showed that King would receive little support over all, even among black voters. This encouraged the media and some white politicians to question both the seriousness and the actual electoral threat of Mel King's candidacy. Not until the last few weeks before the preliminary mayoral election in 1979 did the media conglomerates begin to suggest that King was indeed a serious candidate, and that he was the only candidate who had developed an issue- rather than personality-oriented campaign.

As mentioned earlier, in some sectors of the black community of Boston there exists a myth of black political impotency. This myth suggests that black citizens cannot change their political condition. Either because they are too poor, too few in number, or simply not aggressive enough, black people will not be able to "rock the boat" in this city. To some this means that blacks should seek acceptance, even if in an inferior position, with the established power structures rather than attempt to change it to their benefit. As one older black citizen told a campaign worker, "Mel King is ridiculous to think he can do something in the capital of white America." King has written of the effects of this myth on issues outside the electoral arena:

> This persistent message that white society does not believe in the commitment or the capability of the community of color to improve its situation has seriously damaged the self image of people of color. The constant refrain "there's no way" increases the anxiety and frustration of those who care. Pressure builds and the confidence to proceed with community building and development processes is inhibited.[114]

The White machine began to encourage black voters to accept this myth in the 1971 mayoral campaign. The campaign staff of the mayoral incumbent announced in advertisements that a vote for Tom Atkins would be a wasted vote. Black voters, these campaign ads suggested, could not realistically hope to elect a black mayor.

The belief that black voters cannot be an effective force in Boston politics was expressed in a number of circles during the 1979 mayoral campaign. In the summer and fall some people in the black community stated that they could not participate effectively in the electoral and political processes of Boston. They felt that not enough voters would support a black mayoral candidate. There was a feeling in many parts of this community that the racism pervading Boston life and the numerical size of this community would inhibit a black individual from garnering more than 10% of the vote. The perception held by some potential King supporters that he could not win prevented them from supporting him aggressively. One religious leader commented that King should not run, because "there is no way that he can win," and another offered, "He will embarrass the black community." This type of attitude was not overcome until late in the campaign. What made it difficult for King's campaign organization to destroy this view was his lack of visible support in the early and middle phases of the preliminary election race.

Overcoming a low level of efficacy among potential supporters is crucial for black electoral aspirants—more important for black than white candidates because the former seem to rely on "unorganized" support to a greater extent than white politicians. In a nationwide survey of white and black elected officials, Conyers and Wallace found that 87% of the latter compared to 69% of the former responded that the "unorganized population" of their respective communities were very important to their electoral success.[115] Black voters—especially those who may not be "touched" by white political actors—must be convinced that a black candidate has a chance for electoral success before they will support him or her. But this is where electoral activism under a progressive banner is superior in possibilities to traditional electoral activism. Progressive activism offers not only an opportunity for substantive change in a neighborhood's life, but also new approaches by which to realize these opportunities in the electoral arena.

As a progressively oriented candidate, Mel King was directing his appeal to those voters who were not as "visible" as other citizens. Therefore, his support was not reflected easily in the media and this tended to obscure what support he had. As King's support became more visible, more grassroots support was generated. A momentum developed in the last two or three weeks of the campaign among this part of the electorate.

Blacks seem to be willing to believe that they can participate effectively in the electoral process if black leaders express and act on this belief. The greatest momentum of support for King was generated after black students and a few black civic leaders and ministers publicized their support for Mel King. The political efficacy of blacks, this effort seems to suggest, is partially dependent upon the position adopted by black professionals. If support in this area had been tapped and publicized earlier, support at the grassroots level would have been greater. The results of the 1983 preliminary election proved this. It is almost as if grassroots elements wanted to help in pushing for King's platform by participating in the electoral processes but would not do so until they saw evidence of participation among some black professionals. It may be the posture of this sector in the black community that determines the saliency of the myth of black political impotency, which suggests that it is crucial to involve the black professional and student sectors in progressive strategies of electoral activism.

Sectors in the black community that have been ignored by elected officials, such as the growing underclass and students, must be encouraged to participate in progressive electoral activism. But the registration of these potential new black voters presents another organizational difficulty to the development of black political power. By efforts to register sympathetic voters, the King organization was able to pick up about 1,000 votes. Citywide, this organization was able to register about 2,000 new voters.

Voter registration was not only important in the black community, however. In Jamaica Plain, where less than 10% of the total electorate is minority, Mel King received 17% of the total vote in 1979. This is almost twice the support King received in the citywide vote among white Bostonians. This was accomplished by strong efforts to register progressive voters in this neighborhood. For black candidates advocating a progressive agenda, registration of new voters is crucial.

The "race" issue did not seem to be as important a factor among whites as may have been expected given Boston's recent history on racial matters, in either the 1979 or the 1983 preliminary elections. There are probably two reasons for this. One factor is the campaign waged by Mel King. He ran not necessarily as a black candidate, but as a progressive one. The second

factor may have to do with the perception that the black electorate is not capable of threatening white voters or various
powerful groups in Boston. The media encouraged this particular perception in 1979. By portraying King as a "non-serious"
candidate in the early and mid-phases of the 1979 campaign,
they discouraged the development of a "racial" perception of
this candidate on the part of white voters. Pettigrew pointed
to the importance of the media in determining the influence
of race: "A positive candidate image is a necessary ingredient
in a black candidate's campaign for black and white voters alike,
but it is especially critical for white voters, since it can mediate
and modify the effects of their racial attitudes in their voting."[116]
By not treating King's platform seriously, the media in effect
told white voters: "you don't have to worry about Mel King—he
can't win!"

That race does not have to be an overriding issue when
a black candidate's electoral bid is innocuous to white opponents
is supported by empirical studies of this question in cities like
Cleveland, Gary, Los Angeles, and Newark. Pettigrew found
that race was a salient electoral consideration of whites in these
cities because black voters represented an electoral threat. He
writes, "There are numerous uniformities that appear across
these cities and elections. One is race. Many Blacks view the
mayoralty contests as the sine qua non to representation in
city government. Many whites feel strongly threatened by the
prospect of a black mayor. In short many Blacks and Whites
perceive these contests in largely racial terms."[117] The degree
to which black voters are considered threatening will affect
the relative importance of race. Thus, in the general election
of 1983, after King did so well in the preliminary election six
weeks earlier, many anti-black voters decided to turn out in
order to stop the black candidate.

This dynamic was reflected in Assemblyman Arthur Eve's
1976 mayoral campaign in Buffalo, New York. Although he came
in first in the Democratic Party's primary election, he was soundly
defeated in the follow-up election because white voters were
"alerted" by his early success. His ethnicity became impor-

tant to white voters after they realized that he had a good chance of becoming the next mayor of their city.[118] A similar development took place in Gary, Indiana, when Richard Hatcher won the 1967 mayoral primary. Largely because Hatcher is black, the Democratic Party reacted by "urging voters to vote for the Republican candidate."[119] Dean describes how one black mayoral candidate, although ultimately successful, had to overcome an awakened white electorate and a white incumbent who was so shaken by the black candidate's success in the preliminary election that, "He would now have to go on the offensive at some point during the run-off. . . .The incumbent might introduce race as a divisive issue and would probably begin a quiet intimidation effort in black neighborhoods. While the incumbent and his forces had been totally unprepared for the efficiency of Cooper's organization and thoroughness of its trained workers, particularly on election day, he would not be caught off guard again."[120] The mayoral campaign of Harold Washington in Chicago also witnessed this phenomenon. These instances illustrate how the race of a black candidate will be used within a context of traditional electoral activism. Mel King was treated as not being capable of electoral harm—this is one reason race was not as salient as it could have been in a city like Boston in the preliminary election of 1979.

Race is important in the black community—but so are issues. After the 1979 campign King wrote,

> The racial climate in this city did have a very real impact on the campaign. However, I also believe that the issues were most important. When you compare our performance with the performance of previous black candidates, the difference is in increased voter registration. People who hadn't voted before came out and voted for our candidacy. People who hadn't registered came out and registered. That's an indication that people were identifying around the issues. A survey after the election determined that more than half of the people who voted for me did so because they identified with the issues.[121]

Progressive black candidates must appeal to voters on the basis of issues *and* race. While Mel King reminded voters that blacks enjoy very little power in a city like Boston, at the same time he also asked these voters to organize around issues that concerned them and other poor and working-class people. This is a difficult organizational dilemma for black candidates. If they concentrate too soon and too much in the black constituency, they are likely to be labeled as having a limited or "narrow" base, meaning, of course, that they can only appeal to black voters.[122] On the other hand, not doing this may offend black voters, who feel their candidate is taking their votes for granted. This kind of criticism was heard during the 1979 campaign, but it was overcome by emphasis on a progressive agenda.

The results of the mayoral campaign in 1979 show that organizational problems facing black progressive campaigns can be overcome. Despite the mayor's claim that he would carry the black community, made at a press conference sponsored by the *Boston Herald* in the early part of September 1979, and the findings of numerous newspapers and radio polls, black voters supported state Representative Mel King. These same claims were made in 1983. Many political observers boldly predicted that Ray Flynn and David Finnegan, two of King's white opponents, would carry a significant number of black votes. A few newspaper reporters argued that black churches and other groups in the community were not behind King. Through the efforts of grassroots organizers—many of whom had rejected traditional electoral activism—the majority of precincts in the black neighborhoods in 1979 delivered significant levels of support to King. Precincts 2 and 3 in ward 9 (Roxbury), for instance, delivered approximately 64% of the vote to King; this was similar to the support in precincts 2 and 8 in ward 14 (Mattapan). And in 1983, King carried the black community overwhelmingly by 95%, both in the preliminary and general elections.

There were various reasons blacks supported Mel King. Some viewed his candidacy as an opportunity to react to City Hall's lackadaisical attitudes toward the black community. One Roxbury campaign worker in 1979 explained that she had had enough of Kevin White's arrogance toward the black community; she pointed out that the mayor's belief that black voter support was automatic was reflected in his campaign strategy of not visiting the black community as frequently as other areas of the city of Boston. Another individual pointed out that a vote for King was an opportunity to advise City Hall of the general dissatisfaction of black citizens. Based on a number of interviews with King supporters in 1979 and on a September poll conducted by his campaign organization, it was discovered that blacks were also attracted to this candidacy because it reflected the issue concerns that they held and wanted their leaders to express. Although King's vote was a reflection of a broad-based coalition, it seems that the black community in particular used the preliminary mayoral election to express dissatisfaction with the White machine.

The vote in the black community also illustrated the influence of grassroots organizing around a progressive platform. The importance of effective grassroots organization for challengers with relatively little campaign resources has been witnessed in other cities with strong political machines. In a study of a number of these cities Solomon found that grassroots organization is a viable resource for countering the machine's army of loyal workers.

> A large volunteer, grassroots campaign force has to be organized to compensate for the numerous workers the machine has. The larger the force organized the better. Whereas it is easier for an organization candidate or an incumbent to attract volunteers, if you're a likeable person and bring out the right issues, you should be able to organize an adequate staff. It's better to have a few dedicated workers than to have twice as many volunteers who aren't helpful.[123]

After the 1979 preliminary election, the Boston Globe reported that campaign workers for the major white candidates were stunned by King's campaign in some parts of the city. Although King did not make it into the general runoff, the 1979 election represented a victory of grassroots mobilization over money and personality-oriented campaigns. This was repeated in the 1983 preliminary election.

Although Mel King finished third with 15% of the preliminary vote in 1979, many individuals inside and outside the campaign organization viewed the campaign as a success for a number of reasons. First, it represented a victory over opinion polls. Except for the polls King sponsored and an early Becker Poll reported in the *Boston Herald*, others did not accurately assess the grassroots sentiment for King. This election confirmed the tenuous nature of "outside" polls as instruments for measuring black attitudes. Black citizens may give "publicly acceptable" responses to anonymous or white interviewers; but interacting with black interviewers, they may be more open and honest about their feelings and thoughts on various issues.[124] This has important implications for budgetary decisions in progressive campaigns. The "grassroots grapevine" may be more important to assess the sentiment of black voters than "fancy" polls conducted by experts.

The preliminary election in 1979 was also a victory over the organization of City Hall's political machine—in a limited sense, of course. Despite the decentralized and democratic style of King's campaign structure, certain important precincts were won. Campaign strategists in the King organization targeted 80 precincts for intensive organization; 56, or 70% of these, were actually won. Another aspect of this victory involves the amount of money spent by the four major candidates and the results. Each vote King received cost him about 45¢; each vote Kevin White obtained cost his organization approximately $11.00. A progressive campaign is far more efficient than a media- or personality-oriented one in a black community like Boston.

Victory, then, need not be defined narrowly. This campaign presented important opportunities to develop experience in the techniques of political mobilization, which represents another type of victory. Individuals not only became familiar with the electoral processes, but also came to know what weaknesses and strengths they had in this area. Other researchers have pointed to the importance of this education. In studying the poor performance of state Representative A.W. Willis in his mayoral primary race in Memphis, Tennessee, Stone has suggested that the knowledge of electoral politics gained by blacks is important for future black electoral attempts. Willis received only 12% of the vote, placing fourth in a field of seven. The two leading candidates, both white, received more votes than Willis. But, writes Stone, as "demeaning as Willis's crushing defeat was, his political baptism in the higher councils of powers still left its imprint on the black voters. . . .The educational benefits of this political exercise will not be lost on black people."[125]

In another instance, former mayor of Cleveland Carl Stokes conducted a weak campaign in his first attempt to obtain political office, in order to develop an effective strategy for his second attempt. Finding out what obstacles he would have to overcome to realize electoral success was important:

> The seriousness of my effort lay in finding out how many people would vote for Carl Stokes just in the pull of name alone. This was part of the political groundwork I had to do. I had to find a control factor, a base figure for any serious analysis of my political chances. . . .Without any visible campaign, I pulled 5,000 votes. The man who won the nomination received 53,000 votes. But now I had something to work with.[126]

Similarly, Mel King's race helped to provide a foundation for future progressive mayoral campaigns in Boston. The fact that individuals realized that they could actually deliver a certain number of votes to King tended to raise the level of political efficacy of blacks and whites seeking to develop a progressive political orientation in that city.

The 1979 King campaign was very effective in influencing the platforms of the two runoff candidates. Because of King's preliminary election results, Joseph Timilty, White's challenger in the general election, adopted a stance favoring rent control, in anticipation of the black vote mobilized to support King. Thus some things were indeed won by powerless voters organized to support a progressive platform.

The 1979 preliminary election results showed that in black citywide electoral attempts to dislodge power and ultimately challenge powerful interest groups, the effective approach is two-pronged: first there must be consistent and aggressive voter registration drives. This produces sympathetic new voters, and at the same time is an opportunity for potential voters to become educated about various issues salient to blacks and poor and working-class people. Voter registration also provides a specific objective to the campaign organization and sympathetic groups, allowing them to "role-play" and resolve organizational weaknesses. The Mel King organization became familiar with the intricacies of citywide phone lists and mailing techniques as a result of its voter registration drive. Indications of potential problems on election day were important information that could be used to strengthen the campaign organization.

The second strategy that black electoral campaigns must pursue in Boston is the development of long-term grassroots mobilization. The voter or potential voter who has consciously or unconsciously made a decision not to participate in the city's electoral processes must be tapped. This campaign discovered that the individual who has not been invited to participate in the city's political processes may be inclined to vote the issues rather than the personalities. But contacting this kind of voter requires a grassroots-oriented campaign, which means using "out-moded" methods of electoral mobilization, such as knocking on doors, attending small community meetings, and talking with individuals. It also may mean that resources devoted to "outside" polls, public image specialists, and superficial advertisements may be misspent. But for this approach to be effective, there must be enough time for the candidate to make his or her appeal and to educate the voters. The lack of long-range planning for black electoral mobilization—especially necessary under a progressive platform—was perhaps the greatest weakness of the King organization. A strong, organized campaign structure did not take form until two months before the preliminary election. This mistake was not repeated in 1983.

1983 PRELIMINARY ELECTION

The results of the 1983 preliminary election showed the importance of Mel King's first run in 1979. King pulled together the most effective and issue-oriented campaign in a field of nine mayoral candidates. The decision by incumbent Mayor

White not to run created an electoral vacuum for hopeful candidates to seek to fill. King was the only black candidate in the 1983 preliminary race, and the one with the most identifiable bloc of voters. By late night on October 11, 1983, history had been made in Boston. Mel King came in second place with 47,800 votes, or 29% of the total vote cast. Ray Flynn, recognized as a populist candidate, came in first with only about 400 more votes than King. David Finnegan, long-recognized as the leading contender, outspent Flynn and King combined by about $600,000, only to lose the election. The turnout for this preliminary election was phenomenal for such elections in Boston: about 164,000 voters, or 63% of the electorate, turned out.

Approximately 30,000 of King's votes came from the black, Latin, and Asian communities; the remainder came from liberal and progressive white voters in neighborhoods situated between predominantly black areas, and conservative white working-class and middle-class neighborhoods. In fact, the 1983 preliminary election could be described as a contest between the inner core of Boston's predominantly minority and liberal white neighborhoods and the outer ring of the city composed of white, conservative nieghborhoods.

The strong voter registration effort in the black community was probably the biggest factor in the King victory. According to some sources, about 10,000 black voters were added to the 40,000 already registered. An overwhelming portion of new voters registered specifically to vote for King. Another significant factor in this victory was the turnout vote in the black community, and the level of support King received. In predominantly black wards like 9, 12, and 14, voters turned out at a rate close to 79%. In these three wards King received approximately 95% of all votes cast in the preliminary and general elections of 1983.

King's emphasis on an issue- rather than personality-oriented campaign, along with a long and consistent progressive legislative record, won him the support of about 13% of the total white votes cast. The themes that King emphasized also ignited a great deal of interest in communities across Boston. In the preliminary election of 1983, the major issues of the campaign were those raised by King. The two major campaign discussions were "linkage" (i.e., forcing "downtown developers" to support neighborhood housing) and racism. All the candidates found themselves discussing issues that King raised, first in 1979 and again in 1983.

The 1983 campaign developed out of the experiences of the 1979 effort. The successes in the 1983 campaign came much faster, and were of a greater significance. Money was not raised in amounts comparable to those raised by white mayoral hopefuls David Finnegan, Larry DiCara, or Dennis Kearney, but King did finish the 1983 preliminary campaign with about three times more funds than he had in the 1979 preliminary campaign. Black church leaders joined the campaign very early in the race—this allowed King to speak to a large sector of the black community without relying on major newspapers or television spots. Thus, while the 1979 King campaign showed some weaknesses in support in the black community, by 1983 this was no longer accurate. The black community and its leaders overwhelmingly supported Mel King's effort.

The established media placed a major hurdle before the electoral movement that King generated. After White decided not to seek a fifth term, the *Boston Globe* attempted to influence the electorate's decision regarding his successor. It became obvious to many that those responsible for editorial policy at the *Boston Globe* were threatened by King and his progressive campaign. Beginning in 1979 and continuing in 1983, the *Globe* published a number of articles that attempted to discredit King's political momentum. King's 1979 candidacy was ignored by the *Globe* until a few months before the September election, when articles began to appear, questioning his sincerity and dress, arguing that there were not enough black voters to put a black person into the general election, showing how the black community was not interested in the King candidacy, and finally, red-baiting by referring to King as a "radical," "militant," or "leftist." None of these tactics worked. King's mayoral effort reflected major support in the black community. It was King's candidacy that molded the tenor of the mayoral campaigns in 1983, and it was the issues raised by King that became the focus for all of the candidates. The *Boston Globe* and the *Herald* were not powerful enough to prevent the Mel King mayoral campaigns in 1979 and 1983 from having a positive and overwhelming impact on the city's political development.

6.
Black Politics
in the American City:
The Next Stage

In a number of major American cities, a new kind of electoral politics is unfolding in black communities. There are increasing examples of black electoral activism substantially different from that of just a few years ago. The elections of Eddie James Carthan in Tchula, Mississippi, Barbara Mouton in East Palo Alto, California, Harold Washington in Chicago, and Gus Newport in Berkeley, California, illustrate a politics quite unlike what has been the usual case in post-World War II American cities. The mayoral candidacies of Mel King in Boston in 1979 and 1983, and William Murphy in Baltimore, as well as the budding organizations of progressive black political independents like elected officials Al Vann and Roger Green in Brooklyn, New York, are additional examples. On a national level, the voter registration efforts of Rev. Jesse Jackson also represent the emergence of a new kind of black politics. Largely because of these developments, when one discusses urban politics today, it is necessary to describe two "faces" of politics, each representing different sets of issues, actors, orientation, and style.

One "face" of local government is quite traditional. It basically seeks to maintain the arrangement of power that has characterized major American cities since World War II. Initially, the important actors in American local politics were private interest groups, the federal government, and mayors and their machines. In the late 1950s, the public service unions were added to this urban "executive coalition."[127] During the 1960s, the black thrust for political participation culminated in the community control movement, and the call for Black Power in American cities. Although the post-World War II urban executive coalition acceded some concessions to blacks and other citizen's groups inspired by the black community, an institutionalization of membership into the ruling partnership was never offered. Local government did not invite blacks, or the poor, to join the partnerships of the powerful; instead, temporary political arrangements and reforms were offered. As we know today, many of these reforms have not resulted in the replacement or qualitative change of the urban executive coalition.

Political participation may be directed either at structural change in the distribution of wealth and power, or at the maintenance of the status quo. The latter is characterized by limited flexibility (liberalism), or resistance (conservatism), but what is emphasized is the maintenance of social continuity and political stability. The emerging progressive face of electoral politics focuses on the well-being of people, regardless of its effect on the executive coalition's political stability. Specific electoral activities under the two faces of urban politics may be similar in some cases; both, for example, call for mass political participation, the utilization of the franchise as a means of holding government accountable, and the mobilization of voter support for candidates of choice. But while the thrust of traditional electoral activism is to secure benefits from those holding wealth and power in this country, the alternative is to dislodge the holders and controllers of wealth; it is to force a more equitable distribution of the wealth created by the people of America. It is this very position that allows the progressive face of politics to raise local issues within national and international contexts. This is seldom done under the old face of local politics. Under the progressive face of local politics, activists understand the fiscal links between the militarization of American society and the quality of life in the city. Under the progressive banner, nuclear proliferation, business investments in South Africa, military adventurism in Central America are, in fact, local issues.

Traditional electoral politics essentially is a "buffer" process. It keeps the populace, the poor, the working class—and blacks especially—from effectively confronting "private" decisionmakers.[128] Traditional electoral activism seeks to manage this natural conflict in a way that renders it innocuous to interests that control wealth and power; leadership operating under this framework perceives itself as controlling, rather than representing, those on the bottom of America's socioeconomic ladder. This leadership uses minor or non-systemic patronage inducements to satisfy the wants of the populace at various levels of society.[129] Traditional electoral leadership behaves as broker between powerful partners of the urban executive coalition and the citizenry.[130]

The questions placed upon a city's public agenda within the confines of traditional local politics are well known and repetitive throughout urban America: How can we attract big business for "downtown" economic development? How can we build more office spaces and highrise luxury hotels? In effect, how can we make life easier for those who don't live in the city, but control the city? Which human and social services can be reduced in order to relieve the partners of the executive coalition of fiscal pressures? How can the public schools become more responsive to the needs of the business community? These are the important questions under the old face of local politics. But under the progressive face of electoral politics, new questions must be raised. Martin Luther King, Jr., in what could easily be one of the most important contributions to the study of urban politics, *Where Do We Go From Here: Chaos or Community?*, offers a framework by which to ask questions about the direction of local politics:

> The stability of the large world house which is ours will involve a revolution of values to accompany the scientific and freedom revolutions engulfing the earth. We must rapidly begin to shift from a "thing"-oriented society to a "person"-oriented society. When machines and computers, profit motives and property rights are considered more important than people, the giant triplets of racism, materialism and militarism are incapable of being conquered. A civilization can flounder as readily in the

face of moral and spiritual bankruptcy as it can through financial
bankruptcy.[131]

This provides progressive activists with an overall conceptual framework by which to select, define, and prioritize the
social and economic issues facing urban America. Issues must
be molded in ways that respect the world community; but
before this can happen, the individual, the family, the community, and then the city must be viewed as an integral part
of the world community. All issues, then, must be responsive
to a "person"-oriented society. Solutions to social and economic
problems cannot be inconsistent with respect for the individual,
family, community, and the world. We must be concerned with
the "giant triplets of racism, materialism and militarism." This
means, for example, that although capital accumulation is vital
for economic development, we do not pursue it in a social
and moral vacuum; as financial giants are allowed to build
office spaces, they must at the same time build housing for
the poor and working class. As real estate interests convert
apartments to condominiums they must also be sensitive to
the needs of the elderly. Crime, as another example, is not
approached by calling for more and more prisons, ad nauseam;
under the new face of politics, the causes of crime are attacked
as a public priority. Issues under the new face of politics, in
other words, are not approached exclusively within a technocratic
or managerial framework. They are molded in ways that seek
to bring people together.

The ruling urban executive coalition of American cities reflects
the "old" face of local politics. Within this context, the problems of the city are approached in ways that do not threaten
or interrupt the distribution or flow of power, money, status,
and privilege. Local politics currently operates within a managerial
or "technocratic" framework; here, the specific distribution of
power and wealth is not questioned. This managerial approach
to local politics dictates the substance and the style of electoral campaigns. For example, electoral challengers to incumbents
usually present themselves as *better managers* or technicians;
under the old face of local politics, seekers of electoral office

do not offer themselves as leaers of the citizenry, but as effective brokers. And as such, the major function of mayors elected within this context is to mediate the needs of various citizen's groups with the wealth and power status quo. In other words, the basic problem faced by these managers is how to accommodate the social and economic problems facing blacks, the poor, and the working class, within the present hierarchy of wealth and power?

We have seen this face of politics in the city of Boston. Political managerialism here, as in other major cities, can offer only two weak responses to the social and economic problems facing the people living in neighborhoods. The established political leadership either argues that better management will solve the problems associated with housing, economic development, crime, and education, or it basically adopts a "non-response" alternative and ignores many serious problems facing the citizenry. Thus, during Kevin White's tenure as mayor between 1967 and 1983, the official response to hundreds of documented incidents of systematic racial violence and harassment was: there is no problem. Incidents of racial violence were only isolated events, according to City Hall declarations.

The "old" face of politics has failed to meet the needs of ordinary citizens; this is most evident when we look at black communities in urban America. Indeed, a depressed socioeconomic status has consistently characterized black city life for generations; and today, conditions are worsening. Because of the absence of a commitment to eradicate poverty and racism, and shifting political winds within a stale conservative-liberal debate, we find that blacks and the poor are losing even the small, token gains made in the 1960s. This is clear in a city like Boston. Segregation, for example, is worse today than in 1970. Increasingly, blacks are being chased from neighborhoods in white areas of the city without any substantive reaction on the part of the local government, thus signalling its approval of racial violence against blacks. Unemployment in Boston is worse today than in 1970. The socioeconomic gap between blacks and whites is wider today. Roxbury, a predominantly black neighborhood, still has the lowest median level of income among all neighborhoods in Boston. Almost half of all black families in this city live below the poverty level.[132] Local politics, up to this point, has failed the black community. The urban executive coalition of mayors, private interest groups representing wealth, and the federal government have not at all responded to the problems of blacks and the poor, and have ignored worsening conditions in the black community. The "old" face of politics represents only the interests of the powerful and their managers.

America has reached a critical stage in the struggle against racism and class exploitation. This study suggests that the electoral arena—especially at the local level—will be ever more crucial in challenging the holders and managers of wealth in this country. Black-led progressive campaigns are introducing a new force upon American politics. This black electoral activism will have significant impact on such developments as the nature of political coalitions at the local level, and on the question of black-Latino political relationships. It will also encourage public debates and discussions of issues usually not raised in local electoral campaigns. In various ways, for instance, the Mel King candidacy in Boston has had a "left-ward" impact on that city's mayoral race. King's presence and platform made the problem of racism a major issue in the mayoral campaign of 1983. King's insistence on governmental access for all people forced the League of Women Voters and major TV stations in Boston to invite the 1983 mayoral candidate of the Socialist Workers Party to a series of planned public debates. Without King's insistence and boycott of the first TV debate, the SWP candidate would not have been included in the subsequent TV debates.

Many of the theoretical questions posed today as a result of the emergence of progressive electoral activism in the black community have been raised by political activists in recent periods of protest. Malcolm X, for example, amply discussed electoral activism as a tool for black liberation in his "Ballot or Bullet" speech in 1964. In fact, within the last 20 years there have been sporadic electoral efforts suggesting the movement emerging today. But what is being described as "progressive" politics can be clearly differentiated from the "traditional" politics that have dominated the black community, and the American city, since World War II. The electoral activism evident in the campaigns of Harold Washington, Mel King, and Jesse Jackson is different from traditional black electoral activism in a number of significant ways.

This new political surge is being led and supported by blacks who have heretofore rejected electoral activism as a tool for substantive change in the black community. Many who are now participating in progressive electoral campaigns rejected electoral participation just a few years ago. Black intellectuals and activists on the left, as well as the black underclass, never fully accepted the use of electoral politics for meaningful change. Electoral politics was dominated by individuals and groups that sought accommodation to the power status quo. But the most that the status quo ever was able to offer was periodic patronage for a few in the black community. Traditional politics cannot respond effectively to the social and economic needs of black youth, the poor, or the working-class sectors of American society. Progressive electoral activism offers a welcome mat to blacks who have found very little use for traditional electoral activism, which keeps the distribution of wealth and power intact.

The magnetism of Jesse Jackson's call for increased black and Latino voter registration can be explained by his offer to those who have rejected electoral activism in the past. Jackson's run for the presidency is important and should be encouraged, because it allows a forum for the millions of blacks and Latinos who have rejected political participation within a framework that supports the wealth and power status quo in this country. The Jackson campaign also provides a conceptual linkage between progressive electoral efforts in the South and major Northern cities. Let us not forget that for many in the black community, the question of a Democrat versus a Republican in the White House is largely irrelevant. Jackson represents a political catalyst, encouraging blacks alienated from the usual substance and style of local American politics to become conscientious supporters of a progressive electoral activism. The new participants whom Jesse Jackson is helping to bring into the electoral arena have great potential—because of their structural position in American society—to recognize as being in their fundamental interest the development of an independent, progressive politics that challenges the basis and structure of wealth.

Unlike traditional black politics, the new progressive electoral activism in the black community does not necessarily focus on access or patronage; it recognizes the structure and organization of wealth as critical in determining the quality of life in black America. Black electoral efforts under the traditional framework have sought access to the structures of wealth and power; these attempts, successful in some cases, historically allowed black officials to call upon white power brokers for favors, or concessions to the black community. Thus some blacks were elected into office because they appealed to voters as managers of patronage rather than as political leaders; or as effective developers of cooperative partnerships with the corporate sector. We see facets of traditional black politics in the campaigns and administrations of Wilson Goode in Philadelphia, Thomas Bradley in Los Angeles, and Coleman Young in Detroit. These black leaders present themselves not as challengers to the power status quo but as effective managers of the status quo. Although they may capitalize on nationalist sentiment in the black community, they do not pursue public policies that might be inimical to the interests of powerful white groups and organizations. Progressive electoral activism seeks to assault the City Halls of America, not to obtain the relatively few jobs that might be available, but rather to implement public policies that would have meaningful impact on black unemployment, crime, and social alienation.

The examples of electoral accomplishments cited earlier illustrate the crucial role of black political leadership in the development of progressive politics at the local level. This is a logical extension of the socioeconomic status of black urban life. In other words, it is based on the fact that, "Blacks are at the

center of basic conflicts in most Northern cities. . . .They constitute the racial group whose interests and activities have been
most antagonistic to established institutions and better-off
strata."[133] It is the black community that has the most to gain
from raising fundamental questions about the values and
assumptions that underlie our society. Blacks will be in the
forefront of this, because the contradictions between these values
and socioeconomic realities are most evident in black communities. The development of the progressive face of politics
in urban America signals the emergence of black political leadership as a major force in our society. This leadership has been
thrust upon blacks by American history. The strength and vitality
of the new face of urban politics will come from the black
community—quite a different role than the one reserved for
blacks under the old face of urban politics. But this means
that the clash between the old and new faces of politics will
take place also within the black community. Calls for black
unity notwithstanding, two kinds of black electoral activism
will vie for support among voters. Black political activity in
American cities today must be discussed in the context of this
emerging conflict. Some black leaders will continue to pursue influence within traditional electoral activism. They will
continue to ask: How can we get a piece of the pie? How can
we become a partner in the urban executive coalition? How
can we be given access to the powerful? How can we assist
in reforming white power structures that manage American cities?

Other black political activists are rejecting this framework.
The new face of local politics is encouraging many in the black
community to ask different kinds of questions. Progressive
activists want to know how the pie can be changed so that
blacks, whites, and Latinos can enjoy a cleaner, safer, and more
economically secure life in the American city. Black progressive
activists are not interested in partnership with groups who
seek to strangle and suffocate the city. They ask instead: How
can people at a grassroots level organize to protect themselves
against the excesses of the urban executive coalition? White
power structures must be transformed, not reformed—how

can this be accomplished? How can black, white, and Latino
youth be encouraged to participate politically in these important issues? How can community-based power, rather than personal influence, be developed? More and more people in the
black communities of America are asking these kinds of questions, rather than those raised by black supporters of the old
face of politics.

As conditions for blacks continue to worsen, we will see
more clearly the two faces of urban politics. While one kind
of black politician will seek quick accommodation with corporate America, other black politicians will become more
vociferous *and* sophisticated in their challenges to the powerful. It is the latter face of black and urban politics that will
be able to mobilize the masses of blacks and the poor in the
electoral arena to push for public policies that respond to the
needs of poor and working-class citizens rather than those
of powerful and wealthy interests.

Black progressive politics, as a relatively new kind of electoral activism, is groping for clarity regarding many theoretical
questions. As this movement grows, it will test the flexibility
of American political institutions and processes. It will also
test the American left. In a few instances, white "leftist" groups
have failed the test. For example, despite the appeal of Barry
Commoner, the Citizens Party refused to endorse the proposed
candidacy of Jesse Jackson; it did not do so because such an
endorsement might delay the party's emergence as an alternative to both major national parties. This position reflects greater
concern for organizational interests than for the development
of a progressive politics. In the 1983 Boston mayoral campaign,
in another unfortunate example of the unreliability and con-
fusion of some white groups on the left, a few unions and
a white-led tenants' group did not endorse the candidacy of
Mel King. King was clearly the most progressive of all the
mayoral candidates, and had the most consistent, positive record
on labor, women's, and tenants' issues. This was implicitly
recognized by Local 26 and the Massachusetts Tenants Organization, when some of their leaders privately explained their decision

by rationalizing that since Mel King could not win the preliminary election in Boston, an endorsement of his candidacy would be wasted. This in itself was a subtly racist position. The claim that King could not win the preliminary was quite empty; a thorough analysis of Boston's electoral patterns and characteristics showed that he could, and in fact did, win! Yet some "leftist" groups refused to do their homework on the new face of urban politics.

There is indeed a new stirring in urban America. People from poor and working-class backgrounds, but especially blacks, are becoming disillusioned with simple "piece of the pie" approaches to their social, economic, and educational concerns. Black voters, in particular, are seeking to use the electoral arena not in ways dictated by the old face of politics, but in new ways that maximize their interests. Inevitably, the two faces of urban politics will clash; this will first crystallize in the electoral arena. Perhaps some early examples of this conflict can be seen in the contest for black votes in the recent Democratic Party presidential primaries of Alabama, Georgia, New York, and Pennsylvania. In these and other states, progressive activists supporting Jesse Jackson were pitted against some black elected and party officials supporting Walter Mondale. Thus the old face, useless to blacks and the poor, will be challenged by supporters of the new face.

The new face of politics in urban America does not focus merely on winning elections. Electoral activism under a progressive framework is not an end in itself; rather it is a means, a tool by which to mobilize the black community against the wealth and power status quo. It is not an attempt to share opportunities for exploitation; it seeks to develop public policy alternatives that will enhance the quality of urban life for all people. Under a progressive framework, electoral activism is approached as an educational process, dialectical in nature. It is becoming an important means for raising the political and social consciousness of blacks, the poor, and the working class in the cities of America. The electoral activism unfolding in black America is a new stage in the struggle against racism and economic exploitation. It is an extension of earlier periods of black protest. If the lunchroom counter was a major battlefront for equality in the 1950s, and the streets of the ghetto represented the battlefront in the 1960s, then the battlefront in the 1980s for black and working-class people will be the electoral arenas of American cities.

Acknowledgements

Thanks are in order for individuals who were helpful to me in the development of this study: Vivian Morris, Robert Hayden, Toni Chapman, Mezchui Lui, Carlton Gibbs, Ken Haskins, Mel King, Manning Marable, Chuck Stone, Jim Jordan, Carmelo Iglesias, Martin Kilson, Eileen Southern, Nathan Huggins, Ewart Guinies, Caren Betts, Marcelyn Dallis, and Marilyn Poston. Special thanks to my wife, Lenora. (J.J.)

NOTES

1. Harold X. Connally describes persisting depressed conditions in his historical study of the black community in Brooklyn, New York. He argues that "blacks in Brooklyn or elsewhere were, relatively speaking, as deprived in 1977 as in 1900." He continues, "The relative gap between black and white income, wealth, employment, educational achievement, housing, political representation, and power will persist in the foreseeable future as it has persisted historically." See *A Ghetto Grows in Brooklyn* (New York: New York University Press, 1977), pp. 227 and 233.

2. Manning Marable, "Question of Genocide," *The Nation* (January 27, 1982), p. 11.

3. Norman I. Fainstein and Susan S. Fainstein, *Urban Political Movements: The Search for Power by Minority Groups in American Cities* (New Jersey: Prentice-Hall, Inc., 1973), p. xiii.

4. Nelson Johnson and Phil Thompson, "Which Way Forward for the Black Liberation Movement," *Black Scholar* (March-April 1980), p. 54.

5. Charles V. Hamilton, "New Elites and Pluralism," in Richard M. Pious (ed.), *The Power to Govern: Assessing Reform in the United States* (New York: The Academy of Political Science, 1981), p. 172.

6. Fainstein and Fainstein, op. cit., p. 3.

7. See Richard J. Meister, "Ethnics, Blacks and Machine Politics in Contemporary America," in Scott Greer (ed.), *Ethnics, Machines and the American Urban Future* (Cambridge, Mass., Schenkman Publishing Co., 1981).

8. Ronald Walters, "The New Black Political Culture," *Black World* (October 1972), p. 6.

9. Black Power within this particular framework has not been discussed fully in the literature of urban politics. "Mainstream" literature has overlooked the possibility of black electoral activism within the framework suggested here. Richard J. Meister, for instance, wrote recently that the possible electoral strategies open to blacks include integrationist, separatist, reformist, ethnic, and pragmatic ones. His last one seems to be a combination of the reformist and ethnic strategy. He does not at all discuss the possibility of a revolutionary-based electoral activism in the black community. But even the more progressive literature on black politics has failed to adequately discuss this possibility. Many studies that begin by analyzing black-white relationships as colonial in nature end by calling for Black Power based on the traditional separatist mold; other writings, while decrying the conditions of black life, do not consider fully the role of electoral activism in changing their conditions. The following works reflect the criticisms made here: Richard J. Meister, "Ethnics, Blacks, and Machine Politics in Contemporary America," op. cit.; Francis F. Piven and Richard

Cloward, "What Chance for Black Power?" *Politics of Turmoil* (New York: Vintage Books, 1969); Robert C. Smith, "Black Power and the Transformation From Protest to Politics," *Political Science Quarterly* (Fall 1981); Nelson Johnson and Phil Thompson, "Which Way Forward for the Black Liberation Movement," op. cit.; William Nelson and Phillip Meranto, *Electing Black Mayors* (Columbus: Ohio University Press, 1977). Other works could be cited, but I have found these to be particularly interesting.

10. See E.V. Essiem-Udom, *Black Nationalism: A Search for an Identity in America* (New York: Dell Publishing Co., 1964; 1969) for a concise history and definition of the myriad expressions of black nationalism; especially see his chapter "The Nationalist Tradition."

11. Manning Marable, *From the Grassroots: Social and Political Essays Towards Afro-American Liberation* (Boston: South End Press, 1980), p. 15.

12. H.V. Savitch, "The Politics of Deprivation and Response," in Harrell K. Rodgers, Jr. (ed.), *Racism and Inequality: The Policy Alternatives* (San Francisco: W.H. Freeman and Co., 1975), p. 6.

13. The following table illustrates the distribution of wealth among families in the U.S.:

U.S. Distribution of Family Wealth, 1962

% of Total Families by Wealth	% of Total Family Wealth
Lowest 25.4	0.0
Next 31.5	6.6
Next 24.4	17.2
Top 18.7	76.2
(Top 7.5)	(59.1)
(Top 2.4)	(44.4)
(Top .5)	(25.8)

Thus, the lowest 25% of all families do not own any wealth; and the top 0.5% of all families own 25.8% of all the wealth in America. This information was compiled by Lestor Thurow and is discussed in Michael Harrington, *The Twilight of Capitalism* (New York: Simon and Schuster, 1976), p. 228. One of the classical works on the lopsided distribution of wealth in America is Gabriel Kolko's *Wealth and Power in America* (New York: Praeger, 1962).

14. Robert C. Smith recently argued, for example, that opportunities for black inclusion in American politics have become available at the national level:

The most important consequence of the developments arrayed in this article is the entrance of black interest organizations into the competitive, pluralist interest-group system characteristic of the "middle-level" of power in the U.S. This is particularly evident at the federal level. As late as 1968, studies of the process of formulating federal policy found an absence of access by blacks. Very few blacks were found among the policy-making elites, and blacks did not on the whole possess access to centers of decision making in the federal policy process. A principal reason for this lack of access was the relative absence of effective black interest organizations and elites at the federal level. Since the late 1960's, however, blacks have made significant progress toward the development of a political voice of their own in Washington, that is, political organizations and leaders actively involved in the articulation of black interests.

"Black Power and the Transformation from Protest to Politics," *Political Science Quarterly* (Fall 1981), p. 441.

15. William E. Nelson, Jr., "Cleveland: The Rise and Fall of the New Black Politics," in Michael B. Preston, Lenneal J. Henderson, Jr., and Paul Puryear (eds.), *The New Black Politics* (New York: Longman, 1982), p. 189.

16. Ibid., p. 205.

17. Robert Dahl, *Who Governs: Democracy and Power in an American City* (New Haven: Yale University Press, 1961), pp. 94-95.

18. Ibid., p. 95.

19. James Jennings and Mel King, "Politics and Morality in Boston," *Debate and Understanding* (Summer 1983).

20. Harrington, op. cit., p. 223.

21. Ibid.

22. Ibid., p. 237.

23. Piven and Cloward, op. cit., p. 269.

24. Ralph Otwell, "The Negro in Boston," in Edward Banfield and Martha Derthick (eds.) *A Report on the Politics of Boston, Massachusetts* (Cambridge,Mass.: Joint Center for Urban Studies, 1960), p. 46.

25. Edward Banfield, *Big City Politics* (New York: Random House, Inc., 1965) p. 49.

26. Interview conducted by the *Dorchester Community News* (January 22, 1980).

27. Interview with Pearl Shelton, president, Black Political Task Force, April 10, 1980.

28. Adelaide Hill, "The Negro Upper Class in Boston" (unpublished dissertation, Harvard University, 1952), p. 198.
Jennings, chap 6, pg 103.

29. Stephen Thernstrom, *The Other Bostonians* (Cambridge, Mass.: Harvard University Press, 1973), p. 178.

30. Charles Trout, *Boston, the Great Depression and the New Deal* (New York: Oxford University Press, 1977).

31. Thernstrom, *Other Bostonians,* op. cit., p. 180.

32. The Boston Redevelopment Authority (BRA) lists 16 neighborhoods in the city; only four of these can be described as "integrated," based on the black/white population for the entire city in 1980. The four neighborhoods are South End, Fenway/Kenmore, Jamaica Plain/Parker Hill, and North Dorchester. The white population of these neighborhoods ranges from 40% for the South End to 65% for Fenway/Kenmore; the combined black, Latino, and Asian-descent projection ranges from 36% for Fenway/Kenmore to 60% in the South End. See *Characteristics of Boston's Population and Housing, 1980* (Research Department of the Boston Redevelopment Authority in Boston, Feb. 1982).

Based on my own study of 1970 and 1980 census data, it seems that the problem of segregation is worse in the 1980s than in 1970. If we look at the population changes of Boston neighborhoods that could be classified as "lily-white" in 1970, for example, we find that in only one of these neighborhoods, Hyde Park, has there been any kind of significant change in the racial composition of the neighborhood. These neighborhoods include: Beacon Hill, Charlestown, East Boston, Hyde Park, North End, Roslindale, South Boston, and West Roxbury. In all of these areas the white population in 1970 was approximately 97 to 99% of the total neighborhood population. By examining 1980 census tract data we find that the increased numbers of blacks and Latinos in these neighborhoods are not at all significant, as the following table illustrates. As a matter of fact, the number of blacks in some of these neighborhoods (South Boston, East Boston, and Charlestown) has actually declined.

Hyde Park is the only "formerly white neighborhood" in 1970 that has experienced a significant increase in the black population; in 1980 it was reported that 4,434 blacks, out of a total population of 31,526 persons, reside in Hyde Park. But close examination reveals that most of this growth occurred in only one small section (census tract no. 404), where from 36 blacks in 1970, this population increased to 3,128 blacks 10 years later. Thus, even in the only formerly white neighborhood that experienced a notable influx of black people, we find this development occurring via a segregated path. Hyde Park was not integrated between 1970 and 1980, since only census tract no. 404 experienced this kind of change.

Black population growth in Boston between 1970 and 1980 was quite interesting; generally, the black population did not increase in the white areas of the city. Even though a significant proportion of the black population increase took place outside of Roxbury, it was still primarily within black neighborhoods (South End, parts of Mattapan and Dorchester) where most of the growth occurred.

Population Change in Selected* Boston Neighborhoods by Race and Ethnicity, 1970 and 1980

Neighborhood	Number Blacks 1970	1980	Number Latinos 1970	1980	Number Whites 1970	1980
Beacon Hill	284	445	161	284	13,124	14,058
Charlestown	74	26	46	124	15,134	13,118
East Boston	583	311	649	964	39,441	31,913
Hyde Park	409	4,434	287	658	37,722	27,481
North End	14	169	225	226	11,031	11,339
Roslindale	473	839	376	1,065	39,100	31,333
South Boston	389	105	288	187	37,813	30,854
West Roxbury	77	179	33	368	30,987	28,145

Source: U.S. Bureau of the Census, 1970 Census of Population and Housing: Census Tracts, Final Report PHC-1-29, Boston, Mass., SMSA; and 1980 Census of Population and Housing: Census Tracts, P.L. 94-171 Counts, Suffolk County Mass.

*Only neighborhoods with less than 2–3% black residents in 1970 were selected; the data were derived by aggregating census tract data pertaining to these neighborhoods.

33. Susan Welch and Albert R. Karnig, "Representation of Blacks in Big-City Boards," *Social Science Quarterly* (June 1978).

34. *Characteristics of Boston's Housing and Population, 1980,* op. cit.

35. This is extrapolated from information presented in the BRA study; see Tables B-2, B-3, B-4, B-7, and B-8 in *Characteristics of Boston's Housing and Population, 1980,* op. cit.

36. See James Jennings, "The Black Voter in Boston" (Boston: Black Political Task Force, 1982).

37. This is similar to the method used by City Hall; according to a mayoral memorandum, city departments are to refer to "the composition of the minority population" and "the size of the minority population within the city" in determining the employment progress of blacks. See, "Memorandum to All Department Heads" May 25, 1976.

38. These particular measurements have been suggested by a number of political scientists; see Lucius J. Barker and Jesse J. McCorry, Jr., *Black Americans and the Political System* (Cambridge, Mass.: Winthrop Publ., 1980), p. 11; Stephen Nord and Hollis Price used this measure to assess the degree of integration of racial minority groups in Miami in "Refined Racial Discrimination: A Case Study of Public Employment in a Southeastern City," *Review of Black Political Economy* 9,3 (Spring 1979). In studying New York City, Joseph P. Viteritti also used similar indicators in his *Bureaucracy and Social Justice: Allocation of Jobs and Services to Minority Groups* (Port Washington, N.Y.: Kennikat Press, 1980). Also see Scott Greer, op. cit., p. 36; and Chuck Stone's

path-breaking *Black Political Power in America* (New York: Bobbs Merrill Co., 1967), p. 147.

39. *Boston Globe* (August 31, 1977).

40. This figure is cited in Phillip C. Clay, "Boston's Housing Trends and Outlook" (Cambridge, Mass.: Joint Center for Urban Studies, February 1982).

41. *Boston Globe* (July 23, 1982).

42. Clay, op. cit.

43. For various investigative reports, see the *Bay State Banner* and the *New England Black Weekly* between 1978 and 1981.

44. Mel King, *Chains of Change* (Boston: South End Press, 1980).

45. "Black Political Task Force Will Not Endorse White or Timilty," press release, November 2, 1979.

46. Edwin R. Lewinson, *Black Politics in New York City* (New York: Twayne Publishers, Inc., 1974) p. 199.

47. Ibid., p. 200.

48. Bertram M. Gross and Jeffrey F. Kraus, "The Political Machine Is Alive and Well," *Social Policy* (Winter 1982), p. 38.

49. Ibid., p. 41.

50. Jack Newfield and Paul Dubrul, *The Permanent Government: Who Really Runs New York* (New York: The Pilgrim Press, 1981), p. 63.

51. Edward Greer, *Big Steel: Black Politics and Corporate Power in Gary, Indiana* (New York: Monthly Review Press, 1979), p. 12.

52. Ibid., p. 13.

53. Nelson and Meranto, op. cit., p. 23.

54. Gross and Kraus, op. cit., p. 44.

55. Ibid., p. 46.

56. Ibid.

57. For a discussion of this point, see "The Bankers Take Over," in Newfield and Dubrul, op. cit.

58. See *In These Times:* "Chicago Blacks Test Independence" (June 16, 1982), "Brooklyn Blacks Fight City Hall" (May 25, 1982), and "Revenge of the Good Ole Boys" (Jan. 20, 1982).

59. Interestingly, a few observers have argued that a political machine does not exist in this city; Eric Nordlinger in *How the People See Their City* (Cambridge, Mass: MIT Press, 1972), claims that "Boston does not have a machine, or anything remotely resembling one. Even James Michael Curley's machine was largely a loyal personal following rather than a powerful political organization, as widely believed. Curley, who lost more mayoral elections than he won, left behind a machine too fragile to be passed on to a successor after his death despite the absence of an internal feud over the succession." But seemingly contradictory to this is his observation that the mayor's "Little City Halls"

project was easily used to maintain his political organization:

> Many...OPS (Office of Public Services) staff worked on the mayoral campaign. At least three-quarters did so; and to a far greater extent than in the gubernatorial campaign. The work was done on the city's time. Staff persons in secretarial and administrative positions collected, organized and typed up lists of potential supporters and campaign workers; staff members sent out direct mailings and worked as interviewers on public opinion surveys; managers and high level administrators in OPS central worked closely with the Mayor's office and campaign staff on a wide range of activities. (p. 87)

Kevin White's political machine may have been his own, and did not reflect the style of previous powerful urban machines; but the essential features were present. The White machine could organize between 2,000 and 3,000 workers for any city election, as was done in the 1979 mayoral campaign (*Boston Globe*, September 7, 1979, and *Boston Ledger*, February 29, 1980). White's machine was even able to provide Louise Day Hicks, a staunch anti-busing leader perceived as anti-black, with black city employees to assist her in an election bid to the City Council. The White machine suffered a few setbacks; in 1981 only one of its seven endorsed City Council candidates won election to this body, for example. The mayor frequently found himself at odds with a number of state legislators in Boston. But all of this only meant that the White machine was not perfect. Until White's announcement that he would not seek a fifth term, it was the most organized and consistent political force in Boston. See the following for standard descriptions of a political machine: Raymond Wolfinger, *The Politics of Progress* (New Jersey: Prentice-Hall, Inc., 1974), p. 99; and Hanes Walton, *Black Politics: A Theoretical and Structural Analysis* (Philadelphia: Lippincott Co., 1972), p. 56.

60. Newfield and Dubrul, op. cit., p. 279.

61. Chuck Stone, op. cit., p. 81.

62. *Boston Phoenix* (November 6, 1979).

63. Peter Bachrach and Morton Baratz, *Power and Poverty: Theory and Practice* (New York: Oxford University Press, 1970).

64. Ibid., p. 43.

65. Ibid., p. 44.

66. Alberts, op. cit., p. 2.

67. *Boston Globe* (June 13, 1982).

68. Nicholas Danigelis, "Black Political Participation in the United States: Some Recent Evidence," *American Sociological Review* (October 1978), p. 757.

69. Ibid., p. 760.

70. The mayor proposed similar reforms in 1977, but much suspicion about his motivation was generated; black and white groups accused him of political opportunism. State Representative Thomas M. Finneran (15th Suffolk District, Mattapan) expressed the reasons for this: "It is no secret that Kevin White has advocated charter reform only when it would further his own political goals and machinations. . . . Faced with [sic] a vigorous and independent council, White is now pushing for 'reform' again. Those of us in the local political arena are quite familiar with the power of the mayor's machine. It is well-oiled, fueled by illegal patronage and in a commanding position to seize every single one of the district-level council positions" (*Boston Globe*, July 28, 1980). The reform thrust of 1977 was also open to suspicion from certain white sections of Boston. The *Boston Globe* reported around this time that "Just below the surface of the low-key debate, however, is a concern with white voters in such neighborhoods as South Boston, Charlestown, West Roxbury, Hyde Park and much of Dorchester that they will consider the referendums the 'black question' and vote no to increasing black political influence on those bodies" (*Boston Globe*, Nov. 2, 1977).

71. See Section 24, Chapter 3 of Revised Ordinances and Chapter 236 of the Acts of 1966.

72. See "The Racial Composition of Boston's Neighborhoods: 1980" in *Characteristics of Boston's Population and Housing, 1980*, op. cit., p. A-1.

73. In New York City, too, voter registration sometimes has been used as a political resource. In an interview with Professor Arthur Klebanoff concerning the significance of poverty, apathy, and fear as an explanation for the low rate of voter registration among blacks and Puerto Ricans, the *New York Times* was given the following response: "All those factors were at work, and more so all through the South. The truth is that the political leadership in this town doesn't want more registered voters, because they prefer small, controllable constituencies. Even the black district leaders face this—they want to be able to beat insurgents, and if they let the rolls increase with all these strange voters, they'll lose control of the process" (*New York Times*, January 13, 1974).

74. Penn Kimball, *The Disconnected* (New York: Columbia University Press, 1972), p. 297.

75. Ibid., p. 295.

76. *Boston Globe* (September 11, 1971).

77. *Boston Globe* (September 8, 1971).

78. Conceivably, it could be argued that the discrepancies between the voter registration rates of white and black neighborhoods reflect socioeconomic differences; in other words, poorer areas would not

exhibit the level of voter registration found in better-off areas. If this were the case, however, the gap between white working-class neighborhoods and the black community should not be as large as it is. In addition to this, it has also been discovered that black political characteristics are not as influenced by social and economic attributes as are white political characteristics. This is generally true of urban communities in the North and the South. One early study discovered that, "The level of Negro voter registration in Southern counties is far less a matter of the attributes of the Negro population than of the white population and of the community." Donald Matthews and James Protho, "Social and Economic Factors in Negro Voter Registration in the South," *The American Political Science Review* (March 1963), p. 34. This study concluded that "the personal attributes of Negroes— their occupations, income, and education as reflected in county figures— were found to have relatively little to do with Negro registration rates" (p. 41). In *Participation in America* (New York: Harper & Row, 1972), Sydney Verba and Norman Nie report that when socioeconomic status is controlled, blacks participate in the electoral processes to a greater extent than whites. They discovered that based on the socioeconomic levels they used, "At five out of six socioeconomic levels blacks participate more than whites" (p. 156). They continue, "Rather than the average black being an under-participator, we find that he participates in politics somewhat more than we would expect given his level of education, income, and occupation, and more than the white of similar status" (p. 157). Considering this, it would seem that white working-class areas should not be expected to have voter registration rates much greater than the rates found in black neighborhoods. This all suggests that relatively poor white areas should not have a voter registration rate of 22 to 25 percentage points higher than the average rate for the black community (50.7%) unless there is some "intervening" explanation. The way in which voter registration was approached by City Hall is such an intervening variable.

79. James Q. Wilson, *Negro Politics: The Search for Leadership* (Glencoe, Ill.: The Free Press, 1960).

80. Ibid., p. 257.

81. Ibid., p. 261.

82. John Daniels, *In Freedom's Birthplace* (New York: Arno Press, 1914; 1966), p. 292.

83. Ibid., p. 268.

84. Ibid., p. 282.

85. Charles J. Hamilton, Jr., "Changing Patterns of Negro Leadership in Boston" (unpublished honors thesis, Harvard University, 1969), p. 8.

86. Ira Katznelson, *Black Men, White Cities* (New York: Oxford Univer-

sity Press, 1973), p. 68.

87. Ibid., p. 118.

88. Ibid., p. 84.

89. Ernest A.T. Barth and Baha Abu-Laban, "Power Structure and the Negro Sub-Community," *American Sociological Review* 24 (February 1959), p 75.

90. *Boston Globe* (November 30, 1979).

91. Interview with state Senator Bill Owens, June 15, 1980.

92. This term is borrowed from Wilbur C. Rich, "Special Role and Role Expectation of Black Administrators of Neighborhood Mental Health Programs," *Journal of Community Mental Health* 2, 10 (1975).

93. For one excellent discussion of the relationship between anti-poverty structures and their impact on politics in five cities, see David Greenstone and Paul Peterson, *Race and Authority in Urban Politics* (New York: Russell Sage Foundation, 1973).

94. Stephen Thernstrom, *Poverty, Planning, and Politics in the New Boston: The Origins of ABCD* (New York: Basic Books, Inc., 1969), p. 163.

95. Ibid., p. 190.

96. Charles V. Hamilton, "The Patron-Recipient Relationship and Minority Politics in New York City," *Political Science Quarterly* (Summer 1979), p. 21.

97. Ibid., p. 224.

98. Ibid., p. 225.

99. Ibid.

100. John Mollenkopf, "The Post-War Politics of Urban Development," *Politics and Society* 5,3 (1975), p. 228.

101. Greenstone and Peterson, op. cit., p. 24.

102. Harry A. Bailey, Jr., "Poverty Politics and Administration: The Philadelphia Experience," in Miriam Ershkowitz and Joseph Zikmund II (eds.), *Black Politics in Philadelphia* (New York: Basic Books, 1973), p. 184.

103. Stewart E. Perry, *Building a Model Black Community: The Roxbury Action Program* (Cambridge, Mass.: Center for Community Economic Development, 1978), p. 57.

104. Nelson and Meranto, op. cit., p. 26.

105. Ibid.

106. *Boston Globe* (August 29, 1971).

107. Eric Nordlinger, *Decentralizing the City* (Cambridge, Mass.: MIT Press, 1972), p. 74.

108. Steve Lithenthal, "Candidates and Their Strategies" (unpublished paper, Boston University, Spring 1980).

109. Chuck Stone, op. cit., p. 229.

110. Charles J. Hamilton, Jr., op. cit., p. 19.

111. Banfield and Derthick, op. cit., p. 56.

112. *Boston Globe* (September 10, 1971).

113. *Boston Globe* (September 11, 1971.)

114. Mel King, op. cit., p. xix.

115. James E. Conyers and Walter L. Wallace, *Black Elected Officials: A Study of Black Americans Holding Governmental Office* (New York: Russell Sage Foundation, 1976), p. 105.

116. Thomas Pettigrew, "Black Mayoral Campaigns," in Herrington J. Bryce (ed.), *Urban Governance and Minorities* (New York: Praeger Publishers, 1976), p. 22.

117. Ibid., p. 15.

118. For a fuller discussion of this campaign, see Robert Gilliam, *Black Political Development* (Port Washington, New York: Dunellen Publishing, 1975).

119. Edward Greer, op. cit., p. 46.

120. John Dean, *The Making of a Black Mayor* (Washington, D.C.: Joint Center for Political Studies, 1973), p. 27.

121. Mel King, op. cit., p. 274.

122. Charles V. Hamilton, "Blacks and Electoral Politics," *Social Policy* (May-June 1978), p. 21.

123. Noel Solomon, *When Leaders Were Bosses* (Hicksville, N.Y.: Exposition Press, 1975), p. 185.

124. See the following for a discussion on interviewing problems in the black community: J.A. Sattler, "Racial Experimentation Effects in Experimentation, Testing, Interviewing and Psychotherapy," *Psychological Bulletin* 73 (February 1970); A. Rudushin, "The Racial Factor in the Interview," *Social Work* 17 (May 1972); and G.P. Banks, "The Effects of Race on One-to-One Helping Interviews," *Social Science Review* 45 (June 1971).

125. Chuck Stone, op. cit., p. 216.

126. Carl B. Stokes, *Promises of Power* (New York: Simon and Schuster, 1973), p. 48.

127. The term "urban executive coalition" is borrowed from Robert H. Salisbury, "The New Convergence of Power in Urban Politics," *Journal of Politics* (November 1964).

128. See Harrington, op. cit., p. 223.

129. Ibid., p. 327.

130. On this idea, see Piven and Cloward, op. cit., p. 261.

131. Martin Luther King, Jr., *Where Do We Go From Here: Chaos or Community?* (Boston: Beacon Press, 1967), p. 186.

132. This information was derived from figures extracted from the 1980 census data for Boston, and *Characteristics of Boston's Population and Housing, 1980,* op. cit.

133. Fainstein and Fainstein, op. cit., p. xiii.

OAKLAND

Grassroots Organizing Against Reagan

Rod Bush

1.
Introduction: Black Politics and Oakland Development

In the June 1984 California presidential primary, Jesse Jackson swept the eight delegates elected in the Eighth Congressional District, of which Oakland is a part. Jackson supporters each polled more votes than any of the Hart or Mondale contenders, including popular liberal state Assemblyman Tom Bates, who was running for Hart. This strong support for Jackson can only be explained in the context of decades of progressive electoral activism within the black community of Oakland, which is the subject of this chapter.

Since the 1960s the most consistent and militant opposition to U.S. policies of domestic austerity and foreign intervention has arisen from the black community. Albeit repressed and contained during the last decade, such opposition, expressed as anti-Reaganism in the last three years, has more and more found an outlet of expression in the electoral arena. In this study we will analyze the widespread sentiment in the black community against Reagan's policies of forced unemployment at home and militarism abroad, focusing on the organizing experience of the Peace and Justice Organization (PJO) in Oakland, California. While there are clearly limits to which such opposition can be developed beyond electoral politics, this study shows how progressive politics, articulated by elected officials, such as Congressman Ron Dellums (D-California), and expressed through grassroots organization, can be considered extremely relevant to black people in our search for equality and justice.

PJO, a community organization based in Oakland, was actively involved in four campaigns of local black progressive candidates during 1982-1983, in which a variety of electoral and non-electoral activities were used to activate voters in black and Latino communities. The Peace and Justice Organization began as an outgrowth of the Grass Roots Alliance, a multi-racial, multinational working-class organization, which had conducted three popular initiative campaigns to tax the corporations of San Francisco in 1979-1980.[1] In repeated campaigns, the people-to-people methods used by the GRA were highly successful in mobilizing progressive working-class voters, particularly those who had been forced out of or excluded from the electoral process. The successes of the GRA were based on both its grasp of the political economy of the late 1970s (as articulated in the writings of Marlene Dixon, director of the Institute for the Study of Labor and Economic Crisis) and its political insistence on the need to organize among, unite with, educate, and learn from the people most affected by the conditions that an organization is trying to change. PJO organizers, using these same methods, were able to turn certain specific working-class districts, which had historically been "swing" districts in their support of progressive issues, into a constituency who could be counted on to turn out for progressive candidates in repeated elections.

While the electoral campaigns of PJO learned many lessons similar to those of the Washington campaign in Chicago and the Mel King campaign in Boston, such as the need for organization, the importance of multinational support, and the critical role of the struggle for black empowerment in galvanizing response for a particular candidate, this study also highlights some of the organizing unique to the PJO work in Oakland. We will first look at the historical and economic factors that condition Oakland's electoral arena, and then, in Chapter Two, examine some of the issues upon which PJO based its electoral and non-electoral agitation. Chapter Three analyzes more closely four local campaigns and their cumulative effect on a particular black working-class district of Oakland. Finally, in Chapter Four we will try to understand this experience in Oakland in the context of "the new black vote" and its relation to the world economic crisis.

Oakland, California is a typical U.S. central city, with a large minority population and a high unemployment rate. According to the 1980 census, Oakland is 47% black and 9.6% Hispanic.[2] Since at least 1960, Oakland's unemployment rate has been substantially higher than the U.S. national average.[3] Unemployment among Oakland's minority population in 1983 was estimated at 30%, and among minority youth at 54%. In one predominantly black neighborhood of Oakland, the California Employment Development Department estimated the minority youth unemployment rate to be 98%.[4]

At the same time, Oakland is the home for a number of transnational and multinational corporations, the site of a 420-acre redevelopment area, and one of the major ports on the Pacific Coast. Since World War II, regional planning through the Bay Area Council (a regional organization of corporate leaders) has developed Oakland into the industrial and manufacturing center of the Bay Area, while San Francisco became the region's insurance and banking center, Berkeley the academic center, and the South Bay the locus of high-technology research and development.[5] In this process Oakland drew longshore and warehousing activities away from San Francisco. This, however, did not spur employment in Oakland because the growth of containerization in fact meant a net decrease in longshore jobs in the overall area. Moreover, the recent development of more corporate headquarters has not lowered the unemployment rate, since only one third of all Oakland jobs are now held by Oakland residents. Racism, combined with the planned development of commercial and financial headquarters to replace the light manufacturing sector, has meant that any new employment opportunities are not slated for Oakland residents, at least its black or Latino working class.[6]

The development of urban capitalism played a crucial role in Oakland's early history, but under somewhat different circumstances than in the industrialized Northeast. Like other

Western cities, Oakland has always had small-propertied mayors since its early days, but it lacked the affluence to develop any prestigious elites until the growth of industrialism in the region after World War II. Also, in its early years, Oakland did not face an influx of immigrant Europeans. Thus, the contention of white ethnic forces, which heavily affected so much of the political development of large Eastern cities, was absent. This accounts for the lack of significant white ethnic voting blocs in Oakland, of Poles or Irish or Italians now waiting to take "their turn" in City Hall, as in Chicago or Boston. Instead, the vast majority of the early white population came from third- and fourth-generation Americans, who came West to make their fortunes in gold.[7]

Much of the industrial development of Oakland proper occurred during or just after World War I. As World War II approached, its economy was further stimulated because of its status as a port and naval shipyard. It was during this period that many of the large manufacturing and transportation-related industries, particularly those which thrived on military contracts, became established in Oakland. Many of these corporations, such as Kaiser Industries, Bank of America, and Safeway Corporation, have continued to play an important role in local and regional politics, often fielding their own executives for elective office.[8]

At the same time, Oakland has always had a multinational working class, reflecting its early days. Since the Spanish occupation and deeding of land to the church missions, there has always been a large Mexican/Chicano population in California, whose members have been increasingly drawn into the city from rural areas in search of jobs. Since the building of the railroads there has been a substantial Chinese community in Oakland, kept out of the political process and deprived of their rights through anti-Chinese prejudice. Prior to World War II, the black population in Oakland remained small, but the advent of war meant marked expansion of employment opportunities in the port and shipyards, far more than could be filled by local residents. Black workers were recruited from the South to take these jobs; at the same time, the Oakland establishment hired Southern whites as their police force to keep the new black populace in line.

Since the 1930s, the *Oakland Tribune* has played a central role in Oakland politics, through the domination of its owner and publisher, J.R. Knowland, and later his son William. The paper came to speak as the voice for reaction, reflecting the most conservative forces within the Republican Party on a state and national level. During the postwar period, William Knowland, elected to the U.S. Senate, was one of the mainstays of support for Chiang Kai-sheck and a leading advocate of the anti-union Taft-Hartley Act.[9]

Thus black electoral politics in Oakland, as in other central cities, must be understood to have a contradictory character. On the one hand, electoral politics has been shown to be one arena through which black people can be mobilized to express their opposition to the status quo; at the same time, corporate capital (both nationally and transnationally based) is vying to ensure that its interests are preserved. While its black mayor, Lionel Wilson, embraces the interests of Kaiser and Clorox Corporations, Oakland also has one of the most progressive representatives in Congress (Congressman Ron Dellums) as well as local representatives (such as Alameda County Supervisor John George), who have demonstrated their commitment to serving the needs of their black and working-class constituents.

POSTWAR OAKLAND MEETS ECONOMIC DECLINE

In postwar Oakland, many of the public policies initiated in its earlier decades were no longer suitable to the metropolis of heavy industry in the 1950s. The war had brought a severe housing shortage and a serious transportation crisis. Factories, housing, parking, and highways were so inadequate that workers often arrived four or five hours late to work. Factories were short of key parts and materials because trucks were delayed on the heavily congested freeways.[10] Most of the housing had been built prior to World War I; but no new housing was being built to meet the needs of the burgeoning black work force.

The post-World War II housing conditions for black Oakland residents were abysmal, in the face of a home construction industry totally dependent for real estate loans on a racist banking industry. This same banking industry perpetuated discriminatory loaning practices and segregation, policies that the city government was happy to overlook.[11]

During this postwar period, the Oakland economic infrastructure was allowed to falter, in the midst of the overall expansionary period of U.S. capitalism. This seems illogical, unless it is understood in the light of several key corporate decisions that led to the economic decline of Oakland. In 1935, the Oakland Chamber of Commerce had established a program designed to locate new industry outside the city boundaries, a policy whose impact was staved off by the intervening war years. Choice locations were used up and national enterprises were looking to suburban areas for expansion. Combined with the fact that most of Oakland's industrial plants pre-dated World War II, the decisions of corporate planners to look for low-wage non-union areas with cheap land meant that Oakland had a net outflow of capital. By 1960, the city was classified as a depressed area by the federal government. Between 1958 and 1963 alone, Oakland's employment dropped by 3,200.[12]

Thus, during the decades of the 1950s and 1960s, Oakland's city government continued its benign neglect. Small and large business alike found their mutual interests satisfied in two main policies: low taxation and low city indebtedness. The tax structure was kept regressive toward the working class, with revenues raised mainly through sales and property taxes (which in the absence of rent control are passed on to renters as well). And, as Hayes points out, the low city indebtedness benefited the corporate class at the expense of the working class being denied vital public services:

> The city has a good bond rating in private markets....Such a credit rating is desired by bond purchasers in the private money markets; but it is largely the result of a low level of bonded indebtedness, well below that allowed by state law. This means that even the finances which could be raised by sale of bonds under present governmental procedures are not

raised; hence the hospitals and public housing and development corporations that such money could support have not been built.[13]

As Oakland entered the 1970s, we find a city with a decaying economic structure, growing unemployment, fleeing industry, and a city government presiding over its demise. It was also no accident that out of these conditions, out of the black community whose needs for jobs and public services had been ignored for decades by those in power, arose the Black Panther Party.

BLACK POWER IN OAKLAND

In January 1972, Huey Newton announced the Black Panther Party's involvement in voter registration in Oakland. The Panther Party was in the forefront of voter activism, becoming a serious oppositional political force at a time when no other organization in the progressive movement was considering electoral methods. The experience of the Panther Party provided a touchstone in electoral activization that would not be seen again in Oakland for another decade. The electoral work of the Peace and Justice Organization continued in the tradition of the Panthers' model, which used non-electoral agitation while running a professional campaign that had to be taken seriously.

In a speech made in November 1972, Elaine Brown explained their electoral campaign as "part of the revolutionary process—to build a base of operations to start talking about seizing power in Oakland, New York, Texas. . . ." The Panthers had already built a strong base of support among the black working class through their Survival programs, including free food, free shoes, legal defense, medical screening, and a busing program to visit relatives in jail. The Panthers were also a strong force calling for unity among all oppressed peoples, and linked their opposition to domestic policies with anti-imperialism and defense of the rights of self-determination for all peoples.[14] When Bobby Seale announced that he was running for mayor at a rally attended by 1,800 people in East Oakland, this indeed marked a new era in black participation in electoral politics.[15]

In the April 1973 mayoral election, besides Seale, the main candidates included John Reading, Otho Green, and John Sutter. Reading, the incumbent mayor, was a millionaire businessman, closely associated with the *Oakland Tribune*, downtown development, and the port.[16] John Sutter was a city councilman, a favorite of the liberal white Democrats. Otho Green was a black businessman, who had cornered the support of the black leadership of Oakland and competed with Sutter for the support of the Democratic Party.

In a joint campaign for Seale and for Elaine Brown for City Council, the Panthers registered 30,000 new voters before the city elections. They had few endorsements from labor or the Democratic Party. Their strategy was to go in a targeted way to the black and non-Republican neighborhoods in the flatlands (which are predominantly working-class), while virtually staying away from the hills and Republican (middle-class) areas. The Panther campaign stressed the need to open up the government to public scrutiny, the issue of community control of police, the creation of jobs that served Oakland residents, and other programs from the Panther platform, such as rent control and public services.[17]

The election results "stunned" the political establishment, according to the *Oakland Tribune:*[18]

John Reading	55,453
Bobby Seale	21,329
Otho Green	17,470
John Sutter	15,361

The Panthers were suddenly a major force to be taken seriously. More importantly, their get-out-the-vote efforts had produced fairly spectacular results, pulling out over 63% of the vote. However, by the May runoff, the Reading forces were now more prepared and, in some areas of the wealthy hills, were able to mobilize over 74% of the voters, who voted 10 to 1 against Seale and the threat they perceived from the Panthers. In May, Seale drew 43,749 votes to Reading's 77,634, which also reflected the level of corporate campaign contributions Reading was able to accrue.

The significant factors of the Panther campaign must be understood in light of the changes occurring in Oakland. In the decade prior to 1973, 50,000 white residents had left Oakland, while 40,000 blacks had come there.[19] This trend in minority and white populations has continued through the present.[20] The fact that the Panthers could sign up over 20,000 people to work on the campaign, and get out over 70% of the vote in an off-year municipal runoff election, demonstrated the potential of black voters in elections to come, a force that every politician would thereafter have to take into account.

The Panthers organized a strong base among black youth, and combated cynicism and the traditional arguments against electoral participation. They gave black people hope and electrified the nation with their courage and steadfastness in fighting for their politics. They showed the people of Oakland that a black progressive candidate was indeed viable, and their electoral organizing was decisive in breaking the hold of the conservative white machine over Oakland politics.

The Black Panther Party, repressed by state forces because of its effective and militant organizing, ceased to be an organizational force in Oakland much after 1978;[21] however, the election of Lionel Wilson as Oakland's first black mayor in 1977 can be directly credited to the electoral thrust by the Black Panther Party. Wilson directly inherited the momentum from the Panther electoral organizing. After Reading announced that he would not seek another term, Wilson, then a Superior Court judge, emerged as the consensus candidate of the Democratic Party, labor, the Black Panthers, the United Farm Workers, and others on the left. He also gained support from black business, as well as significant sectors of larger corporate capital, including Pacific Gas & Electric Co., World Airways, and Clorox.[22] His major opponent, Dave Tucker, had backing from corporate and conservative interests, including Edgar Kaiser of Kaiser Industries, Southern Pacific Railroad, Grubb & Ellis Realtors, and Coors Beer.[23]

Wilson ran on a program of improving the city's economic base by attracting more business, and thereby creating jobs. He took a strong stand against an increased business license tax, which he displayed prominently in his campaign material. Tucker used the issue of crime, proposing to put 150 more police officers on the streets (at the cost of $6 million), and attacking Wilson as "soft-on-crime." However, Wilson could counterattack Tucker for being a big spender; all in all, Wilson was not an extremely vulnerable candidate.

However, neither was Wilson a particularly exciting candidate, nor one who could mobilize the black community. Thus the turnout in the primary was only 46%, and in the runoff only 52%. Wilson drew 42,640 votes to Tucker's 36,925; both candidates received fewer votes in actual numbers than Bobby Seale in the 1973 runoff.[24] Wilson of course drew upon Seale's strength, doing best in North Oakland, West Oakland, and East Oakland, the areas where the Panther campaign had been strongest. There was further consolidation of the working-class vote behind Wilson: in some working-class precincts he polled 97% of the votes cast. At the same time, there was an astounding drop in the conservative vote, from 77,000 votes for Reading to 33,000 votes for Tucker.

In the 1981 elections, Wilson faced no significant opposition, with his opponent polling not even 6,000 votes to Wilson's 33,753. What is most striking, however, is the depoliticization of the electoral process since the Panther campaign. Half as many ballots were cast in 1981 as there were in the 1973 mayoral election, which speaks to the lack of mobilization of the black electorate, the active facilitation, as we shall show, by the mayor to a return to "business-as-usual."

OAKLAND EMBRACES REDEVELOPMENT IN THE 1980s

"Business-as-usual" took on a new face, however, as the interests of national and transnational capital diverged from small and local business interests. It is no longer sufficient to keep taxes and bond issues low; in the late 1960s, transnational capital identified the need to develop Oakland as a major port to serve the Pacific Rim strategy.[25] This was a strategy undertaken by transnational corporations aiming towards Pacific expansion; it was designed to turn Southeast Asia and Japan toward the West and integrate those nations into a market system under U.S. hegemony. Oakland's property was too valuable to waste on low-rent heavy manufacturing and warehousing; rather, the financial and commercial needs of the port and its importance as a transportation center for the whole region required expansion of Oakland's capacity as a corporate head-quarters and as a major convention center.

With this perspective, an ambitious revitalization plan was begun in 1969 to renovate 25 blocks in the city's center, known as the City Center Project.[26] Grubb & Ellis, a local real estate company, won the development contract for this project. It nearly went bankrupt in the process, but since has become the fourth-largest real estate firm in the U.S., based largely on the profits from the City Center Project. The city of Oakland worked closely with Grubb & Ellis, buying land with federal monies, then selling it at a reduced price to Grubb & Ellis. Since 1969, over $300 million in federal grants, municipal loans, and private equity have gone into the transformation of the central business district. The city also enabled Grubb & Ellis to secure loans at 0% interest; the state of California and the Bay Area Rapid Transit Authority assisted by providing funds for transit connections and freeway construction.[27]

A tandem project to the City Center Project was the Chinatown Redevelopment Project, whose centerpiece was the Trans-Pacific Center. This office/commercial complex was built at a cost of $60 million by the Hong Kong-based Carrian Group, headed by George Tan.*

---

*The financial backing of the Carrian Group seemed to "come out of nowhere," as one source put it, suggesting funding from outside sources. Somehow Carrian was able to obtain loans from reputable banks on an unsecured basis; one source reported that 50 banks had lent money to Carrian. In June 1983, shortly after the opening of the Trans-Pacific Center, the Carrian Corporation was reported as having financial difficulties; its Oakland properties, including the Trans-Pacific Center and its 14% interest in the Hyatt Regency Hotel, were being sold to the Darton Corporation, a Liberian-registered firm. *Wall Street Journal*, (June 17, 1983).

Both the capital infused into the City Center Project on behalf of Grubb & Ellis and the financial backing of the Trans-Pacific Center exemplify the influx of transnational capital into Oakland's redevelopment, responsive to enterprises of a far greater scale than the small-to-medium-sized businesses that have occupied its city government. Five major office buildings were opened in 1982, with almost 750,000 square feet of additional office space added to the city inventory. Some 101 new construction projects are planned or under construction. Bechtel Corporation is planning to construct a $100 million office tower to relocate one third of its employees now based in San Francisco. The $40 million Convention Center and adjacent Hyatt Regency Hotel round out a development schema to fulfill Oakland's role as the financial/commercial center of an expanding transportation center to serve the global needs of capital.[28]

It comes as no surprise then that the major transnational corporate interests have embraced Mayor Wilson, as he has taken the lead in promoting downtown development. Wilson reportedly counts among his closest friends Cornell Meier (president, Kaiser Aluminum) and Bob Shetterly (vice president, Clorox Corporation). Clorox and Kaiser have been among the main corporate players in the City Council and Oakland city politics in general. In addition, Bank of America, Pacific Telephone, Southern Pacific, Grubb & Ellis, and Pacific Gas & Electric Company have taken active roles, controlling as well the Oakland Chamber of Commerce, despite its image of representing small business.

There has also been a more conservative wing of corporate interests, represented through such key individuals as attorney Justin Roach, Jr. (Reagan fund-raiser), Emylan Knowland Jewitt (sister of the late publisher and owner of the *Oakland Tribune*), and George Vukasin (owner of Peerless Coffee). This bloc historically was more linked to small business and opposed promotion of black moderates in response to the militant organizing of the Panther period; in recent years, however, the right-wing grouping has seemed quite content to support Mayor Wilson both politically and financially with campaign contributions.

Thus it is that Oakland's first black mayor, elected from the groundswell of militant organizing of the 1970s and the demand for representation from the black electorate, now faces his second re-election in 1985 backed by the combined forces of transnational and national/local-based capital.

THE PROGRESSIVE THRUST OF RON DELLUMS

There is also a progressive aspect of Oakland politics that has grown and matured over the past two decades. Out of the tumult of the 1960s and the opposition to the Vietnam War, voters in the Eighth Congressional District—which includes the communities of Berkeley and Oakland—elected Ron Dellums to the U.S. Congress. Since 1970 he has served as a rock of progressivism in Congress; he has kept the faith and his principles. In the interview with Dellums (included at the end of this section), he describes some of the community forces that came together to propel him into office, forces to which he has held himself accountable politically while in office.

Since his first term in office, he has been an outspoken critic of U.S. militarism and the expansion of the U.S. nuclear arsenal. In 1977, he was the first member of Congress ever to introduce an amendment against all funding for the development, production, and deployment of the MX Missile, an amendment that only mustered 11 votes in its support at the time. As a senior member of the House Armed Services Committee, he convened in 1982 the Special Congressional Ad Hoc Hearings on the Full Implications of the Military Budget, at which more than 40 defense and budget experts were invited to testify.[29] Following the six-day hearings, Dellums introduced into the House (and again in 1983) an alternative military budget that would reduce the Pentagon's budgetary authority by $50 billion in the first year alone. His budget proposal was based on basic principles directly opposed to the foreign policy objectives pursued by the Reagan administration: a noninterventionist foreign policy stressing international cooperation and a firm commitment to human rights; a national security policy based on a rational, restrained deterrent defense of the

U.S., rather than the attempted domination of the world through the covert or overt intervention in the internal affairs of other countries; and a doctrine of nuclear arms "sufficiency" rather than "superiority."

Dellums has consistently defended the needs of his constituents for jobs and public services and argued against the massive military budget undertaken at the expense of domestic spending. His alternative military budget also addresses these issues by incorporating specific economic conversion proposals for a transition from a war economy to a peace economy. These proposals would provide job training and economic assistance to those areas most hurt by reductions in the Pentagon budget.

Another aspect of Dellums's progressive positions has been his internationalism, standing for the common interests shared by poor and working-class people of the U.S. and the majority of the peoples of the world. As the following interview describes, he visited Cuba and Grenada in 1982, and admired the social achievements both countries had made, in particular, the profoundly democratic process being undertaken then by Maurice Bishop and the Grenadan people. He has also spoken out against U.S. trade with South Africa and decried the brutality to which black South Africans are subject. More recently, as chair of the House Subcommittee on Military Installations and Facilities, he has protested Reagan's militarization of Honduras, which thus far has not been authorized by Congress.

Taken together, these positions articulated by Dellums on a national level have been very influential in pushing forward other black politicians to support progressive causes, and in pressuring groups such as the Congressional Black Caucus to take public positions in opposition to the Reagan administration.

On a local level, Dellums and his staff have also provided political space in which community organizations, progressive activists, and aspiring politicians can be effective. Without the continuing support for progressive issues in his home district, campaigns for other black progressive politicians, such as John George (Chairman, Alameda County Board of Supervisors),

Wilson Riles, Jr. (Oakland City Councilman), or even Jesse Jackson would not have been as successful. From the onset of its organizing, the Peace and Justice Organization has been assisted by Dellums and his staff, who opened doors, provided information, and united with the PJO efforts to mobilize the black community in Oakland around the dangers of militarism. It was also at the initiative of Dellums and his staff that PJO entered the Oakland electoral arena in June 1982.

Members of PJO also mobilized electoral support for Dellums, as described in Chapter Three, and held key staff positions in his 1982 re-election campaign. That election posed a particular challenge to Dellums, since redistricting after the 1980 census had added large areas of white middle-class suburban voters (from Contra Costa County), while excluding from his Congressional District portions of the black community in Oakland. His Republican opponent made a special effort to get out the vote in these newly added white areas, and at the same time embarked on a redbaiting campaign against Dellums. Thus PJO organizers particularly targeted black voters in South Berkeley and East Oakland, so that lack of voter participation from his widespread support base in the black community would not spell defeat for Dellums. He won that campaign by 67% districtwide, polling over 90% in some areas of the black community. Following this election, PJO has continued to serve on the Dellums Executive Committee, a broad grouping of political representatives and activists who advise the congressman on local issues and candidates.

Dellums continues to be elected to Congress for the same reasons he was sent in 1970. Although there is no question about his representing the interests of the black community, he has consistently taken the most forward position in the interests of all the people, not only in his district, but across the nation, and internationally. Repeatedly in our interview he refers to the refusal of most elected officials to see the world as a community of nations, and not just the U.S. and the U.S.S.R. He has consistently been a model of political integrity even when it was not "politic" in the narrow sense. He exposes the myth that only commercially packaged slick politicians who emphasize personality and ignore issues can be elected to public office.

PROGRESSIVE POLITICS ON A LOCAL LEVEL

In Oakland's local politics there is the example of John George, chairman of the Alameda County Board of Supervisors, who sees his role as part of the struggle for black empowerment. George came out of the civil rights movement of the late 1950s and 1960s, drawn to law as a way to mix rebellion with profession. As he said in a recent interview, "There I was, trying to figure out how to bring about a revolution by being a physical education instructor. Then someone said to me, 'Brown vs. the Board of Education will require a generation of litigation.' One of our rationalizations then was that blacks should become lawyers. Then Kennedy came into office and there was hope on the part of the masses of people. Under Eisenhower, and then Nixon, and now Reagan, the objective conditions may be as bad, but you may not have the same optimism, the same hope to keep on struggling."

From legal work with the NAACP on de facto school segregation to legal defense of Huey Newton and the Panthers, he came in 1968 to run for Congress in the Eighth Congressional District. In 1966 he had actively supported a white progressive anti-war candidate, Bob Scheer (former editor of *Ramparts*) who had come close to winning with 45% of the vote, in particular drawing upon liberal Berkeley and Oakland. By 1968, as George puts it, "I had reached an anti-war position, although I came to it not out of alienation (like white progressives did), but out of the conditions of oppression. I decided to run for Congress, in order to use the resources of that position to try to do something about those conditions. At that time, many blacks, including many middle-class blacks, would have thought my running was idiotic. I was not well known at the time, but there was no one else, in terms of black established politicians, available or willing to run."

In the 1968 race there were many factors that ran counter to George's success, factors that in the recent period have been reversed. First, redistricting had tended to increase the number of conservative voters in the district. Second, blacks, especially working-class blacks, had at that time turned to the Panthers as a viable organizing vehicle. The Panthers were not yet involved in electoral politics: the energy of the Panther youth was directed to "Free Huey." While George's position was "Save Huey Newton," black youth did not identify with his candidacy enough to engage them actively in support of his electoral campaign. Third, the Peace and Freedom Party had just been formed, attracting much of the white progressive anti-war vote; even though it did not yet have ballot status, those registered in Peace and Freedom Party could not vote in the Democratic Party primary. Yet despite all of these factors, John George won 45% of the Democratic primary vote, a showing that he regarded as a "miracle" and that was sufficient to convince Ron Dellums to run in the 1970 primary. According to George, Dellums felt that if George could do that well without the white progressive vote, it was time that the Eighth Congressional District had a black congressman.

Today George represents the Fifth Supervisorial District of Alameda County, which encompasses Albany, Berkeley, North Oakland, West Oakland, Emeryville, and certain portions of the Lake Merritt area of Oakland. This is said to be a progressive district, covering the same area that Dellums represents in Congress. George describes his politics as "the politics of neighborhood and community empowerment: Nothing can be done solely by elected officials. You have to catch up with the people, get in front of them, and try to lead them."

While many people think of the state as providing schools, open space, recreation, and museums, there is another side of the state, its coercive arm, which is carried out through the county apparatus: "The city police arrest people, but it's the county who jails and prosecutes them." The function of the county, in George's view, is to process the poor, for it is to the county that the superexploited of the black community must turn in the end to meet their needs for housing, health care, emergency services, etc. He describes a week in the life of a typical poor single mother:

> On Monday she will have to be processed by the county welfare bureaucracy to get Aid to Families with Dependent Children. Then on Tuesday that same mother may have to take her child on county transportation to the county hospital, where she will have to be processed by the health care bureaucracy. That same woman may on Wednesday have to appear in municipal court with her son, where the public defender will provide his legal defense. They may wait around all day: the court system is one meant especially for processing the poor. Her son may end up being taken away by the county sheriff. Then on Thursday she will have to visit him in the county jail. On Friday she has to go to the county probation department. By Saturday, left alone and without any childcare, she is taken away screaming to the county emergency psychiatric service. On Sunday she still has to feed her kids, but she tries to rest in quiet desperation, the only way she can survive.

George sees his constituency as the segment of the population that has to deal with the county, and his role as attempting to deal with the "tangle of pathologies" that come together in this context. As he says, "I need the resources to do something, so I join with the black people of my district to say that the preparation of war is killing us." He confronts the day-to-day realities of federal policies on his locality, which have led to a cascade of state and local budget cutbacks and massive unemployment. In the end, he believes, all politics is local: "Have you ever walked a precinct on a federal level?" He argues against those who claim that the threat of nuclear war is not a local issue; the county board has had to consider such issues as the location of population in a nuclear war, and the preservation of the county hospital for military purposes. George says: "Ask the mayor of Hiroshima if nuclear war is only on a national level."

He also sees the duty of elected leaders to educate their constituency about the relation between conditions they face locally and conditions in the rest of the world: "We've got to think globally, but we can only act locally. We can see the forces struggling in Central America, and then we hear the people in East Oakland asking for the same things, for housing, schools, health care. I wonder who's putting them down—it's the same corporate forces who are putting them down in El Salvador and Nicaragua. I'd like to be able to break down the mystery so that people can fully understand the linkages."

It is the history of decades of electoral organizing in the black community which then accounts for the sweep of the primary delegates by Jackson in the Eighth Congressional District. In George's view, "For whatever their motives, black working-class people are voting and it is this black unity which must be transformed into organization. And now certain professional/middle-class types are joining them, too. That's what happened in Chicago, and what's really been going on since Reagan. Jackson didn't make this happen, but he could see that it was happening."

There are no easy answers to the question: how do progressive politicians remain responsive to their constituency? But throughout his public service, George, like Dellums, has maintained his commitment to the struggles of black and working-class people, and has welcomed and assisted progressive organizations working in Oakland. He lent considerable time and energy to the electoral campaigns in which the Peace and Justice Organization was involved (described in Chapter Three). And he continues to be involved, to lend his presence, and to be accessible to the constituency he serves. The search for black empowerment requires both local leadership of this caliber and the organization of the constituency to whom these politicians must hold themselves accountable.

2.
"Money for Jobs, Not for War"

While the immediate period in Oakland has welcomed a development boom, a highly significant fact remains that only one-third of Oakland's jobs are held by Oakland residents. There are more jobs than resident Oakland workers, but two thirds of these jobs are held by commuters.[30] According to a study by the Oakland Planning Commission, racial discrimination in hiring is at the root of Oakland's unemployment, and causes businesses to hire non-Oakland workers: "Minorities and low-income persons have been denied equal employment opportunity either intentionally or institutionally."[31]

Plant closures and runaway shops have also affected the city of Oakland, just as they have devastated millions of families across the U.S. Between 1980 and 1982, Alameda County, of which Oakland is the largest city, led the state of California in plant closures, with Oakland the hardest-hit city in the county.[32] Within the past few years alone, 11 plants have been shut down, including World Airways, Del Monte Cannery, and the General Motors Parts Plant.

It is no secret to the people of Oakland, particularly its black community, that Reagan's federal policies have directly exacerbated the lack of prospects for jobs. While social programs contracted or disappeared under his budget cuts, the Reagan administration slated Oakland as one of the touted sites for an "urban enterprise zone."[33] Under this schema—reminiscent of South African bantustans—workers would be recruited to low-wage, non-union jobs without protections, while capital would be lured in with local incentives and federal tax credits. While Reagan's urban enterprise zones never materialized, he achieved a semblance of political mileage by proffering the prospect of jobs to a depressed area whose social services his administration had decimated.

As Reagan's militarism has channeled a larger and larger percentage of federal revenues into the Pentagon and its associated military-industrial complex, as his policies have precluded detente and jeopardized already-strained U.S. diplomatic relations around the globe, the threat of war, most especially nuclear war, has become a more considered possibility within the Reagan administration. The cost of Reagan's militarism has been borne by working-class and middle-class taxpayers—for example, in the forms of soaring unemployment, reductions in available public services, and decreases in Social Security and other benefits. At the same time, there have been corresponding transfers of wealth to benefit corporate interests, through, for example, tax credits, incentives, and deregulation of critical resources.

In 1982, the Peace and Justice Organization initiated a 24-month campaign within the largely black working class in Oakland to oppose Reagan's policies, with a specific demand for jobs. The political strategy underlying its approach was inspired by analysis done by the Institute for the Study of Labor and Economic Crisis, whose research on urban taxation, runaway industry, and voter participation showed the need for organizing among the most exploited sectors of the working class, i.e., the worst-paid, least-organized, often unemployed "lower-and-deeper" working class, which has a high proportion of minorities and women. It is this sector that has been excluded from the political process in this country, and whose mass participation—both in the electoral and non-electoral arenas—could profoundly alter the entire political landscape of the United States.

Despite the potential for developing a progressive political movement centered on the consciousness and militance of the black working class, there are many reasons for this stratum of the population to be wary of those who have traditionally been posed as its allies. First of all, there is the shameful experience of organized labor, which for decades has stood for the interests of the skilled, white male sector of the labor force in opposition to the interests of the majority of the work force. Second, the Democratic Party has consistently taken the support of the black electorate for granted, despite the fact that the black community has been among its most loyal supporters. Third, white liberals who have been progressive around issues like segregation, which did not threaten their interests, could not be depended on when their interests were threatened (e.g., Oceanhill-Brownsville). Fourth, the decimation of the Black Panther Party itself is an obvious example of what happens to black working-class people when they do build effective organization.

For these reasons, PJO attempted a variety of organizing methods, including electoral work and non-electoral organizing. This strategy had a dual purpose: it could assist progressives to be elected to government positions; but also could be used to pressure these officials once in office, since officials have a tendency to forget rapidly who actually elected them.

Thus PJO undertook several activities simultaneously: popular rallies, support for local candidates pledged to full employment goals, work on an electoral initiative campaign to increase jobs, direct pressure on the local government for jobs, actions against corporations that refused to provide jobs, involvement in full employment legislation in the U.S. Congress, and door-to-door organizing that linked jobs and U.S. foreign military intervention. It was this series of electoral and non-electoral activities that brought a new style of politicization to the Oakland scene. The level of education, mobilization, and activization, sustained over a 24-month period on a wide range of progressive issues, meant that the voters were already identified and knowledgeable about many of the issues that most touched their lives. While PJO was a very different organization from the Panther Party in that it was multi-racial, its style of activism and concern for classwide unity meant that PJO engaged many of the same issues and built upon its legacy.

The Peace and Justice Organization initiated its Oakland activities by organizing a march to oppose the rise of militarism engendered by Reagan's policies. Organizing for this march was in itself a lesson in how closely people identified their lack of jobs with Reagan's warring postures. The original conception of the Oakland march was based on a very successful rally held earlier in San Francisco, whose central theme was "Peace and Disarmament." The leaflet written to publicize the San Francisco rally was designed to reach the predominantly white, liberal, middle-class constituency there. When this same leaflet was distributed in Oakland, however, PJO leafleters found that people would not take them. When PJO organizers analyzed the response, they found that the reception to the event's initial publicity was cool at best. This rapidly changed when the rally's focus was changed to "Money for Jobs, Not for War"; rally organizers reported an overnight change to great enthusiasm, tapping the depth of opposition to Reaganism within Oakland's black community. The spirited march and rally held April 17, 1982, attracted over 3,000 people, 50% minorities, who turned out to the beat of high school bands and filled the streets of downtown Oakland. The rally was also unique in its breadth, being one of the first in many years to bring together speakers from the revolutionary movement in El Salvador and the anti-nuclear movement, as well as progressive black politicians and religious leaders condemning Ronald Reagan.[34]

PJO then launched its Full Employment Project, a broadly conceived campaign with many layers of activities and tactics— local and federal legislative proposals, demonstrations, civil disobedience, guerrilla theater, "open mike" rallies, and street-corner speeches, among others. This project was designed to reach out to many diverse types of people who would be willing to participate in a wide range of activities. One tactic used by PJO was to address those politicians and corporations that refused to provide jobs to Oakland's chronically unemployed. This tactic was used in the Oakland Jobs Petition, which demanded that 80% of the new jobs at the Hyatt Regency Hotel, a major downtown development, go to Oakland residents; that the mayor's summer jobs program, funded by Oakland corporations, be expanded from 1,000 to 5,000 jobs; and that a tax be levied on downtown businesses that refused to hire Oakland residents. Petitions bearing 16,000 signatures in support were presented to the mayor and City Council on June 21, 1983, after a colorful rally, at which the petition signatures, joined together in a scroll, were unfurled in front of Oakland's City Hall.[35] The process of gathering signatures drew in people from many areas of the city, including many unemployed youth, going door-to-door in the most dilapidated housing projects, setting up tables in areas of heavy street traffic, and driving car caravans through Oakland's neighborhoods.

Part of the signature-gathering effort was a series of street theater actions, demonstrations, and "open mike" rallies at which anyone could take the microphone and talk. All of these events were covered to some extent by the local media. One demonstration at the Clorox Corporation demanded more jobs in the mayor's summer jobs program, noting that Clorox had pledged a mere 15 jobs in the program, while earning $42 million in profits in 1982.

PJO also canvassed the Chicano/Latino community in Oakland with literature opposing U.S. intervention in Central America, linking the use of militarism and the lack of jobs. PJO extended its analysis of unemployment in Oakland to a national perspective and the responsibility of the federal government to provide jobs to its residents. Local work was aided by researchers from ISLEC, who participated in the drafting process of a wide-ranging piece of federal legislation, the Income and Jobs Action Act of 1984, being introduced by Congressman Charles Hayes Jr. (D–Illinois) and Congressman John Conyers Jr. (D–Michigan).[36]

These issues of Reaganism, jobs, and militarism were also central to the education done in the course of campaigns for specific local candidates. When meetings were held in housing projects to teach people the mechanics of voting, these were also opportunities for PJO organizers to discuss other avenues of struggle beyond electoral methods.

It must be emphasized that all of these efforts were conducted prior to the current mobilization for a national black presidential candidate; black people were just beginning to become activated electorally to express their long-standing opposition to reaction, represented by Reagan's election, and its consequences for both domestic and international relations. The 1982 elections were the first opportunity following Reagan's ascension to the presidency for an anti-Reagan sentiment to be registered electorally. It was in this context of opposing the rise of reaction that PJO took on its electoral campaigns.

3.
Four Campaigns: The Role of Anti-Reagan Sentiment

No one needs extensive electoral analysis to show that black people don't like Ronald Reagan. What these studies on the new black vote do point to, however, is the degree to which black people have come to identify the search for black empowerment with opposition to Reagan and a program for progressive change on a variety of domestic and international issues. As in Boston and in Chicago, black enfranchisement became identified with a particular candidate or candidates, for whom voting was not just a lesser of two evils but a statement against the continuation of inequality, injustice, and racism.

In the case of the Peace and Justice Organization, this fact was demonstrated over the course of numerous campaigns conducted over several years. From June 1982 to May 1983, PJO carried out extensive electoral work in East Oakland, an area that is predominantly black and Latino. Its organizing aimed to activate the working-class electorate, first through a voter registration drive in which 15,000 new registrants were added to the rolls, and then in four campaigns to support local black candidates, who were running on progressive programs. PJO organizers stressed issues about which black people were expressing concerns: unemployment, housing, crime, schools. On the one hand, people had a large degree of cynicism towards how much change could be accomplished within the existing system. On the other hand, organizers encountered an eagerness to discuss politically the situation in East Oakland and the possibilities for change.

The electoral methodology used by PJO was based on the experiences of the Grass Roots Alliance (GRA), which had organized three initiative campaigns in San Francisco to tax the major corporations based there. The experience of the GRA showed that through sustained organizing efforts and people-to-people techniques, the working-class electorate could be mobilized to vote in its self-interest:

> An organization using people-to-people methods can counter over time the commercial strategies of established politics. Personal contact methods (e.g., street work, canvassing) are labor-intensive and time-consuming, but used properly they encourage people to participate in the electoral process. The success of such personal contact depends very much on access to residents, which may be influenced by such practical factors as traffic patterns, language of residents, and type of housing. However, in comparison to consumer marketing approaches (such as direct mail and radio ads), whose effectiveness can be very immediate but transient, the people-to-people approach builds long-lasting support.[37]

The Tax the Corporations movement organized by the GRA faced well-financed opposition, which they countered through the use of street work, leafleting, canvassing, phone-calling banks, and the involvement of thousands of activists. The first two initiatives were narrowly defeated; the third, Proposition M, was finally passed as a policy statement in November 1980.

Key PJO organizers had gained considerable campaign experience through the GRA Tax the Corporations campaigns, and these same organizing methods were applied by PJO in East Oakland. In the candidates' campaigns, they particularly used canvassing, a system of identifying supporters throughout a precinct by going door-to-door, talking with residents and convincing them to vote. Activists were identified and trained as precinct captains, who then were responsible from the beginning to the end of a campaign to work their precinct and bring out the vote. Voters were identified in the classic method as supportive of the candidate ("1"), undecided ("2"), or opposed ("3"). Then on Election Day, both "gross pull" and "select pull" methods were used to get-out-the-vote: "gross pull" (bringing out the "1's" and "2's") was used in very supportive areas, while in "swing" areas "select pull" (doing the utmost to bring out all of the "1's" without contacting the opponent's supporters) was more effective. This method of canvassing in itself is not new and is a standard method of electoral organizing. However, what was unique about the efforts of PJO was the volume and intensity of activity, the number of times each precinct was visited. A precinct was not considered "fully canvassed" until two thirds to three quarters of all registered voters had been reached—which sometimes meant going through precincts 6 to 10 times! (This compares to the standard campaign practice of canvassing 10-15% of a precinct's voters.)

Prior to beginning their electoral campaigns, PJO activists had also spent nearly a year going door-to-door, talking with residents about the need for organization, about why it was important to "vote working class," and about the need to get involved. There were car caravans through the neighborhoods every weekend, "open mike" rallies in the unemployment office, and a very visible presence in the community. Then, when organizers came around during a campaign, many people were already familiar with PJO and the issues.

We will now examine highlights of four electoral races in which PJO campaigned and sample the impact of its organizing on the progressive vote in the precincts in which it worked.

SANDRÉ SWANSON CAMPAIGN: PRIMARY AND RUNOFF

PJO entered electoral work in Oakland in June 1982, working for Ron Dellums's aide, Sandré Swanson, who was running for the Alameda County Board of Supervisors. This campaign would be the first in many years to mobilize voter activism in Oakland's black community, to call upon black voters to support the struggle for black empowerment in a concrete way through their vote for a young black progressive against an entrenched 12-year white incumbent who had significant ties to the moderate/liberal wing of the Democratic Party and organized labor.

There was already one progressive black supervisor on the Board (John George) and it was PJO's assessment that the election of Swanson would build a George-Swanson bloc that could be responsive to and held accountable to a mobilized black and Latino working-class electorate. Both George and Swanson took strong positions against Reagan's policies of promoting domestic unemployment and militarism abroad. While Swanson was in the end not to win, his coming within 3% of defeating the incumbent signified the beginning efforts to build this movement of progressive voters who could be called upon in future elections.

The Third Supervisorial District, in which Swanson was running, is made up of the neighboring city of Alameda (32% of the registered voters in the district) and East Oakland (68% of the registered voters in the district). While East Oakland working-class voters generally vote progressively, the city of Alameda, composed predominantly of white middle-class and upper-working-class voters, tends to vote more conservatively. Even though the preponderance of registered voters live in East Oakland, the voter turnout is historically much higher in Alameda. In the June primary, Swanson ran first in a field of three candidates, receiving 38% of the vote. The other two candidates, both white, were incumbent Fred Cooper and Chuck Corica, mayor of the city of Alameda. Cooper barely edged out Corica for second place with 31% of the vote; however, analyzed by area, Swanson received 58% of the Oakland vote while Cooper and Corica together took 90% of the votes cast in Alameda.

Cooper's campaign was typical of commercial politics, relying on misleading information and playing to racism, while avoiding stands on issues. Two examples bear out this point. He had two sets of campaign materials, one for white voters in Alameda and another for blacks in Oakland. The East Oakland brochure showed a black man on the cover with Cooper's name under the picture, clearly intended to give the false impression that Cooper is black. On the day before the election, the Cooper campaign hung doorhangers, labeled "Vote Democrat" and listing

Cooper's name alongside well-known black candidates, such as Tom Bradley and Ron Dellums—as if they were running as a slate, and as if Cooper was officially endorsed by the Democratic Party (neither of which was true in the primary). One of Cooper's main supporters was Carter Gilmore, the city councilman from Oakland's District 6, who happened to be black. Cooper was also endorsed by the United Auto Workers, in repayment for political debts. He had clearly called in favors owed to him by significant parts of the black establishment and the Democratic Party, but even given this, he was unable to win a majority in the June primary.

We examined a sampling of 13 precincts in the Fruitvale area of East Oakland, which were among those canvassed by PJO in the June election. These 13 precincts were considered "swing" areas, based on the 1978 election where a black progressive only received 53% of the vote against Cooper in the same area. This sampling was indicative of the success of the grassroots methods PJO was able to employ; with an intensive people-to-people campaign, PJO brought out 65% of the primary vote in these sample precincts for Swanson.

Between June and November, PJO conducted a two-month voter registration drive in areas considered to be the most progressive, primarily black, working-class sections in East Oakland. A roving car equipped with a sound system traversed the main thoroughfares in the area, and reached into the housing projects along with stationary teams. The drive resulted in 15,000 registrants added to the rolls, with approximately two thirds coming from East Oakland. This was significant in that the number of registered voters in Oakland in November 1982 was 23.6% higher than in November 1978. This was in contrast to the city of Alameda, where the number of voters rose by only 10% in the same period.

Get-out-the-vote efforts were similarly intense in the work done by PJO; in one sample of 16 precincts on Election Day, there were 90 campaign workers walking these precincts during peak hours, which had the effect of drawing out 68% for Swanson in this area. Both primary and runoff campaigns had shown that intensive efforts to engage black working-class people in the issues, to identify the candidate as a progressive black, and to link his election to opposition to Reagan had turned this particular set of "swing" precincts into a set of progressive precincts whose vote could be called upon in repeated campaigns.

**Table 1. THIRD DISTRICT,
ALAMEDA COUNTY SUPERVISOR RACE, GENERAL ELECTION, 1982**

	PJO* Sample Precincts	Oakland	Alameda	Total
% Turnout	61.1%**	59.7%	68.6%	62.5%
% for Swanson	68.3%	62.4%	20.1%	47.4%
% for Cooper	31.7%	37.6%	79.9%	52.6%

*Based on analysis of 16-precinct sample worked by PJO.
**This percentage includes a factor for absentee voters based on the countywide proportion of absentee to nonabsentee voters.

Racism in Alameda, and the lack of an effective strategy to counter this racism, resulted in Swanson losing to Cooper by 3,000 votes. Swanson received 62.4% of the vote in Oakland, compared to 20.1% of the vote in Alameda. The PJO campaign staff had estimated that Swanson needed 65% of the total Oakland vote and 25% in Alameda to defeat Cooper, who accrued the bulk of the white vote from Alameda and Oakland.

The importance of this progressive voting pattern can be seen in the light of congressional elections and their effect on a progressive like Ron Dellums. Since the Swanson campaign was conducted in some areas also shared with Dellums's Eighth Congressional District, the electoral apparatus of progressive voters was also infused with support for his re-election in 1982. One example is shown in Table 2, which examines a sampling of five "swing" precincts worked by PJO in the Dellums district. While the overall Oakland average for Dellums was 67%, the average in these five precincts was 91.5% for Dellums. When we compared control precincts chosen for demographic similarity, the five PJO precincts showed a 2-3% increase in their support for Dellums from the June primary to the November runoff. The control precincts, on the other hand, showed a slight decline (averaging 0.6%) in support for Dellums over the same period.

Dellums has strong support in his district, receiving 90% of the overall vote in these five precincts; however, in that light, convincing 3% of 10% opposition to vote for Dellums is significant.

Table 2. SAMPLE ANALYSIS OF DELLUMS SUPPORT IN "SWING" AREAS, NOVEMBER 1982

	PJO* Sample Precincts (N=5)	Control Precincts (N=20)
% Dellums, Nov. 1982	91.5%	90.5%
% Dellums, June 1982	89.5%	91.1%
% Difference Nov.-June	+2.0%	−0.6%

Much of the excitement and mobilization around the Swanson campaigns came from the fact that he was clearly running as a progressive black candidate against a white conservative incumbent. The issue of black enfranchisement was a strong mobilizing force in involving working-class residents in the campaign. Even though he did not win, the fact that he came so close, in a race where it had seemed so unlikely that he would be able to capture the seat in a three-way contest against two well-known established white politicians, was seen as a forward thrust for black political power in his district. Also, his association with Dellums was viewed as a powerful factor in his favor, continuing the progressive representation fielded from the black community. For no one had forgotten that Dellums himself had started his political career on the Berkeley City Council.

WILSON RILES, JR., CAMPAIGN FOR CITY COUNCIL

PJO next managed the campaign of Wilson Riles, Jr., for re-election to the Oakland City Council in April 1983, using the same people-to-people methods. The campaign was conducted out of the PJO office at the same time as the Full Employment Project petition campaign, which meant that the office was a constant center of activity involving people of all races and ages. Of important significance in the Riles campaign was the reversal of the historical voting pattern by which middle-class voters turn out at a higher rate than working-class voters. In the course of the campaign, hundreds of volunteers contacted over 13,000 of the 21,000 registered voters in the district.[38]

As a result, Riles was re-elected by a landslide of 66% in Oakland's most racially mixed district. This election was the first in which the City Council was elected by district rather than citywide. Riles's district in central Oakland has large black, Latino, Asian, and white working-class populations. In fact, few of the precincts in the district have a majority of any one race; to reflect this, PJO produced Riles campaign literature in English, Spanish, and Chinese.

Riles campaigned on a platform of fighting unemployment, increasing citizen participation in city government, organizing neighborhoods to fight crime, and rent control. In particular, he called for higher taxes on local corporations that refuse to hire Oakland residents and for immediate expansion of the city's summer jobs-for-youth program.

Riles was opposed by pro-business Mayor Wilson and major corporate interests in Oakland, which (as has been shown in Chapter One) have been pursuing a course of major expansion. They preferred a City Council that would remain subservient to their corporate needs. The fact that six other candidates entered the race against Riles was seen in progressive circles as a downtown strategy aimed at preventing Riles from obtaining a majority vote in the April election. Had this happened, Riles would have been forced into a runoff, in which corporate resources could be concentrated behind one opponent who, theoretically, could have defeated Riles through sheer force of money and media. The likelihood of this occurring was predicted by most political observers to be extremely great, considering that if each of his opponents took only a small percentage of the vote, Riles would be forced into a runoff. In fact, because of the people-to-people organizing by PJO campaign workers, Riles surpassed his 1979 vote of 56.6% in that district, when he had only faced one opponent. In the 1983 race, he ran strongest in five predominantly black precincts, receiving 75% of the vote, even while running against three other black candidates.

PJO organized the Riles campaign by reaching out to a broad cross section of forces throughout Oakland—churches, labor, democratic clubs, community organizations—to involve them in the campaign. This outreach resulted in one of the most impressive coalitions in Oakland's recent political history. The coalition itself reflected the multinational constituency in the district. Among those participating in the campaign were Democratic clubs, including the Niagara Movement, Muleskinners, La Raza, and Montclair-Greater Oakland clubs; ministers such as Bishop Martin J. Clifton and Rev. Herbert Guice; the Alameda County Central Labor Council and unions including SEIU locals and the United Farm Workers; the Black Political Alliance, the National Women's Political Caucus, and the Oakland Progressive Political Alliance.

The extended support through this widespread coalition built upon the electorate already mobilized by PJO through the Swanson campaigns and his appeal for black empowerment. While Riles's appeal was broader, PJO was able to continue the process of identifying progressive voters and building a progressive bloc of precincts: 70% of the top-ranking precincts for Riles were directly canvassed and organized by PJO activists. An additional comparison can be made to the vote in that district for Swanson, who received 59.5% in the runoff, which indicates that the Riles campaign built upon and extended the progressive voting patterns in these precincts.

Another point of significance was the response to Riles in the Latino precincts. In 1979 he had received only 40.9% of the vote in those precincts with predominantly Latino voters, and only 36.9% in the three with the most heavily concentrated Latino residents. In 1983 he received 65.1% and 63.3% of the vote, respectively, in these groupings. A graphic illustration of the swing toward progressive voting in the Latino precincts was seen in one precinct, which had previously gone 31% for Riles in 1979 and only 44.5% for Swanson in 1982. This precinct (which has the highest Latino population in Oakland—over

50%) went 59.6% for Riles in 1983. This is just one example of areas that were previously unorganized, which through a variety of organizing methods—Spanish-speaking canvassing, churches, tables, Spanish literature—could be clearly responsive to progressive issues and candidates.

Over all, the PJO grassroots campaigning increased voter turnout districtwide by 4-6%, which is generally considered to have made a significant impact. This percentage is based on using the middle-class precincts near Lake Merritt as a standard; historically the Lake area has a 4-6% higher turnout than the district as a whole. In this election, the turnout in the Lake area was equal to the district as a whole. Voter turnout in the Latino precincts was actually higher than the turnout in the Lake precincts or the district as a whole, reversing traditional voting patterns. In the predominantly black areas, voter turnout was 2% lower than the Lake area in April 1983, a marked increase over June 1982, when black voter turnout was 12% lower than in the Lake area.

Table 3. VOTER TURNOUT IN LATINO PRECINCTS, DISTRICT 5 CITY COUNCIL RACE, 1983

	June 1982	*November 1982*	*April 1983*
Latino Precincts	36.8%	53.9%	30.5%
Lake Area	46.0%	63.3%	27.7%
Overall District	37.5%	56.1%	29.9%

At the time of Riles's re-election bid, he began to raise the issue of jobs for Oakland residents. ISLEC proposed a "Jobs for Oakland" ballot initiative, for which it prepared the major research and documentation.[39] PJO organizers publicized the jobs initiative as a major theme in Riles's campaign. The proposal would have increased local taxes on Oakland corporations that continued to refuse to hire Oakland residents. Corporations that increased their hiring of chronically unemployed Oakland residents, without displacing other workers, would receive tax rebates. In this way, more jobs would have been created, either through direct hiring by the corporations or through more local

tax funds for the hiring of more public-sector workers. The
initiative specifically addressed the key fact that only one third
of Oakland jobs are held by Oakland residents.

As we have shown, unemployment is one of the most critical
issues facing Oakland's working class. The racism of the corporate interests stands all the more evident with the current
development boom. The new office highrises are occupied by
employees translocated from San Francisco: the transformation of Oakland into a commercial/financial hub has little prospect
for employment of black and minority unskilled workers. At
the same time, plants and warehouses are running away to
nearby non-union states, such as Nevada and Utah; employment in these states is in reality not available for these workers,
compounded by the racism they would face, moving into rural
communities with few black residents and entrenched white
chauvinism towards Chicanos/Latinos.

Therefore, the "Jobs for Oakland" initiative proposal presented
a concrete approach toward the problem of unemployment.
Introducing it at the time of his re-election campaign, Riles
also gave the image of a politician more than willing to take
an anti-corporate position and willing to oppose the mayor
and the dominant corporate interests. It also distinguished Riles
from the other black and Latino candidates for City Council
in his district, making his re-election not an issue of race, but
one of class interest. This election represented a victory for
black progressive forces in Oakland, a significant victory for
multinational grassroots organizing.

Riles as candidate must be distinguished, however, from
Riles as elected official. The Jobs for Oakland Initiative appeared
to be facing legal entanglements; Riles no longer pursued it
once he was re-elected. He no longer consulted with those
organizations that had, in the main, returned him to office;
and the broad-based coalition of progressive forces built during the campaign was allowed to disintegrate. He did not see
himself as accountable to or responsible to the larger movement that had fueled his campaign, a key lesson understood
by other progressive politicians, that they are ineffective without

a base of popular support and mobilization. While Riles has not kept his campaign promises, he now has his eye on the mayor's job in 1985, and it remains to be seen (as with Lionel Wilson) whether he will continue to move to the right or be more accountable to his constituency. Riles's particular shortcomings, however, do not detract from the progressive impulse represented by the voters who came out in his support, and who embraced an anti-Reagan program in this campaign.

DARLENE LAWSON CAMPAIGN FOR SCHOOL BOARD

Within a few weeks of Riles's re-election, the Peace and Justice Organization was asked by Darlene Lawson to help elect her to the Oakland School Board, representing the same district as Wilson Riles, Jr. In a very brief campaign, by activating its precinct workers and supporters who had already been identified, PJO was able to transform this election from one based on race alone to one in which positions on progressive issues were decisive. Lawson, a black woman, had come in second during the April 19 election, but neither she nor her Latino opponent Noel Gallo had received a majority, which forced a runoff election May 17. In entering this election, PJO emphasized political differences between the two candidates, so that the race would be decided on progressive politics, not on whether the person was Latino or black.

Lawson's campaign focused on increasing Oakland's summer jobs-for-youth program, stopping layoffs of teachers and other cutbacks in the school budget, shifting more of the burden of supporting public schools onto large corporations, stepping up bilingual education programs, and creating a safe learning environment for students and teachers alike. When PJO entered the campaign, she was trailing and not expected to win; in fact, many observers said that she didn't have a "ghost of a chance." Within four days, this situation was reversed. PJO undertook a door-to-door canvas in the district, seeking out existing Lawson supporters and persuading others. By Election Day, the number of identified Lawson supporters had increased from less than 100 to almost 3,000, thus laying the basis for an extensive get-out-the-vote effort.

By a narrow margin, Lawson did win the election, becoming the first black woman elected to the Oakland School Board. Working-class voters in Latino precincts gave stronger support to Lawson (42%) than Gallo (38%), while middle-class whites were Gallo's strongest base of support. This election was won on the basis of class, not racial interests, another example of the depth of opposition to Reagan policies existent in both the black and Latino communities.

Table 4. COMPARISON OF LAWSON AND GALLO VOTE IN DISTRICT 5 SCHOOL BOARD RACE, 1983

Precincts	Lawson	Gallo
Latino/Working-Class		
April 1983	38%	62%
May 1983	42%	58%
Black/Working-Class		
April 1983	57%	43%
May 1983	71%	29%
White/Middle-Class (Lake Merritt Area)		
April 1983	25%	75%
May 1983	27%	73%

The electoral efforts of the Peace and Justice Organization ultimately went on to contribute to the campaigns of Ron Dellums, John George, and other progressive Oakland candidates, culminating in "Run, Jesse, Run." The Jackson sweep of the Democratic presidential delegates in the Eighth Congressional District must then be understood within the fabric of progressive unity that had been built up over this series of campaigns. It is significant that the progressive black leadership—such as Ron Dellums and John George—took a strong stand against the mainstream Democratic Party support (black and white) for Mondale and organized for Jackson, even when it was almost certain that Mondale would get the nomination.

While the PJO electoral energies were subsequently assimilated into the Jackson campaign, the style of political mobilization that PJO brought to Oakland elections remains as something very unique. The level of electoral activism, voter education, and linkage to a broad program of progressive issues in opposition to Reagan have moved whole districts of the city to vote in a progressive direction. PJO did not build just another effective "machine," but sought to link an efficient organization with the struggle for black empowerment, the search for the broadest aspirations of our people for equality and justice.

4.
Conclusion:
Black Enfranchisement
and Beyond

The 24-month campaign studied here, conducted by the Peace and Justice Organization in Oakland, brought a new vibrancy to the Oakland political scene, which many observers agreed had not been present since the Panthers' organizing in the 1970s. Arising in the advent of growing opposition to Reagan, this phenomenon parallels the Panthers' opposition to domestic and military policies of the 1960s. But the new black voters have perhaps indeed learned their lessons, not to just get transmuted into another Lionel Wilson or a subsequent black face doing the beckoning of those in power. The electoral work by PJO also demonstrated that multinational organizing was essential in winning an election in Oakland, for the populace is and always has been racially and culturally very diverse. While Oakland is nearly 50% black, the fact that white turnout is generally so much higher than black turnout means that it would be difficult for a black candidate to be elected on the basis of black support alone.

But the issue is not just one of electing black candidates. What do they stand for? Are they out for "a piece of the pie" for themselves? We would submit that progressive black candidates must speak to the aspirations of all black people, which includes those on the very bottom. And there cannot be "more" for everyone without a radical restructuring of the wealth and power in this country, a restructuring that speaks to the needs not just of blacks but of Latinos/Chicanos, Asians, Native

Americans, working-class women, the unemployed, and underemployed—all who are forced into the lower reaches of the working class.

While it is likely that those in power will be forced to accommodate in some way the rising demands of the masses of black people, that will not come about without hardship. The problems faced daily by black people—lack of jobs and social services, dilapidated housing—are not ones that local or even national governments can solve. Since 1967, as a consequence of the steady expansion of production in all of the major productive areas after 1945, the world-economy has entered a period of stagnation—the result of a classic worldwide crisis of overproduction. It is the combination of this contraction and the loss of U.S. political hegemony that makes the current U.S. unemployment crisis such a deep and long-term phenomenon.

In response to the crisis of stagnation, oligopolistic producers have attempted to maintain their profit margins by increasing prices amidst competition with each other for markets. At the same time, many of the largest firms have sought to solve their immediate problems through cost reduction by relocating parts of their production processes to low-wage areas of the world. Thus, since the 1960s and the 1970s, a significant amount of mechanized production has been shifted out of the core countries (e.g., U.S. and West Germany) to the free-trade zones in the periphery, to the so-called newly industrializing countries (e.g., Taiwan, Singapore, South Korea), where wage rates are considerably lower than in the core countries. As we have written elsewhere,

> The core zones of the world-economy are no longer sole supplier of manufactured goods, while the periphery provides raw materials. Under the emerging new arrangements, the core zones will provide the plant and the know-how while the periphery provides the primary products and manufactured goods. . . .What the restructured world-economy portends for the working classes of the core zones, especially the United States, is increased polarization. The outlines of such a polarized work force are already extremely clear: a small technological elite and a large number of unskilled, unemployable workers.[40]

The process of reindustrialization will not return U.S. workers to their former standard of living; rather, it is a program designed to transform increasingly larger portions of the population into superexploited workers.

The importance of the new black vote then takes on broader importance in the context of the social crisis being forced upon the black and other minority communities. As of yet, there are no large uprisings occurring in the streets; because of both the chronicity of the crisis and the hope that things may improve, the worsening social conditions have not produced even the tumult of the 1960s as yet. But the aspirations for empowerment, the sentiments for equality and justice that reside among the minority working class are being expressed electorally, particularly when they are accompanied with organization. This vote has elected Harold Washington and supported Mel King and Jesse Jackson. This is the sentiment that returns Ron Dellums to Congress with 90% of the vote in some areas. This is the locus for the broadest opposition to Reagan's policies, both in domestic and foreign affairs. Whether this expression of social outrage can be contained in the electoral arena remains to be seen in the coming decade.

Of course, there are limits to which black progressives in office can achieve significant social change outside of the context of a broader social movement. That movement for black empowerment has witnessed the repression of the Panthers, the containment of its protest through accommodation to its moderate leadership (such as Mayor Wilson), and the rollback of most of its hard-won gains in civil rights. Today this search for black equality and justice is being expressed in the electoral arena, electing black progressive candidates to office and challenging the Democratic Party to represent the interests of that movement. Until conditions exist within the U.S. for a broader movement to press beyond the limits of electoral reformism, black progressives in office, just like white, Latino, and Asian progressives, cannot be expected to achieve more than the social movement that placed them in office.

The experience of the Peace and Justice Organization in Oakland speaks to the potentialities of electoral organizing. Until the emergence of the "new black vote," the black community in Oakland had viewed the electoral arena with a healthy and realistic skepticism. The assassinations of King and Kennedy, the destruction of the Black Panther Party, the predominance of Reagan in national politics, and the ineffectiveness of the Democratic Party locally—all of these cooled any enthusiasm for electoral politics. The black candidate had to be more than black to fire people's imagination. The Black Panther Party, the Peace and Justice Organization, and other comparable organizations around the country were able to involve black people in electoral politics because they offered more than "good candidates"—they promoted candidates who actually talked politics and debated the burning issues of the day, a far cry from the commercial politics of slick brochures and packaged media campaigns. They linked candidates and propositions with broader political issues and emphasized the interconnection of voting and educating; they talked about power and the necessity to build power by mobilization of the community, not just through the political representation of one person; and they recognized that electoral politics is only one of many arenas for political mobilization.

PJO and other similar grassroots organizations also learned about the limits, the constraints, and the potential treachery of electoral politics. First, it is increasingly difficult/problematic for local politicians, however progressive, to exercise political control over a political economy that is increasingly regional, national, and transnational. Secondly, the track record of progressive politicians, once elected, is often not impressive. The constraints of political office, the conservative lure of upward mobility, and the lack of formal and real mechanisms of accountability to their constituency—all of these factors account for the to-be-expected "defection" of "progressive" candidates once in office. In this sense, politicians like Congressman Dellums and Supervisor George, who have remained both progressive and accountable for many years, represent a unique political animal.

PJO made it clear to its constituency that the solution to their problems was not ultimately to be found in the election of this or that person. It encouraged people to vote in their class interests and for candidates who might reduce the burdens of Reaganism and provide space and support for progressive community organizations. It did not promise pie-in-the-sky. PJO recognized but did not solve some major dilemmas: 1) How do we keep honest politicians honest? 2) How do we ensure that community organizations maintain a spectrum of political activities and do not become totally absorbed into the electoral arena? 3) How do we develop electoral strategies that take into account the growing contradiction between local politics and regional/national/global power? These are the questions that must be addressed by future Black Panther Parties, by future Peace and Justice Organizations, and by future Rainbow Coalitions.

5.
Peace, Justice and Politics

An Interview with Congressman Ronald V. Dellums

This interview* with Congressman Ronald V. Dellums (D-California) highlights some of the issues that progressive black politicians must address, to remain responsive to and representative of the movement that keeps them in office. While the interview was conducted in 1982, in these times of mean-spirited Reaganism, many of the same policy issues—such as Central America, the threat of nuclear war, and unemployment—are even more urgent today.

Bush: Could you describe how you got into politics and your political evolution?

Dellums: How I got into politics? I literally was talked into going to a meeting one night. This was in January of 1967. The occasion was a discussion among black community leaders in Berkeley to determine how many black candidates they wanted to run in the upcoming city council election, and who that person or those persons would be.

A number of candidates came. A few of my friends literally took me to the meeting, although I told them I was not interested in political office. When it was my turn to speak, I got up and said why I wasn't particularly interested in politics; I said which issues I thought were important, but I was not sure they'd *ever* get talked about in *this* country.

---

*Interview first published in *Plain Speaking* 6, 10-11 (May 16 and June 1, 1982).

Later, when it was time to select the candidate, somebody said, "Take Dellums's name off the list, because he's not interested in running."

There was a woman in that room. Her name was Maudelle Shirek. She turned to me and said, "Son, I heard what you said, and I want to ask you this question. Now that I've heard what your thoughts are, would you run on your own terms?"

I turned to her and said, "That's the only way anyone ought to be in public office—on their own terms—not owned or controlled or manipulated by anyone, but on their own integrity."

And so she said, in a very motherly way—because since then she's become like one of my mothers—"You leave his name on the list, because he's going to get one vote."

When she made this statement, I literally did not know how to respond. In that moment of hesitation, my whole life was changed. I then won the majority of the votes cast that night, and thus became a candidate for the Berkeley City Council by no design of my own.

Bush: Do you regret having made that decision at that time and place?

Dellums: If I had to have a baptism of fire in politics anywhere in the country—anywhere—I would not exchange the experience of that time, at that moment, in that place. There was incredible energy in this community—tremendous intellect, outrage, principle—a genuine desire to really change society. And a very serious concern about people dealing with each other as equal human beings, and people trying to move away from the incredible power of materialistic values.

So I had an interesting opportunity to grow up black in the Bay Area, in a place where people are trying to address those problems in some genuine way. I also was able to develop politically in the left wing of the body politic. And that clearly is a result of my being in Berkeley and my political evolution in Berkeley.

Martin Luther King is the other very powerful reason why I am in politics. If you can understand Martin Luther King, and where he was going at the time he died; if you understand the passion of what was happening in the 1960s and in the early 1970s in Berkeley, then you can understand me and my politics. It was the peace movement that gave rise to my going to Washington, D.C.

Bush: What are some of your main concerns?

Dellums: I'm still in search of peace. When I went to Congress, the issue was withdrawing from Vietnam. The issue today is withdrawing from the mentality of war. And so I still essentially have the same constituency. I feel that this same constituency is raising the same questions. They are still raising the issues of war and peace. They are now raising them in a larger context than Vietnam. They are raising them in the context of El Salvador, in the context of Cuba, in the context of Europe, the context of the Middle East. They are raising these issues in a global context. People are still concerned about peace in this area. And I see myself still as an advocate of peace, and as a person elected to office to seek peace.

To me, it was not enough to just stop at getting out of Vietnam—it always had a larger context. I came into politics at a time when people were struggling around the issues of justice and equality, and I think that those are still issues that have to be struggled around. They have not been achieved fully in this society.

Bush: Why do you think it is necessary to fight for peace year in and year out?

Dellums: Our foreign policy continues to mirror the fact that we have not clearly addressed ourselves to the problems of international relationships. We find ourselves in bed with South Africa, a very racist regime. We find ourselves propping up military dictators around the world. We're involved in El Salvador in an inappropriate way. So I think that what brought me into elective office in the late 1960s are still very important matters in the early 1980s.

The only difference is that maybe, in the 1980s, people will begin to see that they have to look to the progressive wing of the body politic for the leadership of the 1980s. I think that when one looks across the political spectrum, the only wing of the body politic that is not bankrupt at this point, and that has new ideas and new approaches, is the progressive wing of the body politic. We are the only ones who have the audacity to offer a different analysis of America's problems, and a different role that government ought to play in our lives.

Ronald Reagan has established what he perceives to be an appropriate role of government in our lives in the 1980s. That is a stripped-down version of the federal government—taking programs back to the 50 states with his so-called "New Federalism." This only brings us back to states' rights, which raises all the regional, racial, and potential class clashes that could occur as a result.

The only other competing analysis is a progressive analysis of the role of government in people's lives. And I think that in the 1980s debate has to occur around that question. My advocacy in that debate is that, at a minimum, the government, as the collective expression of people's will, should guarantee the basic necessities of life.

We have to expand, in certain areas, the role of government in people's lives. I just don't think that one ought to have to shop for the basic necessities of life the way you shop for luxury items in a supermarket. Eating should not be a complex economic consideration. Neither should whether one has a functional and aesthetic place to live, nor whether one is able to matriculate in a high school or a university. Nor whether a person will have appropriate health care and preventive care, and health education. These things ought to be basic things of life, guaranteed by the government.

In the 1980s, I see that debate: What is the appropriate role of government? Reagan is saying: Get government back out of people's lives; let corporate policy and other economic considerations be the cornerstone of public policy.

Bush: Many people are saying that the danger of nuclear war is the issue of our time. How would you respond to that?

Dellums: To me, the number one issue of the 1980s is to move back away from the brink of nuclear disaster. And if there is going to be a slogan for the 1980s, it needs to be: "From

confrontation to negotiation." That has to be the cornerstone
for foreign policy in the world.

We have taken nuclear power and nuclear technology to
a very frightening and very dangerous level. We are now forcing each other to react within a matter of minutes—20 to 40
minutes. If we deploy the Pershing II missile, we will bring
the Soviet Union within four minutes of a nuclear weapon.
And a Pershing II is in many ways, as I perceive it, a cheap
way to purchase a forwardly deployed ICBM system, because
you can have it sitting there.

But you've got it sitting there, within four minutes of
the Soviet Union. Now *what* were we prepared to do—only
a few short years ago—when missiles were within four minutes of the United States in this hemisphere? We were prepared to go to war—nuclear war—over the issue of missiles
in Cuba.

If the American people can understand and go back in history,
and recall the fear and anger that we felt at the danger of nuclear
weapons that close to us; if we can remember that this country was prepared to go to war over Soviet missiles in Cuba;
what makes anyone think that another society of people would
not react essentially the same way?

It's a moral imperative that the world decides that nuclear
weapons have to go; that human life and nuclear weapons
are not compatible. And we have to begin the process, to start
talking about negotiation as opposed to confrontation.

Bush: The nuclear arms race has been going on for some time
now. How do you think it has changed under Reagan?

Dellums: We started off talking about nuclear weapons to be
used. We dropped a bomb on Hiroshima and Nagasaki. And
then we developed a policy of deterrence. MacNamara defined
deterrence as that point at which you reach the nuclear capacity
to destroy 30% of another nation's population and 70% of the
economic infrastructure—factories, plants, and what have you.
At that time, this capacity was 400 strategic nuclear weapons.
We now have 10,000 strategic nuclear weapons and the Soviet
Union has 7,000. This administration has gone beyond the concept

of mutually assured destruction and is saying that we must have the capacity to fight and win a nuclear war.

Bush: Many members of the Democratic Party are taking positions not too different from Reagan. How do you explain that?

Dellums: Congress is made up of representatives who've campaigned on various gradations of political ideology. In Congress, the only time party becomes a relevant factor is when we organize the Congress. Whoever has the majority organizes the Congress. Once you begin to talk about issues, you don't have parties, you have politics. You don't have a Democratic Party position and a Republican Party position in Congress. You have ideological perspectives.

Tip O'Neill, for example, got up on the floor one day in the midst of a debate over the budget. He turned to the Republicans and said, "Your proposal cuts the little people off at the hips." Then he turned to the Democrats and said, "But the tragedy is that the Democratic Party's program is cutting them off at the knees, so they're still being cut down."

The majority of the Democrats are to the right of Tip O'Neill. That leaves you 30 to 60 Democrats that you could call progressive. That's 30 to 60 people who would be willing to challenge on important foreign policy matters, and not play games or engage in shady language, or in compromises that end up watering down resolutions so that they lose their integrity. I'm talking about people who are willing to go to the essence of the issue and take a very clean stance—30 to 60 people—whether you're talking about foreign policy or domestic policy.

That's a very frustrating thing for me in the Congress. Most politicians are trying to be mainstream; trying not to be a lightning rod; not to create too much controversy; not to be too far out there, to attract challenges.

You know, there's a joke in the House that the best vote for a politician is when he casts a vote, and goes home and says, "I voted 'yes' and 'no'."

And sometimes they actually construct votes to be able to say that they voted "yes" and "no." And so from that kind of mind-set, you're not going to get leadership moving us through the dangers and the imperatives of the 1980s.

Bush: And these are the top leaders of our nation?

Dellums: Two weeks ago, in the midst of all these polls about people being concerned about the military budget, my colleagues, in four hours and 40 minutes (with time off for lunch in the middle), passed a $255.1 billion military budget. Now, you tell me anybody can intelligently debate a quarter of a trillion-dollar budget in four hours and 40 minutes?

The vote was 40 to 3. Now you tell me that 40 to 3 votes really reflects where the American people are? Do you think, on a ratio of 40 to 3, that the American people want to spend a quarter of a trillion dollars on the military budget? But that's how far away my colleagues are from the American people. I think that maybe we've arrived at a point where this system does not serve us well. I don't see anything sacrosanct about the two-party system. I am in the Democratic Party because the majority of our people are in it.

Bush: There is some talk about a filibuster in the Senate to block the extension of the Voting Rights Act. What would be the implications of this for black people?

Dellums: First of all, I think we will have communicated again to black and Third World people in this country that we're really not talking about an egalitarian society, but a society where people are still ranked at the level of their citizenship on the basis of race. Secondly, we will be saying to people that we talk about the franchise as significant, but we really are not trying to make it the easiest thing in the world.

Just the fact that we even have to be debating this bill is a sad commentary on our time. That we are not prepared to extend the full weight of the law to guarantee that every human being is able to exercise the franchise is, to me, an incredible indictment of the political moment that we're in.

It is an encumbrance for us even to have to debate this question. Psychologically, it keeps us in a position of having to debate civil rights matters that we ought to have been years beyond, while other major important issues that we are not involved in are being decided on a daily basis. So you keep black and Third World America upset about the Voting Rights Act, right? We are conspicuously silent and absent from the peace movement because our energies are over here with civil rights.

Meanwhile, a number of white male Americans over 50 are making life-and-death decisions about the quality of life today, tomorrow, and decades into the future, or if indeed there's even going to be a future.

Bush: Would you comment on your role in local politics and how you affect the local political process?

Dellums: I am not involved in power politics, and my mission in life is not to control the political flow of life in the Bay Area. That's absurd. My responsibility is, as clearly, cleanly, and articulately as I can, to take the concerns of the people in this area to Washington, D.C., where madness reigns on a daily basis, and to try not to become as mad as that situation often dictates. So I don't see my job as trying to control the flow of political life in this community.

I just feel that my responsibility is to project a set of ideas cleanly to the people, and say, look: I stand in the left wing of the body politic; I stand as a progressive human being; these are my views on foreign policy; these are my views on domestic policy; these are my views of the world. If you have become more conservative than me, then elect somebody else.

Bush: In terms of local issues, where do you stand on a controversial issue like rent control?

Dellums: We've supported every rent control measure that's come here. And that's not even to say that rent control is the way of solving the problem, because we all know that it's not. But it's the only way people at the local level are able to respond in an atmosphere of economic chaos, and in the absence of any kind of national policy.

People at the local level are faced with some very simple options and some very simple realities:

"My rent is going up and I can't afford it going up. For

me to have to pay $100 a month more for rent in this situation means that I can't take care of something else."

Clearly those persons are going to vote for rent control, because that's the only method they see that can help them. And clearly I am going to stand with those people.

We've had urban hearings in different parts of the country, trying to look at the problems of urban Americans. When we looked at housing, we came up with an interesting finding: The tax laws, for example, don't support people who live in, who own, or who construct rental housing. So if there were commitment to expand rental housing in our society, there would be no law to support it. There's literally no national housing policy.

Bush: You recently returned from a trip to Grenada. Would you tell us something about the trip?

Dellums: Grenada has a provisional revolutionary government. Their prime minister is Maurice Bishop, a very bright young black man who is trying to bring about some major changes in that society. Defense Secretary Caspar Weinberger, in his report to the U.S. Congress, raised some questions about Grenada being a military threat to the U.S. He charged that an airfield is being built in Grenada which could be used to land Soviet MIGs, so that it would be a military base. He also tried to claim that there is a deep water harbor at which the Grenadans are in the process of developing a Soviet submarine base. So I went to Grenada to investigate this.

When I talked to Prime Minister Bishop about this, he explained that Grenada is one of the most beautiful islands in the world, and for them a top priority is the development of tourism. This means that they have to build this airfield and have to use the deep water harbor as a yacht harbor. But for Grenada to be seen as a military threat to the United States seems to me to be a case of the elephant and the flea. As Maurice Bishop said,

"I've 110,000 people and I have to respond to a challenge from the President of the United States, one of the great superpowers. Now let's suppose military motivations here. And let's just suggest that in a crisis a ship is floating along the horizon past my island bound for the United States, filled with strategic materials or oil or whatever, or leaving the United States in support of their troops. Now suppose I fired a missile off my tiny little island and blew that ship out of the water." He said, "Now the important question is, *what would I do next?* Would I run back and try to hide my island somewhere out here in the middle of this water?"

The United States has also raised the issue of the Grenadans not having elections. Their response is,

"Look, we have a number of priorities. One is to build this airport for development purposes. Another is to rewrite our constitution because we don't want to just have free elections in the context of the constitution that has dominated our lives for a number of years. And so we seek to rewrite the constitution democratically, adopt the constitution in a democratic way, and have free elections based on a new constitution."

Now I mentioned to you that in the Armed Services Committee, we passed a $255.1 billion military budget in four hours and 40 minutes. The Grenadans just passed their budget or are in the final stages of approving their budget for this year. For an island of 110,000 people, you know that it's only a very few million dollars. For three months, they went to every community and every area on this tiny little island where debates and discussions could occur on that national budget. Now, where is the democratic practice?

I think there's a major effort on the part of these people to develop a very exciting, vibrant society in Grenada. We as American people have an opportunity to embrace some young people who are really trying to do something.

Bush: We understand that you also went to Cuba.

Dellums: I decided for myself that in order to have a more comprehensive understanding of what was happening in Central America and in the Caribbean, that I wanted to get Fidel Castro's perspective—just so that it was another part of my thinking. I wanted to understand from his vantage point how he saw the tightening up of relationships and the building of tension between our two countries.

The key to intelligent and sensitive U.S. policy in the Caribbean, and the key to lowering of tension and moving toward political solutions in Central America is the U.S. relationship with Cuba. At the government level, we find ourselves unable to even talk about these matters because we're locked into this propaganda struggle with Cuba.

Bush: What is the key task for you at this time?

Dellums: At this particular historic moment 1982, I feel that my responsibility is to try to heighten people's awareness: a) to the danger of the nuclear arms race; b) to the need for embracing a foreign policy that, at its base, says we embrace the notion of world peace, that we embrace the notion of an immediate freeze on development of all new nuclear weapons.

We should immediately begin at this point to seriously negotiate significant reductions with a view toward the eradication of nuclear weapons from the face of the earth. We should embrace a foreign policy that states that the problems of the world are not military, but are political, economic, and social. A foreign policy should respect human rights, human dignity, human freedom, human life, and economic justice. Foreign policy should not be dominated by our international, multinational corporations now invested in self-interest. Our foreign policy should go beyond seeing only the Soviet Union, to see a complex world of some 160-odd nations, where open communication is required.

We need to develop a domestic policy that begins to talk about the federal government guaranteeing the basic necessities of life. At a minimum, we should discuss the role of government in people's lives. In the 1980s, that debate has to go forward.

Secondly, we need to build a coalition toward getting beyond symptoms to causes. We need to talk about advocating a domestic economic policy that provides a broader range of people participating and benefiting from the economics of the country. I think that America has enormous potential to develop a magnificent society, one unheralded on the face of the earth. But it has to be in relationship with other nations in the world, within the framework of world peace, and within the framework of human rights and justice in the world. Against that backdrop,

I think we can evolve a society that would be terribly exciting.

But I think that we are going to have to look at both the inevitability and the desirability of change in a variety of areas of our lives. That's my responsibility, to get out there and to say we have to debate these questions. So my role is twofold—to demand that there is a process of open debate and open discussion, to try to be effective as an advocate in that debate for a political perspective where the solution goes toward the cause of the problem and not the symptoms. In general terms, that is where I'm supposed to be.

Then in that context we can talk about specific issues: about housing policy, about the deployment of the Pershing II, or the purchase of the B-1 bomber. And so it's about being part of the educative process and trying to the best of my ability to be out there clearly focusing people's attention on the critical issues.

NOTES

1. The electoral work of the Grass Roots Alliance is more fully analyzed by the Institute for the Study of Labor and Economic Crisis in *Grassroots Politics in the 1980s* (San Francisco: Synthesis Publications, 1982). This study also showed that over a four-year period of organizing in San Francisco, there was a significant rise in progressive voting, particularly among voters in working-class neighborhoods where the GRA had been most active.

2. *Oakland Tribune* (April 8, 1981).

3. Oakland Study Center, "Oakland: The Jobs and the Jobless" (May 1977).

4. Data from the California State Employment Development Department, February 1983.

5. For further historical detail on Bay Area development and the origin of the Bay Area Council, see "Regionalism and the Bay Area," special issue of *Pacific Research and World Empire Telegram* (November-December 1972), published by Pacific Studies Center, East Palo Alto, California.

6. Rod Bush and Thomas Bodenheimer, "Full Employment: Prospects for Organizing in the 1980s" (ISLEC paper presented at the Society for the Study of Special Problems, August 1983).

7. Edward Hayes, *Power Structure and Urban Policy: Who Rules in Oakland?* (New York: McGraw-Hill, 1972), pp. 186-87.

8. Ibid., pp. 6-7.

9. The role of the Knowland empire in world affairs is well described in Franz Schurmann, *The Logic of World Power: An Inquiry into the Origins, Currents and Contradictions of World Politics* (New York: Pantheon, 1974); also see Hayes, op. cit., pp. 14-15.

10. "Regionalism and the Bay Area," op. cit., p. 6.

11. Hayes, op. cit., pp. 43-71.

12. Ibid., p. 49.

13. Ibid., p. 192.

14. To understand the Black Panther Party history, program, method, and analysis, see Bobby Seale, *Seize the Time* (New York: Random House, 1968); Huey Newton, *Revolutionary Suicide* (New York: Harcourt, Brace, 1973); Philip Foner (ed.), *The Black Panthers Speak* (New York: Lippincott, 1970).

15. *San Francisco Examiner* (May 14, 1972).

16. *Oakland Tribune* (March 2, 1966; September 8, 1976).

17. The following news sources of that period provide information on the Panther election strategy: *Oakland Tribune* (May 20, 1973); *Liberated Guardian* (January 20, 1973); *San Francisco Chronicle* (April 12, 1973); *Daily Californian* (May 7, 1973).

18. *Oakland Tribune* (April 18, 1973).

19. *Jet Magazine* (March 1973).

20. As documented in the *Oakland Montclarion* (April 8, 1981).

21. Repression of the Black Panther Party is analyzed in: Institute for the Study of Labor and Economic Crisis, *The Iron Fist and the Velvet Glove* (San Francisco: Crime and Social Justice Associates, 1982), which describes the extensive FBI COINTELPRO operation targeting the Panthers for disruption and assassination. Also see Robert Justin Goldstein, *Political Repression in Modern America: From 1870 to the Present* (New York: Schenkman, 1978).

22. Data from campaign financial statements filed at the office of the Oakland City Clerk; *San Francisco Examiner* (April 4, 1977).

23. Data from campaign financial statements filed at the office of the Oakland City Clerk; *Bay Guardian* (April 15, 1977).

24. Election data from Oakland Registrar of Voters.

25. The Pacific Rim strategy and its relation to U.S. intervention in Vietnam are explained in Peter Wiley, "Vietnam and the Pacific Rim Strategy," *Leviathan* (June 1969).

27. See files on Grubb & Ellis at the Oakland Data Center, Oakland, California; see also *Oakland Montclarion* (April 1977).

28. "Oakland '83," op. cit.

29. Excerpts of testimony from these hearings and Dellums's alternative budget proposal are included in Ron Dellums, *Defense Sense: The Search for a Rational Military Policy* (Cambridge, Mass.: Ballinger, 1983).

30. Data from the Association of Bay Area Governments and Oakland Chamber of Commerce.

31. *Oakland Tribune* (January 12, 1978).

32. *Oakland Tribune* (April 8, 1982).

33. For further analysis of the urban enterprise zone within the context of the world economic crisis, see Marlene Dixon et al., "Reindustrialization and the Transnational Labor Force in the U.S. Today," *Contemporary Marxism* 5 (Summer 1982).

34. *Oakland Tribune* (April 19, 1982).

35. *Oakland Tribune* (June 22, 1983).

36. This bill has been introduced as H.R. 5814 by Hayes and Conyers into the 1984 Congressional Session.

37. ISLEC, *Grassroots Politics in the 1980s*, op. cit., p. 21.

38. Data for this campaign from "Oakland Election Analysis: 1982-83," issued by the Peace and Justice Organization, May 1983.

39. Institute for the Study of Labor and Economic Crisis, "The Feasibility of a 'Jobs for Oakland' Ballot Initiative," April 1983.

40. Rod Bush, "Racism and Changes in the International Division of Labor," *Crime and Social Justice* 20, p. 42.

INDEX

About the Editor

Rod Bush is a member of the research and editorial board of the Institute for the Study of Labor and Economic Crisis. A graduate of Howard University, he has written extensively on the black political experience in the U.S. He has taught black history and black studies, and been a columnist for the *California Voice*, a black newspaper. He has worked as an urban planning analyst and a psychologist, and was a candidate for the San Francisco Board of Supervisors in 1980. Bush was formerly a member of the Youth Organization for Black Unity and the African Liberation Support Committee.

Contributors

Abdul Alkalimat (Gerald McWorter) is Professor of Afro-American Studies and Sociology at the University of Illinois and is active in the black liberation movement. He is a member of Peoples College and senior author of their text, *Introduction to Afro-American Studies*.

Ken Cockrel, currently a trial attorney in Detroit, served as a member of the Detroit City Council in the 1970s.

Doug Gills is a black activist intellectual, working on a doctoral dissertation in political science at Northwestern University.

James Jennings is Dean of the College of Public and Community Service at the University of Massachusetts. He has taught courses in black and Puerto Rican political experience at Harvard, Cornell, and other universities. He is co-author of *Puerto Rican Politics in Urban America*. Dr. Jennings has worked with community organizations in Brooklyn, New York and Boston, Massachusetts.

Other Titles from Synthesis Publications

ISBN Prefix: 0-89935
Order from your local bookstore or directly from the publisher. Send payment plus $1.50 for the first book, 50¢ for each additional book to **Synthesis Publications**, Dept. 131, 2703 Folsom St., San Francisco, CA 94110